Social Content Marketing for Entrepreneurs

First published in 2015 by
Business Expert Press, LLC
222 East 46th Street, New York, NY 10017
www.businessexpertpress.com

ISBN-13: 978-1-63157-212-8 (paperback)
ISBN-13: 978-1-63157-213-5 (e-book)

Business Expert Press Digital and Social Media Marketing and Advertising Collection

Collection ISSN: 2333-8822 (print)
Collection ISSN: 2333-8830 (electronic)

Cover and interior design by S4Carlisle Publishing Services Private Ltd., Chennai, India

First edition: 2015

10 9 8 7 6 5 4 3 2 1

Printed in the United States of America.

Abstract

This book will provide a practical overview of how digital content, social media and search engine optimization work together in driving website traffic and sales leads. The goal of the book is to educate readers on the new mindset and social technologies required to drive this traffic in a timely and non-intrusive way. Readers will benefit from a comprehensive but succinct overview of how social networking, search friendly blogging, trustworthy content, contextually-targeted online campaigns and mobile marketing techniques are transforming companies that embrace inbound marketing.

Targeted for business professionals and students that are saturated with social technology updates, the book offers a more strategic orientation to these subjects as they relate to sales nurturing and thought leadership. And unlike books that cover social media one platform or technology at a time, this book is organized for readers to master elements of strategy in the order of their implementation. In so doing, it will help order the steps of professionals in the midst of launching new digital marketing initiatives as well as students tasked with completing social media marketing plans.

Keywords

Inbound marketing, content marketing, social media marketing, blogging, online marketing, social networking, thought leadership, search engine marketing.

Praise for Social Content Marketing for Entrepreneurs

"James Barry nails the details on how to build trust-based relationships through social content marketing, including how to stand out from the noise in the marketplace. Keep this book close to your side—and give it to everyone on your marketing team!

—Charlene Li,
founder and CEO of Altimeter Group,
coauthor of *Groundswell* and author of *Open Leadership*

"Moving beyond mechanical marketing tactics into creating more meaningful content and social experiences differentiates success from failure in today's digital world. Social Content Marketing for Entrepreneurs by Dr. Jim Barry is a comprehensive, can't miss guide for developing credible, authoritative marketing that connects with buyers intellectually and emotionally."

—Lee Odden, CEO,
TopRank Online Marketing and author of *Optimize*

"Social content marketing takes more than posting to online channels. Getting your audiences to know, like, and trust you requires new skills, strategies and tactics. Dr. Jim Barry makes all of them accessible and actionable in Social Content Marketing for Entrepreneurs. Do yourself a favor and make this book your guide for building business relationships."

—Ardath Albee,
B2B Marketing Strategist and author of *Digital Relevance: Marketing Content and Strategies that Drive Results*

"I've been asked to preview a lot of books, but Social Content Marketing for Entrepreneurs is one of the few to hook me and keep me interested all the way through. Jim has successfully and comprehensively organized a large, diverse, and heavily discussed field. The charts and diagrams are fascinating and useful. As a comedian who's read much of the research and books about why comedy works, I think his section on humor is an exceptional summary."

—Brian Carter,
comedian and international bestselling author of
*The Like Economy: How Businesses Make
Money with Facebook Marketing*

"I've had the opportunity to review James Barry's book 'Social Content Marketing for Entrepreneurs' and I have to say, I'm so impressed with the design and content. This book was constructed in a very unique way. Each chapter is organized for deep learning. I have written books that were used in college classrooms, but this is the one I would recommend to any teacher if they want information that is evergreen and not tied to User Interface changes on each social site. In other words, this book can be used for years in the classroom. Entrepreneurs need to know that this book will give them that 30,000 foot view of online marketing and why they need to deeply understand and participate in the structure. Mr. Barry deeply understands the social environment and he shares his wisdom freely in this book. I highly recommend it to my students and to all social media managers, consultants and business owners looking to understand social media marketing."

—Phyllis Khare,
cofounder of Social Media Manager School,
founder of TimeBliss.ME, and author of *Social Media
eLearning Kit for Dummies* and co-author of
Facebook Marketing All-in-One for Dummies.

"The number 13 has long been held to be one of the most powerful and mystical numbers. Dr. Barry has added to that lineage in this book; a simply extraordinary guided path for entrepreneurs to evolve their marketing. Each of the 13 incredible chapters are powerful, yet pragmatic, lessons. Taken as a whole, they will focus the entrepreneur to build trust, appeal emotionally and align with the customer's values—all in the name of moving business forward in today's world. Kudos to Dr. Barry for making the way forward so clear."

—Robert Rose,
chief strategy officer of Content Marketing Institute,
author of *Managing Content Marketing*

"It's been said that teaching social media is not unlike running on a sidewalk while you're paving it. But somehow James Barry has managed to wrap his arms around the rapidly changing landscape, providing readers with intuitive and useful frameworks to think about the value and application of all things social to their business. What I perhaps like most, however, is how Barry keeps the customer squarely in the center of it all, marrying old school trusted marketing principles with new school social tools. Sure the most popular platforms will no doubt change as will the top-performing tactics, but the fundamental need for entrepreneurs to break through the noise and reach their customers in a meaningful way will remain. Barry's book will help point you in the right direction."

—Sima Dahl,
America's personal branding champion,
Sway Factory, Inc.

"In this book, James covers 13 tenants crucial to successful inbound marketing. This is not a glossy overview of inbound marketing, but instead a detailed look at every step and every issue you will face as you develop your inbound strategy. Gamification? Covered. Social Media? Covered. Promotion and amplification? Covered. Email? Covered. And on and on. Whether a student or an entrepreneur this book belongs in your arsenal. And not just on your bookshelf, but right on your desk within arm's reach."

—Arnie Kuenn,
CEO of Vertical Measures and
author of *Content Marketing Works*

"I have been in sales and marketing for over 20 years, and have owned a digital marketing firm for almost 8 of those years. I am looking for great resources to help small business owners and those new to digital marketing. There are very few that are as thorough and relevant to today's marketer as Dr. Jim Barry's, Social Content Marketing for Entrepreneurs. This is a wonderful resource for anyone wanting to understand not only today's changing marketing environment, but more importantly, today's tech-savvy consumer. This should be a guidebook on every entrepreneur's bookshelf."

—Gina Schreck, president,
CEO, SocialKNX

"Jim Barry has made the subject of Relationship Marketing through Social Content easily understandable for entrepreneurs who don't have backgrounds in marketing or advertising. Devoid of jargon and hyperbole, Barry's book lays out a simple, step by step, road map which business owners can immediately implement and execute in their businesses. This practical read will replace dozens of other Social Media books full of hype but little meat. Thanks for writing this gem, Dr. Jim!"

—Kevin Knebl,
coauthor of *Social Media Sales Revolution* and
Learn Marketing with Social Media in 7 Days

"James Barry guides current and aspiring business owners through the myriad maze of social media and content marketing using easy-to-recall terms and visuals. From lead nurturing to personas to in-depth analysis of content channels like podcasts, you'll find content ideas springing up and you'll know where to promote them—and ultimately solve prospects' problems by earning their trust and respect, driving sales and brand loyalty."

—Suzanne McDonald,
new media strategist and education expert, professor,
2014 "Internet-New Media Company of the Year"
International Business Award winner

Forward by Rich Simmonds

This book will be amongst my most read . . . It has become my textbook!"
—Rich Simmonds,
voted by *Forbes* as a leading social influencer

The digital age has brought many challenges to the way we think. In fact, it asks more questions of us than we have ever imagined and constantly disrupts our thinking. Social media has become an integral part of our lives and there are people who still think of it is a virtual world, when in fact it is real life playing out in front of us. Our effectiveness in this game of life is paramount to our success. The challenge of understanding what we should be communicating and how we should be communicating remains our biggest hurdle to success.

Fortunately, we have visionaries like Jim Barry who, through his new book *Social Content Marketing for Entrepreneurs*, has had the foresight to anticipate our needs. This book has everything you need to know about social media in it.

Jim simplifies the concept of social content marketing by using acronyms like my personal favorite R-E-I-M-A-G-I-N-E-D (Repurposed to macrocontent, Expertise driven, Integrated into content platforms, Miniaturized for microcontent, Adapted to media formats, Google search friendly, Integrated in mobile platforms, News feed friendly, Engaged with others' content, Discussion framed). In my opinion, this book can be viewed as an academic masterpiece, and I am sure it will be.

This book is more than academic, however, as Jim has managed to capture the real-life aspect I referred to earlier. Chapter 3 deals with emotional communication, a factor often overlooked in the corporate world today. If you are an entrepreneur or in the corporate world, take my advice and read this book with the greatest sense of urgency you have ever had. Social media has made it possible for the David's to take on the Goliath's. Jim has provided you with every stone you need to be the most effective entrepreneur you can be.

Acknowledgments

I want to thank my Lord and Savior, Jesus Christ, who guides my every move. And to my wife, Claudia, thank you for your continuous encouragement. I also want to express my gratitude to my Dad, Jim Sr., for your never-ending support and to my daughter, Madison, for your patience during the research phase of this book. Finally, my many thanks to my reviewers and editors, Pam Didner and Dr. Victoria Crittenden, for your generosity and thorough evaluations.

Contents

Introduction

People don't believe what you tell them. They rarely believe what you show them. They often believe what their friends tell them. They always believe what they tell themselves.

—Seth Godin

Relationship Marketing through Social Content

It has been over three decades since relationship marketing has been revitalized. And now with content marketing in full swing, we see it revealed in social-media channels where consumers restrict their attention to those they *know, like,* and *trust*. To relationship marketers, this was no surprise. The move from best bargain offers to a marriage metaphor was merely waiting for a consumer who had the power to tune out marketing messages and engage with those that provide useful, timely, and relevant problem solving. And kudos to those who inspire, humor, or surprise them in the process.

What really changed was a vehicle allowing us to *walk the talk* of relationship marketing. For years, sales and marketers were coached on building trust through what amounts to speed dating. Those well versed in the 10-second elevator speech and pumped up with *sell yourself* confidence had a shot at stealing attention from someone's planned agenda. Conferences and trade shows designed around stalking prospects were a primary venue for building fast relationships. And cold calls were seen as a way to advance your prospect through a sales funnel before they had time to reflect. For many, relationship marketing was essentially a milieu of rapport building behaviors that would set the stage for future business.

Meanwhile, trust building was being examined by academia and practitioners as a smarter way to build retention. Marketers were encouraged to show evidence of their capabilities and competence in addressing their target audience's needs. Eastern and Latin America cultures then taught us to appreciate the role of benevolence, open communications, and socialization in the process.

However, many of us remember pitching these lofty aspirations to our boss as an explanation for why deals did not close. CEOs are not too receptive to ". . . If only we had a bit more time to show evidence of our candor and willingness to sacrifice our interests for theirs . . ." And since these relational attributes are not tangible, measurable, or redeemable in the short term, executives are often reluctant to wait out the benefits of long-term relationship building.

Another obstacle to the adoption of relationship marketing relates to the time and effort required to win over target audiences. When working in international business development, sales personnel used to describe our American base as "hit and run." We like to pitch our solutions and move on to the next deal. To some, it may not be in their DNA to seek out opportunities that demonstrate their helpful natures. This not only takes time, but the path to closure is also far more indirect. And to what degree will the target audience even credit them with relationship building?

This is why social content marketing rules the day. Conference schmoozing, cold calls, and sales visits can't force fit trust especially at an age when prospects conduct between two-thirds to 90 percent of their decision-making research before contacting a supplier. But a timely and relevant blog can start a trustworthy trail of problem solving. And when provided at no cost to the audience, it could signal intentions that the marketer genuinely cares about their targeted audience. What's more, when provided often enough, the blog shows evidence of subject-matter authority while conveying a knowledge of the audiences' pain points.

A challenge arises at this point, however, when brands become content publishers and add to the nearly half a billion registered blogs bombarding us with helpful advice. Add to this the amount of information shared in the past 48 hours exceeding that collected from the history of time until 2003.

How can brands stand out in this noise? It starts with connecting emotionally to our audiences through storytelling, humor, inspirational advice, acts of generosity, and visual content. And if the story sheds light on your values more than your information, audiences will not only identify with what you represent, but they may also even seek you out and spread your message.

At this point, the audience begins to *know* and *trust* you especially when social-media channels expose your intentions to the public. Brands and small businesses that grasp this advantage over a more transactional marketing approach also present themselves as a real voice backed by a real story and culture that exudes its vision and ideals. As a result, they become *likable* as well. Without content and social-media channels, there are few avenues in which to gauge a marketer's trustworthiness. In a B2B world, buyers have to resort to years of face-to-face dealings that permit enough scrutiny of a marketer's opportunistic behaviors and expertise. In a B2C world, this examination of trust often excludes any contact with a marketer or engagement with their messages unless their social followers and connections endorse them.

But when permitted by a target audience to share your expertise online, the rules of competition open new doors for entrepreneurs. Disappearing are the days where deep pockets monopolized us with ". . . buy right now and we will double the offer . . ." Instead, small businesses are discovering ways to compete with better content that is mobilized on more devices and across more relevant social channels. Often described as inbound marketing, this more permissive form of marketing lends itself to more lasting relationships. But more importantly, it opens the door for firms of limited resources to unseat the reigning incumbents of their industry.

Back to Ethos, Pathos, and Logos

Marketers are quickly recognizing that persuading audiences takes more than cleverly timed deals and broadcasted claims of distinction. It takes what Aristotle Rhetoric called ethos (credibility), pathos (appeal to emotions), and logos (authority). And there is no better way to persuade people to release their wallets on your behalf than through a genuine contribution of your social content.

So let's fast forward 2064 years from this ancient Greek treatise. Copyblogger's Brian Clarke and Amy Harrison[1] demonstrate the many parallels with what qualifies today for persuasive content. We first establish our credibility (ethos) or trustworthiness as a *thought leader* worthy of respect from those that share the same values.

With the character approved for worthy attention, thought leaders are in a ripe position to lay out their logical (logos) approach to problem solving. This is why "how to" content pieces, product evaluations, or useful apps have to resonate with what audience's deem as relevant to their pain points. This takes more than supporting evidence; it requires a consistent message. But where the most strides have been made in recent years by brands and small businesses is in the use of stories that help audiences visualize their pain points and promising future. This appeal to an audience's heartfelt emotions (pathos) or imagination creates a more lasting bond than can be made under the best of logical arguments. Moreover, it sets the stage for audiences to identify with the content provider. This is why fan engagement, entertaining content, and brand personality have been the most discussed subjects among advocates of social content marketing.

The 13 E's of Inbound Marketing

Using relationship marketing and Aristotle's *Rhetoric* as an academic foundation for justifying why we are witnessing this current state of inbound marketing, the remainder of this book lays out the strategic guidelines for entrepreneurs to follow in their social content-marketing efforts. One way to manage the progression of social content planning steps is to follow the 13 E's of inbound marketing laid out in this book across three parts described as follows:

- getting audiences to talk;
- getting audiences to raise your content; and
- getting audiences to react.

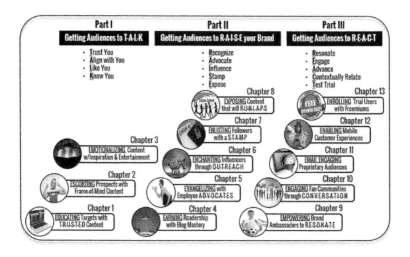

Educating Targets with T-R-U-S-T-E-D Content

Covered in Chapter 1, the start of any social-media marketing planning has to include a roadmap to educating target audiences. As any potential consumer or buyer will gladly let us know, no one wants to be sold. If prospects are conducting their own research online rather than contacting sales personnel, the job of marketers is to educate them in the hopes of moving them further down the sales funnel and getting credit for problem solving in the process. The better the education, the greater the opportunities to showcase expertise. The goal here is to gain credibility as a subject-matter expert by offering T-R-U-S-T-E-D (timely, relevant, useful, situational, transparent, engaging, and deliverable) content.

Escorting Prospects through Frame-of-Mind Connections

Once the content is jump-started in part through search engines and social networks, Chapter 2 demonstrates how to escort your prospects as they advance through their buyer journey. Known in some circles as lead nurturing, this process requires the repurposing and sequencing of content to where it fits the audience's *frame of mind*. And by creating the right e-Books, webinars, podcasts, videos, or case studies, we can begin to connect with our prospects. The goal here is to leverage social CRM, e-mail, and effective lead nurturing strategies to ensure that our prospects are greeted with the right content at the right time. But paramount to success are permission-based marketing practices backed by a provider that audiences *know, like,* and *trust.*

Emotionalizing Content with Entertainment, Inspiration, and Visuals

As discussed in Chapter 3, once the content is crafted along the pain points felt by targeted personas, its mark of distinction and usefulness has to be amplified over the ever-growing noise from content infobesity. This means S-H-I-P-P-I-N-G (through surprise, humanizing, inspiration, playfulness, passion, imagery, narratives, and generosity) your content with an emotional twist. This chapter highlights the growing demand for content that is highly entertaining, inspirational, and visual. It deals with those aspects of your content strategy that get audiences to *like* you.

Earning Readership with Content Mastery

As hundreds of millions register their blogs to begin the courtship with their prospects, we are now witnessing a new generation of spam. Only the spam in this case is the content itself. Bloggers are promoting their posts much like the way ads pummel us with their one-way messaging. Besides incorporating emotion, Chapter 3 discusses ways to captivate your readers through content that is

- T-U-N-E-D (trended, user generated, niched, evergreen, digestible) for audience connection;
- F-O-C-U-S-E-D (frequent, optimized, cross-platform, unique, shareable, eye-catching, documented for SEO) on audience attraction; and
- consistently created with high Q-U-A-L-I-T-Y (quick, unbiased, advisory, lead generating, image intensive, talk-worthy, your voice).

Evangelizing with Employee A-D-V-O-C-A-T-E-S

Successful social-media marketers understand the power of employee advocates. And by adopting a passionate culture within a well-coordinated social business, employees can become your greatest advocates. They are the most trusted and connected source to target audiences at a time when the growing demand for social media is stretching internal resources to their limits. Chapter 5 discusses how companies are evangelizing through employee A-D-V-O-C-A-T-E-S (amplification on personal accounts, delivery of brand experiences, voices, oversight of brand ambassadors, content creation, activism, trusted communications, engagement, and scaling of brand relationships).

Enchanting Influencers through O-U-T-R-E-A-C-H

Much like the role played by these advocates, influencers are key to spreading brand stories that would otherwise stall out. Audience growth at any stage of social-media development inevitably requires the help of key influencers who benefit from big audiences and a lot of clout. But not unlike fans, influencers only stick around for as long as you provide value to them. A key influencer strategy is to cocreate and promote content that helps them with their audiences.

With their reach, relevance, and resonance, Chapter 6 describes how influencers have social capital that lend extensive O-U-T-R-E-A-C-H (organic reach, user relationships, topical relevance, endorsement credibility, authority within a concentrated community, compelling content, and hubs of important conversation) to those that effectively court them.

The chapter also discusses what it takes to discovery and romance influencers through O-U-T-R-E-A-C-H (opportunities for influencer blogging, unique or unannounced content, thought leadership platforms, recognition, easy engagement, authentication through research, common interest pursuits, and helping their causes).

Enlisting Followers with a S-T-A-M-P

Each fan, follower, and connection that touches your content has audiences in the hundreds on average. So when they provide an e-mail address—perhaps through some fan-welcoming incentive—your rolodex can explode. Ideally, we want to exploit social-networking channels for their reach and subscription incentives for proprietary audience development. In Chapter 7, we explain how to enlist followers with a S-T-A-M-P (social networking strategy, thought leadership strategy, advertising strategy, media relations strategy, and profile strategy).

Exposing Content that Will R-U-N-L-A-P-S

One aspect for amplifying your content requires it to be pinned, posted, or updated on channels where fans and followers hangout. And for the content to gain momentum, Chapter 8 shows how it has to be talk-, share-, and link-worthy. Native advertising in particular has shown great promise in promoting content. Especially when hypertargeted or formatted as native advertising, today's audiences often appreciate its contextual relevance. The goal here is to blaze a trail of trustworthy content at the top of the funnel while earning new followers in the process.

Empowering Brand Ambassadors to R-E-S-O-N-A-T-E

Chapter 9 explains how empowering your biggest fans can trigger engagement with your audiences while helping spread a consistent story. Now with the addition of easily shared social content, brands are seeing how this untapped resource is ideal for sharing product information, resolving customer issues, and sharing great customer experiences. Knowing this

power that brand ambassadors have, many are empowering ambassadors to R-E-S-O-N-A-T-E (rally around their mission, embrace their story, share content, offer insights, neutralize negative sentiments, act on their behalf, tap into their own communities, and enlist others).

Engaging Fan Communities through C-O-N-V-E-R-S-A-T-I-O-N

An experienced social-media marketer knows that fans and followers disappear without your relentless engagement. That is why many of them sponsor contest, events, and games to keep their crowds involved. And this goes beyond customer acquisition. Customers need to be turned to fans who in turn drive even more customers. The key to developing the right venue and behavior to engage communities is to understand where they hang out and what they expect on their platform of choice. To be effective, Chapter 10 discusses how engagement has to involve a C-O-N-V-E-R-S-A-T-I-O-N (contests, open dialogs, negative complaint handling, exclusivity, responsiveness, sharing customer stories, ask and answer dialogs, twitter chats, interactive infographics, opinion polls, and networking groups).

E-mail Engaging and Perpetuating Proprietary Audiences

A looming concern of brands and other firms is their vulnerability to social-media platforms that continually change their rules. No longer can firms count on organically reaching their audience news feeds. Platforms like Facebook have forced a "pay-to-play" avenue for fan exposure. As explained in Chapter 11, this is pressuring firms to develop proprietary audiences that wean them off social networks. Using combinations of e-mail addresses and mobile IDs, brands are exploiting the subscription channels to gain control over their audience conversations. In the process, they are exploiting look-alike and other custom audience features from the social networks to continually expand their audience of followers-turned subscribers. Chapter 11 further discusses the types of strategies to adopt—once e-mails are captured—so as to escort these proprietary audiences through a sales funnel.

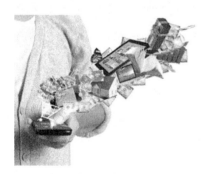

Enabling Mobile C-U-S-T-O-M-E-R Experiences

No doubt the ponential shift from desktop to mobile devices has empowered all of us to demand information on our smartphones, tablets, and even wearable technology. And as big data predictive analytics and geo-located technologies continue to mature, audiences are expecting content to arrive in real time and in the right SoLoMo (social, local, mobile) context. Chapter 12 demonstrates how you can capitalize on the mobile customer experience gap using real-time marketing apps and behavioral data for mobile shopping and context marketing.

Enrolling Trial Users with Freemiums

As consumers get accustomed to their real-time mobile content responses, a question arises as to if and when charges should be applied by marketers for use of the app. Especially when the app provides utility in the form of real-time problem solving, marketers

are faced with a tough dilemma. Given that 90–99 percent of the over 1 million apps are now downloadable free of charge, most brands see the role of freemiums as a wiser choice than charger for apps. Chapter 13 discusses how freemiums can be exploited to showcase brand competence while getting sales-ready prospects to test trial an offer.

Notes

1. "Aristotle's Ancient Guide to Compelling Copy" by Copyblogger's Amy Harrison (bit.ly/1yqnwWU) and "The Force that Powers Persuasive Content (And 3 Ways to Intensify It)" by Copyblogger's Brian Clark (bit.ly/1sdAku0

PART 1

Getting Audiences to T-A-L-K

A good first step in any social content-marketing plan is to lay out the elements required to get your target audiences to T-A-L-K. In the next three chapters, we will find out how social media gets your potential prospects to

1. Trust you (Chapter 1)
2. Align with you (Chapter 2)
3. Like you (Chapter 3)
4. Know you (Chapter 1).

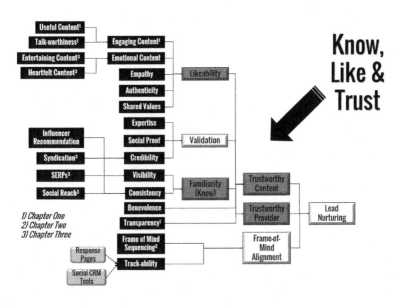

Summary Model of Factors Getting Audiences to T-A-L-K

CHAPTER 1

Educating Targets with T-R-U-S-T-E-D Content

Traditional marketing talks at people. Content marketing talks with them.

—Doug Kessler, Cofounder of Velocity

Did you ever imagine a world without cold calling or interrupting ads? How about one where marketers share their secrets for free? There go all of our textbooks on baiting audience attention and holding them hostage to switching costs and the remorse of lost opportunities.

But in the immortal words of Charles Dickens, these are "the best of times and the worst of times." As quickly as sales personnel and marketing communications departments are departing their professions, brand publishers and entrepreneurs are relishing the opportunity to unseat the big dogs in their industries with content-marketing strategies. Instead of watching deep pocket competitors monopolize billboards, commercials, and print ads, smaller businesses can outflank them in audience exposure and engagement with carefully crafted blogs, webinars, and e-Books that *help* rather than *sell*. In essence, they let their content do the talking and only when asked.

The first stage of any social content plan should begin with discovering and qualifying conversational topics that could stir up the passions of your intended audience while inviting you to demonstrate your trust. This trust with a targeted audience is created to a large degree by the content itself. One way to look at this is to consider the evidence backing a society's migration away from transactional marketing to relationship marketing. The latter is driven primarily by communications, trustworthy actions, expertise, and social bonding. Contrast this with sales offers and promises of great deals often associated with transactional marketing.

Relationship marketing theories posit that trust is the result of benevolent activities—like donating advice without expecting something in return. This implies that new comers to a community must show their willingness to help before promoting any offers. These offers not only suggest opportunism, but they also preempt your opportunities to get invited to communities thriving as much on research advice as on *what to buy*.

But how can this be done online? Why not start with content that benefits your targeted community through education or by feeding a passion? For example, *American Express* hosts an advice sharing platform, known as the Open Forum, which provides valuable information to entrepreneurs on running their businesses. Consequently, they have rejuvenated their credit card image as one that helps start-ups and early business growth. In the process, they entered their audience's sphere of influence.

Once invited to an audience's sphere of influence, relationship marketing theories suggest that these prospects will subsequently subject you to a series of trustworthiness exercises through ongoing communications and information disclosure. This may include a request for more content or an examination of your willingness to participate in a nonopportunistic manner.

In theory, we could build trails of trustworthy blogs at the top of the sales funnel to encourage deeper engagement with audiences as they advance through their buying journey. These blog posts and other forms of light content at the top of the sales funnel allow audiences to test our expertise and helpfulness before diving into more in-depth webinars and e-Books. In the process, we share valuable advice in order to build trust that is worthy of an invite.

At this point, this may sound more like marriage counseling than marketing. Exactly! Imagine your targeted persona starting with: ". . .We don't want to hear from you; furthermore, we don't trust you. Our attention is determined by our peer recommendations and what we read on our own. . ."

Now envision what happens when you continually provide your prospect with information that addresses their job security or ignites their passions. Could they become dependent on that information? Moreover, would they mentally position your brand in a better light? Suppose they see you as a corporate citizen, or a socially responsible, goodwill ambassador, or a charitable community giver? Okay, that might be a stretch, but you get the picture.

Yes, we are asked to share competitive secrets and provide free content while waiting for an invite from our target audience. This would make sense given nearly everyone's aversion to unpermitted marketing messages. However, it obviously raises concerns among marketing traditionalists taught to guard their secrets while holding on to their trump cards. In their mind, overpublicizing their problem solving not only helps the competition, but it also makes the marketer more vulnerable to audiences exploiting their free contributions. Add to this the growing demand to discuss thorny issues like pricing, installation challenges, and competitive comparisons, and you can see why traditional marketers are hesitant to embrace inbound marketing.

Letting Trusted Content Do Your Talking

A question often arises why would marketers spend time and money for target audiences to download the marketer's free content only to wait for an invite? When marketed correctly, useful content during the awareness stage of the buying cycle can leave a trail of expertise backed by a *likable* persona. And if delivered free and without wanting something in return, marketers can be credited with thoughtful contributions and *empathy*. Overtime, the audience may seek out the content provider as a *trustworthy* source of timely, relevant, and useful information.

Now imagine doing this with ads and cold calls or what is normally referred to as *outbound* marketing. Where is the trail of expertise and trustworthiness when the media of communications and delivery channels are inherently one way and rolled out as repeat doses of "call now"? Let's face it. Today's consumers hold little trust in our promises and will demand a trail of trustworthy advice before inviting use to help. What's more, they have the power to ignore our unwanted e-mails and unidentified calls while fast forwarding through our commercials. Instead, they conduct their own online evaluations and consult with social-networking friends as their trusted advisors.

To fit this new mindset, we have to embrace a more *inbound* marketing approach that ultimately creates a higher level of trust between you and your target audiences. And to do this effectively, it's the content itself—not your preemptive call—that has to show evidence of expertise, customer understanding, and impartiality. Otherwise, the audience senses opportunism and a potential supplier incapable of addressing their pain points. To be credited as the favored solution provider, the content not only has to be seen as useful and relevant, but it also has to be seen as trustworthy. Finally, marketers are quickly discovering the merits of adopting content formats that suit their audiences' channel preferences for reading, viewing, or listening to your advice.

Timely Content around Urgencies and Consumption Routines

One way to get your target audience to appreciate your timely content is to address urgent situations early in their buying stage. The example shown in Figure 1.1 illustrates how a real-estate accountant educated his property management and Home Owner Association (HOA) audiences on what to do with a recent county regulation. At the time when condos and housing associations were faced with serious economic issues, HOA boards were looking for sources of cash to offset foreclosures. One method to solve this problem was to liquidate reserves applied against potential property damage. But when a county ruling restricted the use of reserves as a cash source, HOAs faced tough choices on how to fund budget shortfalls.

Figure 1.1 Accounting Example of Exploiting an Urgent Situation

A savvy real-estate accountant used this opportunity to connect with an urgent pain point. Starting with what the ruling implied, and continuing through the decision cycle with alternative workarounds, timely content was aligned with the HOA's frame of mind from awareness to decision. The accountant, in this case, was credited with providing an objective response to an urgent issue.

Another way to ensure a timely consumption of your content is to understand the routine your audiences follow in checking their e-mail, tweets, or posts. Knowing their consumption patterns can make a difference in whether your content gets on their radar at the right time. Many tools like Klout's scheduler shown in Figure 1.2 will let you know when

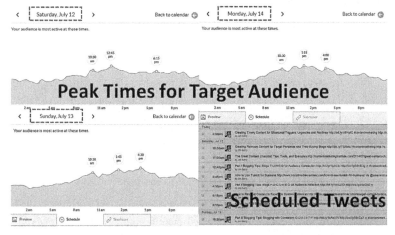

Figure 1.2 Timing Tweeted Content with Audience Peak Activity

your audience is most active across each day of the week. Their scheduler, along with that of Hootsuite, TweetDeck, and others, allow you to tweet your content to meet these peak periods.

Relevant Content for Target Personas and Their Buying Stage

If your content marketing is for everybody, it's for nobody
—Joe Pulizzi, author of *Epic Content*

One of the most common complaints expressed by brands and entrepreneurs is the inability of their e-mail marketing to yield high open and click through rates. Invariably, the low rates are blamed on e-mail content or messaging that failed to connect with the target audience. The same holds true for content postings on blogs or social media. In a growing climate of infobesity, relevance is arguably the most critical attribute of any content intended to educate its target audiences.

For content to be truly relevant, it has to resonate with a persona's pain points or passions. A test of relevance could start with the following questions proposed by content-marketing strategist, Joe Pulizzi:[1]

1. Who is the audience and specific buyer persona you are targeting for each piece of content?
2. What's the pain point you are solving for them?
3. Is what you are saying really that important?
4. Could they find the information elsewhere?

But the process of first discovering the relevant personas is not as simple as framing clients with monikers like "Debbie Downer" and "Soccer Moms." Unless the persona evaluation leads to distinctions on what topics intrigue each persona or where they hang out, the evaluation serves little purpose.

If, on the other hand, an examination is made of the audience subtleties that reveal distinct pain points or passionate interests, any blog post, webinar, or mobile app aimed at these persona nuances has a chance of at least being viewed by a target audience. Where the rubber meets the road on delivering relevant content is when it reveals a rich enough insight into each personas interest that the marketer is credited with intimately knowing the targeted persona as well as speaking their language.

To do this effectively, the following audits and analyses should be conducted as a prelude to discovery relevant topics:

1. An audit of the spending motivations behind current target audiences (i.e., why was your offering selected?).
2. An examination of distinct psychographic personas most associated with each spending motivation.
3. An analysis of the traits, wants, and passions associated with each persona.
4. A translation of these personas attributes need-oriented topics of interest.

Notice how this was down for the case of a custom tailor shown in Figure 1.3. Starting with why target audiences pulled out their wallet, four spending motivations were discovered. Customers of the tailored suits were either seeking (1) perfection, (2) pleasing others, (3) prominence, or (4) posturing. But when further examining the psychographic attributes of personas, 12 distinct personas were discovered, each with distinct traits, wants, and passions.

Although this seems like an overkill, a scan of the 12 personas should convince you that these folks don't hang out in the same circles; nor do they expect the same lifestyle image from their tailored suits. Each one showed distinct enough persona traits and passions to warrant dedicated content topics especially at the top of the funnel (ToFu).

Continuing with the analysis, each persona attribute now allows a consolidation of needs traced back to the spending motivations. This begins the process of defining relevant content without having to build 12 different segment strategies. In this case, 11 topics were compiled for potential blog content that addressed the following pain points:

1. not fitting in desired social circles;
2. inability to exude charisma; and
3. fear of embarrassment from inappropriate etiquette or attire.

Target Audience 1: PERFECTION
Persona 1: Metro Males
- Traits: Narcissistic
- Wants: Admiration
- Passions: Grooming & Fashion

Persona 2: Red Carpets
- Traits: Pampered
- Wants: Entitlements
- Passions: Global Business

Persona 3: Featured Attractions
- Traits: Honored
- Wants: Elegance
- Passions: Performing Arts

Target Audience 2: PLEASING
Persona 4: Father of the Bride
- Traits: Sentimental
- Wants: Unspoiled Daughter Day
- Passions: Weddings

Persona 5: Sommeliers
- Traits: Accommodating
- Wants: Refinement
- Passions: Fine Hospitality

Persona 6: Podium Pleasers
- Traits: Charismatic
- Wants: Inspiring Audiences
- Passions: Motivational Speaking

Target Audience 3: PROMINENCE
Persona 7: Saville Rows
- Traits: Classy
- Wants: Sophistication
- Passions: Luxury Craftsmanship

Persona 8: Polo Clubbers
- Traits: Cultured
- Wants: Etiquette
- Passions: Prestigious Club Events

Persona 9: Monte Carlo Black Ties
- Traits: Extravagant
- Wants: Upscale Nightlife
- Passions: Casinos

Target Audience 4: POSTURING
Persona 10: Proud Patrons
- Traits: Proud
- Wants: Stature
- Passions: High Society Life

Persona 11: Primetimes
- Traits: Boastful
- Wants: Flamboyance
- Passions: Celebrity Mingling

Persona 12: Trump's Apprentices
- Traits: Professional
- Wants: Swagger
- Passions: Fast Track Leadership

Target Audiences (Spending Motivation) / Persona	PERFECTION			PLEASING			PROMINENCE			POSTURING		
	Metro Males	Red Carpets	Featured Attractions	Father of the Bride	Sommeliers	Podium Pleasers	Saville Rows	Polo Clubbers	Monte Carlo Black Ties	Proud Patrons	Primetimes	Trump's Apprentices
NEEDS ORIENTED TOPICS OF INTEREST												
Topic 1: Affirming Society Stature	✓	✓					✓	✓		✓		
Topic 2: Networking in Prominent		✓					✓			✓		✓
Topic 3: Boosting Celebrity Status	✓								✓	✓	✓	
Topic 4: Flaunting Physical Prowess	✓									✓		
Topic 5: Performing for Audiences			✓								✓	
Topic 6: Impressing Clients		✓	✓									✓
Topic 7: Attending Gala Events	✓	✓	✓	✓				✓	✓		✓	
Topic 8: Celebrating in Style	✓	✓	✓	✓		✓			✓		✓	
Topic 9: Closing Deals		✓										✓
Topic 10: Reinforcing Corporate Image		✓			✓	✓						✓
Topic 11: Indulging Fine Taste					✓			✓	✓			

Figure 1.3 Persona Evaluation for Custom Tailors

Topics were developed as a way to brainstorm helpful tips that address these pain points. But without knowing the personalities associated with each spending motivation, pain points are difficult to derive. Consider the case of an organic food supplier whose target audiences include chefs seeking worry-free appetizers; mothers looking for nutrition for baby development; adults seeking hair and skin development; and those suffering from inflammatory diseases. The latter, in turn, consists of three personas: a *Deprived Athlete*, the *Closet Bound*, and the *Les Miserable*.

Each of the personas has highly distinct pain points. For example, the *Deprived Athlete* is mainly concerned with high burst performance in high pollen conditions. The *Closet Bound* is concerned with disguising ailments. And the *Les Miserable* needs energy and lifted spirits to get through the day. Collectively, the target audience (inflammatory diseases) needs relief and could perhaps benefit from natural remedies; however, their specific pains points require very different content. For a more complete evaluation of more small business personas and the process used to derive relevant content, you can download the e-Book found at http://slidesha.re/1mMqovu.

Useful Content for Research, Self-Help, and Decision Tools

Instead of one-way interruption, Web marketing is about delivering useful content at just the precise moment that a buyer needs it.
— David Meerman Scott, author of *The New Rules of Marketing and PR*

Equally as important as content being timely and relevant is the need for it to be useful. For content to be *useful*, you have to be *helpful*. If it doesn't help your audience in their research, decision making, or fixing something on the spot, it gets archived at best and trashed at worst.

At the top of the sales funnel, when audiences are researching solutions to their primary needs (e.g., image, career transitioning, health, etc.), helpfulness can be enlightenment. Content that sheds light on their possibilities for changing their image, improving their health, or transitioning to a new career, for example, could help them in their research. Any assistance you provide in laying out a criterion for solving their problems could be just as helpful as making them decide on a course of action. This is where blogging becomes especially important as an opportunity for you to help them narrow their choices.

In the middle-of-the-funnel (MoFu) consideration and evaluation stages, audiences then begin to seek out product reviews, spec sheets, "how to" demos, webinars, and case studies. The more your content helps complete their compliance check lists, the more useful it becomes when conducting their evaluations. In fact, with audiences now spending upward of 90 percent of their decision-making research before contacting a supplier, it's apparent that MoFu content is considered by many to be useful enough to thwart off sales calls.

But where the usefulness of content becomes especially critical is at the bottom of the funnel (BoFu). Banks, tax accountants, and realtors often provide apps for mortgage calculations in the later stages of buying. Similarly, product suppliers can easily provide usage demos, installation instructions, or nutritional content in digital formats that warns prospects in advance of potential complications. In so doing, the prospect has one more piece to complete their evaluation.

Indium Corporation, a maker of specialty alloys and solder paste, hosts a highly popular blog for engineers talking to other engineers. Rather than pitching the benefits of their solder paste, the firm hyper-targets engineers who have questions about industrial soldering equipment. The 10 blogs and 15 writers always talk about matters relevant to Indium's target audience. As a result, the potential prospects benefit from content useful to their routine practice. And by encouraging comments and dialog exchange, the company has drastically cut their technical support costs in the process.

Add to these decision-making tools the growing reliance on location-based tools, and the growing demand for useful content becomes more evident. Especially in this day of appification, target audiences are accustomed to having apps handle their emergencies and real-time inquires.

As explained well in Jay Baer's book *Youtility*, and in Chapter 9, content marketers are finding clever ways to provide real-time solutions to customers facing urgent pain points. A widely downloaded app for stain removals is sponsored by Clorox. Although much of their researched advice goes well beyond the scope of their offerings, the app addresses some immediate ways to address recently spilled substances like wine before it is too late. Similarly, Ortho has an app that will help you identify and treat harmful weeds before it is too late. In both cases, these brands are counted on target audiences crediting them with real-time responses to urgent problems.

Finding the Useful Content that Strikes a Chord with Targeted Audiences

Knowing what content can be most useful to your audience may seem like an overwhelming task because of the myriad of options to consider in content formats and media tactics. Your content strategy should not only address what content to include, but it should also center on how audiences prefer to access this content. But if you start by answering the what, why, and how content is delivered in your industry, you may discovery a structured approach to managing your content development efforts.

Target audiences in the social-media ecosystem are comfortable with media familiarity; so if these audiences regular tune in podcasts, this would be a good place to start. Similarly, if the communication format is highly imagery based, there is no sense in shifting their attention to fact sheets.

Where many struggle in this area of content defining is in getting the process started. Consider the following three-tiered approach to mapping our content elements. And exclude entertaining content for the moment. This will be covered in Chapter 3.

1. *Defining the purpose*: Is the content meant to instruct, inform, or evaluate?
2. *Selecting a preferred communication mode*: Will the mode of communication be text, audio, image, or video based?
3. *Identifying the right media tactics*: Will the audience expect blogs, newsletters, e-Books, white papers, videos, reports, articles, webinars, case studies, or apps?

Selecting Content Tactics that Balance Expertise, Objectives, and Usability

The process starts with an understanding of content purpose. How does your audience want to be taught? And will they benefit more from learning *how to* do something; gaining *insights* on their business practice; or making quick and accurate *choices* on solving their problems?

In general, educational content used successfully in B2B and B2C arenas tends to be either instructional, informative, or decision helpful.

The informative side can be further divided into insights and intelligence gathering. Collectively, they provide the core of what audiences will find useful throughout their buying stages.

Instructional Aids

One effective way to meet this goal is to use product demonstrations or instructional videos that explain "how to" do something related to some benefits offered by your firm's offerings. Consider how often we use the Internet to accomplish something like training a dog or cooking a meal. In fact, if you search for "how to tie a tie," you'll find videos garnering over 20 million views.

Our target audiences have the same challenges and could benefit from your stepping them through a solution. As a result, tutorials become especially useful in the awareness and consideration stage of the buying cycle. They also allow you to demonstrate your expertise and credibility before committing to the more research-intensive content required in the evaluations and decision-making stages.

A related instructional technique involves the use of checklists, to-do lists, and budget planners. In this case, audiences may appreciate the advice you provide in managing their tasks more efficiently. That is why realtors compile moving and inspection lists or why outdoor recreation suppliers offer lists of items to pack.

Business Insights

To keep up with the latest trends in their field of interests, target audiences often benefit from the latest news or business trends. As a content marketer, you can create or curate content that keeps the audiences well informed. Like instructional aids, these topics provide an opportunity to build subject matter authority.

Most often, these insights are gathered from expert interviews, research, and industry forums. Interviews, in particular, are a great way to provide business insights. By interviewing experts who have professional knowledge in the topics of interest to your audience, you not only provide a fresh perspective but also can take a break from your own content creation efforts. Moreover, the two-party interaction provides a more stimulating listening and viewing environment than even the best of talking head formats.

Other ways to provide expert commentary include the use of discussion forums where threaded conversations help answer your audience's business challenges or personal passions. LinkedIn, in particular, provides a great way for you to build thought leadership by responding to questions posed by members fitting the profile of your targeted audiences.

Oftentimes, these insightful commentaries can be gathered by highlighting main attractions at an event. For example, content marketers often curate news clips of important announcements and expert opinions collected from industry conferences, conventions, and shows. Audiences not only benefit from missed sessions, but they also save time in reading a more condensed synopsis of key takeaways.

Research can also provide opportunities to help audiences seeking insightful business intelligence. Hungry for industry statistics and technology solutions, B2B buyers appreciate the empirical data derived from survey results as well as digital conference papers or technical briefs addressing their operational pain points.

For a less-demanding form of insightful content, content marketers often resort to news reporting. Whether it's an editorial on industry trends, coverage of an event or a breaking announcement about a firm of interest, audiences benefit from time saved in keeping up to date. And by repeatedly releasing insightful news, your audiences eventually look forward to seeing your updates.

Decision Aids

A third way to provide useful content is to help your target audiences with decision making. Starting from the consideration phase of the buying cycle, audiences benefit from your helping them make up their minds. Any content that addresses the evaluation of suitable offerings or permits a test trial saves your audience's time while boosting their confidence in making the right choice.

This is where reviews, ratings, rankings, and buyer's guides become invaluable resources to your target audiences. Assuming that the reviews of solutions relevant to your audience's pain points are not biased toward your own offerings, the recommendations further add to your credibility as a subject-matter expert. The same applies to fact sheets and blogs that address frequently asked questions (FAQs).

Another way to help an audience in their decision making is to provide convincing examples of how an offering like yours can help them. Virtual tours and customer success stories are among the content forms that can provide this evidence provided they are not self-serving. Credible testimonies, especially from notable thought leaders, can also help in this evaluation stage.

But the decision often requires a physical touch and feel before a target audience reaches for their wallet. In these days of *freemiums*, audiences expect branded content tools ranging from product previews to free test trial apps. This is why brands have stepped up to return on investment (ROI) calculators, configurators, trackers, and other interactive content. These mobile apps and widgets provide a real-time examination of what the audience intends to buy. Consequently, it represents one of the most critical components of a content-marketing strategy.

Selecting Content Delivery Formats that Balance Consistency and Audience Familiarity

For content to truly resonate with an audience, its format has to suit their channel preferences and the time they allocate to reading, listening, or viewing it. When used for educational purposes, the following content has a proven track record of success:

1. podcasts
2. explainer videos
3. virtual seminars
4. customer success stories
5. blogs
6. infographics
7. e-Books
8. e-newsletters
9. authoritative articles
10. slideware
11. branded content tools and apps.

Podcasts

Without a doubt, the most popular form of audio used in content marketing today is a radio stationlike podcast, or simply downloadable audio programs that play on a computer, iPod, or smartphones. The digitally compressed files are delivered over the Internet to a subscriber, who can then download the content at a time of their choosing.

The content is often distributed via a really simple syndication (RSS) feed that alerts audiences of updates soon after the release of an episode. This allows audiences to subscribe to and get alerts of new content much like they experience with a new blog post. Podcast episodes can be downloaded to subscribers from syndicated directories like iTunes, Sound Cloud, or Stitcher. Because the downloaded audio clips are released as continuous clips or episodes, marketers have jumped on this opportunity to emulate radio talk shows.

What has created excitement over recent years for marketers is the growing number of audiences who are now aware of podcasting. This year approximately 39 million Americans will listen to podcasts each month, with 1 in 5 weekly podcast users consuming 6 or more podcasts per week. Helping to fuel this growth is a growing number of audiences more inclined to deal with its technical requirements. For example, you can now get your podcast episode delivered direct to a smartphone without having to hook up an iPod to the computer. This comfort with the technology has led to Apple announcing their one billionth podcast subscription logged on the iTunes store. And Pew Research confirms that over one quarter of Internet users listen to podcasts.

Percentage of Internet Users Who Listen to Podcasts

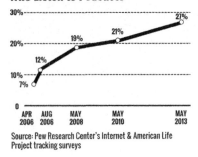

Source: Pew Research Center's Internet & American Life Project tracking surveys

This ability to target anyone through subscription makes this audio content especially suitable to building thought leadership. Successful podcasters will argue that narrowcasting—or targeted your niche to specific personas—is what allows podcasting to overtake radio shows. Compare, for example, the impact a radio broadcast has on its audience. Being limited geographically, they have to appeal to a wide spectrum of interests. Podcasting, on the other hand, can address a worldwide audience that has specific interests. Overtime, the podcast host has an opportunity to build authority and credibility by addressing specific pain points or passions felt by the targeted audience.

For a podcast to be effective, it helps to limit its time to that of an average commute. Venture capitalist, Mary Meeker, says there are 52 minutes of unclaimed time in the car every day, and people are seeking things like podcasts to fill it. As a venue for narrowcasting, it is especially crucial to narrow your audience theme to something very specific. And then stick to the same theme throughout episodes as audiences will know what to expect.

Among the most popular applications for podcasting is the interviewing of experts and other guests. Often through a simple Skype or phone connection, these audiences are sometimes encouraged to share their industry perspectives. Other techniques include a cohosted talk show that regularly updates their audience with trended news and tricks of the trade. Finally, a growing number of podcasters are using their episodes to highlight major industry show activities and events. The audio and video podcast formats, in this case, work well in capturing roundtable discussions, debates, and conference presentations.

As perhaps the one type of content that absolutely needs a scheduled release, podcasting should only be attempted by those who can be passionate enough to host every week. Finally, for a podcast to gain listener insight, it's imperative to link the audio content to a blog that accommodates user feedback.

When produced and distributed effectively, expert podcasters normally cite the following as among the key benefits derived from the use of podcasting:

1. *Super fans*: Podcasting offers far more of a personal connection than what you can get from a blog post. It allows for the show host to convey passions, emotions, and feelings. And especially when mixed with fun facts and motivational speakers, the show can create a sense of loyalty among avid followers. Overtime, audiences begin to share their own stories, thereby creating a sense of intimacy with a tight community. Some podcast experts believe this is the perfect formula for creating brand evangelists.

2. *Audience accessibility*: Audiences unable to attend seminars during their busy work schedules are using commute and exercise time to listen to audio tutorials and business news. Driving a car is prime podcast-listening time where an estimated 15 billion hours of time is spent per year by Americans who drive alone in their cars.[2] And according to Edison Research and Arbitron, 23 percent of existing podcast listeners play digital audio in their car almost every day.[3]

3. *Worldwide narrowcasting*: There is power when your show has a niche focus. You can not only pinpoint your message to qualified listeners, but you can also expand your reach to anyone possessing a smartphone, iPod, or computer. This essentially makes the content marketer a program manager for their own global radio station.

4. *Top to BoFu Relevance*: Dan Miller, an expert podcaster, points out that no other form of content invites people into the sales process like podcasting. Podcasting uniquely fits the early stage of trust and rapport building where the host can walk their audience through common business challenges. Later, the broadcasting of events and highlighting of news can acquaint listeners with your expertise. And as audiences reach the consideration and evaluation stage, podcasters can field FAQs as well as invite audiences to share their successes.

5. *Affordability*: You likely already have the equipment you need to podcast. All that is required is a microphone (including a built-in mike in your laptop) and software or sound-mixing apps for recording and editing audio. Many of the popular programs like Audacity

and GarageBand offer free downloads. Podcast costs normally start at $100 per show. But if you're looking for radio-quality results, expect to pay around $350 per episode.[4]

6. *Competitive head start*: Despite the rising number of podcast listeners, few marketers have taken this route. A study by Social Media Examiner found that only 6 percent of marketers offer a podcast, but 28 percent want to improve their knowledge of podcasting. Moreover, 33 percent marketers want to start podcasting this year.[5] This provides a great opportunity for marketers to gain a competitive advantage.

7. *Mobile*: The number of listeners who access podcasts by mobile device is now higher than the number who downloads a podcast from their desktop computer (Next/Market). And with over 7 billion mobile devices in use around the world (Cisco), it is only a matter of time before the greater population realizes the advantages of narrowcasting for a growing "on the go" society. Add to that the accelerating growth of smartphones, car-connecting devices, and iTunes adoption, and it is not surprise that podcasters are so bullish in their forecasts.

8. *Evergreen content*: The format of a podcasts lends itself well to evergreen content or the type of content that stands the test of time. Shows featuring how-to tips or personal stories, in particular, can maintain their relevancy over several years.

9. *Time-lapsed recordings*: Podcasts are an excellent way to capture lectures, presentations, and even virtual conferences for playback to people who missed the live setting.

10. *Influence marketing*: Including guest speakers with relevant audience expertise is a great way to extend your community influence.

11. *Multimode*: Besides audio podcasts, video podcasts have emerged from MP4 technology. But perhaps more promising for business professionals are "slidecasts" that merge audio files and PowerPoints to form self-contained presentations like webinars.

12. *Repurposed content*: Audio content from a show's episode can easily be repurposed for infographics, e-mail marketing, articles, blogs, and e-Books.

13. *Qualified Listeners*: Unlike traditional radio, podcasting allows you to narrowcast a specific audience so as to address more qualified listeners.

14. *Easy distribution*: Audio content can be readily distributed across different networks. Most podcasts are uploaded through iTunes simply through the "submit a podcast" from the iTunes storefront. Once recorded, podcasters can easily park the episode alongside a related blog post since most blog content management systems accommodate audio files.

15. *Search results*: iTunes is a massive search engine for content that serves 575 million subscribers. Although not as fine tuned as Google search, there are many ways you can maximize your exposure in the iTunes search listings.

Video podcasts, in particular, have shown exceptional performance in search results. These podcasts essentially combine the audio component of podcasting with visual media. You see this quite often on sites that provide quick demos. A dentist in Fort Lauderdale, for example, raised his site traffic dramatically by featuring video podcasts on subjects like "removing a gummy smile." Others use it to demonstrate cooking tips.

The advantage of these video podcasts over YouTube-shared videos is the impact each video episode has on search and website traffic. Although YouTube gains favor with Google search algorithms, podcasting capitalizes on RSS feeds that permit a great deal of exposure on syndicated sites. These sites often link back to your own podcast hosted website—as opposed to delivering traffic to YouTube. Search engines not only award these links with high PageRanks, but credit is given also to the video format. Moreover, there are ample opportunities to feature the video podcast in multiple podcast directories (e.g., iTunes, Stitcher, and Sound Cloud).

Podcasts are not only growing in popularity, but podcast subscribers are now also seen as among the most desirable audiences for podcast hosts to target. Their tuning into a niche-oriented program qualifies them as a potential business prospect. And the personal forum creates an atmosphere conducive to story sharing and ultimately brand evangelism. But besides the growing audience popularity, those entering the podcast arena have a huge opportunity to gain an early competitive advantage. According to Chris Brogan, a world-renowned social-media expert, ". . .It's a pretty open space right now because companies aren't rushing in and figuring it out. . ."[6]

Explainer Videos

A common application of videos for education includes *explainer videos*. This particular content provides an excellent way to introduce your firm and explain what it can do for your viewers. Consisting of "how-to-use" tutorials, demos, trailers, and virtual tours, the format addresses the limited attention span of today's audience demanding a "show me" over "tell me" style of content delivery.

There are a vast number of ways to use explainer videos, but the most common cited include the following:

1. *Demos, tutorials, and how-to's*: Since it is far more effective to *show* than to *tell*, video demos can be highly effective in explaining how a product works or what it does.

2. *Trailers*: According to Moz, you have about 8 seconds to sell yourself and your business to potential customers. With trailers, you can grab the attention of your visitors to introduce yourself or your company in just a few seconds.

3. *Live-event coverage*: From features of fashion shows and conventions to facility tours and expert interviews, these videos take advantage of a captured audience in an energized atmosphere.

4. *Behind the scenes showings*: This technique allows audiences to gain an insider perspective that adds to their feeling included in exclusive communities. Consisting of facility tours, interviews with the core team, and "how it is made" demonstrations, this technique is one of the best for creating intimate connections to your company.

5. *New stories and intelligence*: Video reports on industry news can make content seem more relevant. And by adding statistical information and other marketing intelligence, you can position yourself as a reliable source of information.

6. *Customer testimonials*: Customer reviews of your service as well as their success stories can be highly effective especially when it involves user-generated content.

7. *FAQs*: A common use of videos is for Q&A's where the host reads and answers questions from the membered audience. In so doing, you establish yourself as a thought leader with more recall due to the visual nature of the forum.

Much like the case of podcasts, the key to developing effective explainer videos is to narrowcast in order for attention-deprived audiences to see a clear connection to their specific pain points. Furthermore, many experts suggest that their attention has to be caught within the first 10 seconds. Think "elevator speech time." And to maintain attention, it is recommended that you limit the total length of an explainer video to around 4 minutes.

Another key requirement is to ensure that the video is distributed across a broad range of demographic channel preferences. This includes, at minimum, Vine, Facebook, Instagram, and YouTube. However, baby boomers will prefer YouTube, and millennials will prefer 6 second loops on Vine. More is described on this subject in Chapter 5.

If constructed effectively, explainer videos have some distinct advantages over plain text, audio, and still imagery in terms of engagement, trust building, and overall ROI performance. Some well-proven benefits include the following:

1. *Search engine results (SEO) results*: The chances of getting listed on page one of Google's search engine results increase 53 times with video (source: Forrester Research). Supporting this finding, MarketingWeek found that video results have appeared in about 70 percent of the top 100 search listings on Google. This is not just for entertaining videos. According to Google, there are three times as many searches for the term "how to" than there are for "music video" on YouTube.[7]

2. *Click-through rates and links*: Not only do videos have click through rates over 40 percent higher than plain text, SEOMOZ concludes that video-based posts will attract three times more

in-linking domains than a plain text post.[8] What's more, consumers are 27 times more likely to click through online video ads than standard banners. E-mail, in particular, benefits from having video links. A survey by the Web Video Marketing Council and Flimp Media, for example, found 88 percent of their respondents to agree that campaign performance improved when e-mails included integrated video.

3. *Conversion and purchase*: The same study found that 72 percent of respondents believed their prospective clients are more likely to buy after viewing video content sent via an e-mail. Another recent study by Invodo found that half of consumers claimed YouTube videos influenced their purchase decisions. And some 57 percent of online shoppers said they are less likely to return a product bought after watching it explained via video.

4. *Easy to create and share*: Who could imagine this claim only a few years ago? With the availability of high-quality video production hardware and software, over 100 hours of video are uploaded to YouTube every minute. Using the current generation of smartphones and older, video recording and editing has reached unprecedented levels of simplicity. Sharing videos has become the preferred method of sharing as well. Consider the number of mobile users—who now represent 40 percent of YouTube viewing time—and how easier it is for them to share videos compared to text-based posts.

5. *Purchase impact*: The fact that explainer videos tend to address many of the concerns target audiences have in the consideration an evaluation stages of their buying cycle makes them critical to purchase influence. Many of the applications, for example, include demonstrations of use, client testimonies, and FAQs questions. All of them tend to impact the middle to bottom of the sales funnel.

6. *Engagement*: More than e-Books and white papers, videos make people feel something. And when they feel connected to you, they are more likely to engage with you and share your content. A study by ROI research, in fact, demonstrated that users interact with video at twice the rate of other forms of content.[9] Another showed that 65 percent of online shoppers spend 2 minutes longer on a site after

watching an online video. And when used with rich metadata (e.g., transcripts and tagging), video can drive engagement rates by anywhere from 40 to 300 percent.[10]

7. *Trust*: Video provides the greatest opportunity to showcase who you are in a persona setting. Audiences can connect with you on a far deeper level than can ever be accomplished through words. And given that most of our impressions are derived from body language, videos are uniquely suited to trust building.

8. *ROI*: About 52 percent of marketing professionals worldwide mention video as the online content with the best ROI (CopyPress).

9. *Visual learning*: With a vast majority of the world population being visual learners, video is the best mode of communications especially when used for instruction and decision making.

Virtual Seminars

From a marketing and sales perspective, virtual seminars have been quite popular in providing MoFu content to target audiences. Ranging from simple telephone hook-ups to highly interactive web conferencing, virtual seminars score high on content usefulness as an on-demand alternative to attending costly trade shows, workshops, or conferences. And by offering audio and sometimes video, they allow your audiences to connect with you more intimately.

Some of the more popular ways to conduct virtual seminars are the following:

1. *Webinars*: These collaborative and in-depth presentations permit live interaction with your audience by combining audio and slides through an Internet connection. But they must be recorded to be viewed on demand.

2. *Webcasts*: This streaming media technology adds video as well. They can be viewed on demand, but the transmission of information is one-way from presenter to listener.

3. *Teleseminars*: As an *audio only* venue, these interactive telephone seminars are accessed through a phone or Skype connection. If recorded, the teleseminar can essentially function as a podcast.

4. *Hangouts on-air (HOA)*: Hangouts give users the ability to create instant webcasts over Google+ through a live streaming platform and automatic HD video capture. There is also a screen-sharing option, so you can also present slides or share anything from a Google doc or spreadsheet.

Webinars combine audio and slides where listeners can ask questions and get immediate answers. They are also capable of conducting online polls, chats, and information transfers throughout the live session. This interactive focus makes them especially useful as a tool for collaboration and learning.

A typical webinar session normally lasts between 45 minutes and an hour including a 15-minute live Q&A at the end. Although the webinars must be watched at a scheduled time, they can easily be recorded for those unable to attend. If recorded, however, webinars can be hosted on a website augmented with downloadable slide decks, MP3 audio files, and transcribed narration. As the technology matures for webinar setup, companies like Webex, GoTo Webinar, and Adobe Connect Pro have made the service very affordable.

Webcasts add a video component to a webinar; however, audiences cannot verbally ask questions. These have to be e-mailed in advance to the presenter. But since the platform is not overburdened with data sharing and two-way interactivity, webcasts are more suitable to serving large audiences. Webinar audiences, on the other hand, typically max out around 500 viewers.

Teleseminars resemble webcasts but without the video or screen sharing. In this case, participants are given an option to receive slide decks and other information in advance. It's then up to the audience to synchronize these elements to the presenter's narrative. An advantage of teleseminars over webcasts is the interaction permitted with audiences. For example, listeners can call in with questions during a live session. And like webcasts, teleseminars provide an opportunity for a host to provide information to a large number of people simultaneously.

Google+'s *HOA* have become one of the most popular ways to engage conversations with real people for virtual seminars and chats. Some of the popular applications surfacing across politics and business include its use in the following:

1. *Company news or product announcements*: Hangouts could include company executives hosting a news release. The audience could include members of the press and other stakeholders.
2. *Educational seminars*: Because of their setup flexibility, collaborating options, and an ability to fine tuning the end production, Hangouts have emerged as a primary hosting platform for webinars as well as one of the best mid-funnel content vehicles for building thought leadership.
3. *Peer-to-peer panel discussions*: Industry thought leaders can be assembled into an online roundtable for current event discussions, survey data analysis, and trended news. Similarly, Hangouts can feature users' groups for showcasing customer success stories or Q&A sessions.
4. *Video blog or video podcast episode*: Interviews can be conducted with leading experts as an opinion or advisory piece to host in lieu of a video blog or video podcast episode. This could provide a refreshing changeup if the episode featured new guests and thought-provoking interaction with the right audience.
5. *Virtual summits*: In this case, you could livestream conference events including the presentations of featured speakers.

Depending on the number of participants, hangouts should last between 15 and 45 minutes in a fast-paced setting facilitated by a moderator. Up to 10 participants can collaborate throughout the dialog as it is presented to members of Google+. During the live hangout, text questions can be taken from the audience.

Hangout experts find that a mix of attention getting pattern interrupts and conversation spontaneity work best for HOAs. Although slides provide an opportunity for pattern interrupt, care must be taken to always emphasize conversation over slides. And like all video media solutions, lighting and sound quality are key. So it's advised to use headsets to avoid feedback. For an excellent resource on setting up HOAs, check out *Social Media Week*'s "Google+ Hangouts on Air" at http://bit.ly/1lJvZ3C.

To prepare and promote an HOA, hosts often use a special guest to promote a teaser video. In the trailer, YouTube viewers are told of Hangout time and invited to post a question using a hashtag. Viewers can then be selected to join the hangout based on the thought-provoking nature of their question. Consider how this was down by Facebook expert, Mari Smith at http://bit.ly/1pDlv9B or soccer superstar, David Beckham, at http://bit.ly/1iKd6OJ. Similar 1–2 minute teasers could be offered after posting the broadcast on YouTube with highlight clips to encourage future attendance.

When live, up to 10 members from a Google+ circle can collaborate as an expert panel. But questions can be fielded live from up to a million concurrent viewers. The entire episode can then be recorded, edited, and uploaded on YouTube. And once uploaded to YouTube, you can then host the edited Hangout on blogs, websites, and social platforms. In effect, you have your own TV station.

	Webinars	Webcasts	Teleseminars	Hangouts on Air
Format				
Audio	✓	✓	✓	✓
Video		✓		✓
Slides	✓	✓		✓
Interaction				
One to Many	✓	✓	✓	✓
Live Audience Calls	✓		✓	✓
Interactive Chats	✓			✓
Panel Collaboration	✓			✓
Audience Access				
Live View	✓	✓	✓	✓
Subscribed Recording	✓	✓	✓	✓
Public Recording				✓
Editing				
Highlighting & Muting Speakers				✓
Editing Out Slow Moments/Distractions				✓
Public Recording				✓

Customer Success Stories

Customer success stories, also known as case studies, are arguably the most credible sales content that you have under your control. According to a recent B2B Content-Marketing Trends Report, customer testimonials and case studies are the most effective content-marketing tactics.[11] The study showed that 89 percent of respondents found testimonials to be effective, while 88 percent found case studies to be effective.

By letting your customers tell their stories in their own words, you are adding a human element to your brand. Like any good story, the narrative behind a case study can create empathy with the case study subject. Especially if audiences appreciate the challenges faced by the subject, a personal connection can be made.

Customer success studies become especially useful in marketing when the content does not directly involve your product or service. Instead, it involves a solution to a problem your firm can potentially address. For example, an accounting firm soliciting case studies on how the firm's exemplary tax advice bailed them out would not be as effective as a case demonstrating how a particular asset management remedy or other accounting procedure improved the case subject's net profits. The accounting firm could then feature themselves as an experienced advisor in this field.

But to be truly effective, the case study should follow a familiar story arc with a journalistic tone. This includes you, the hero; a series of obstacles standing in the way of success; and a turnaround in results following the resolution of a problem leading to proven results. And by using video, the case can more dramatically play out the suspense surrounding challenges as well as the excitement of reaching a happy ending.

Overall, some of the key advantages of using customer success stories over alternative forms of content include the following:

1. *Emotional connections*: As discussed more in Chapter 3, storytelling is the key to building an emotional connection with your audience. When a case study is actually told as a story, audiences are more likely to be interested in and engage with the content especially if they can recognize some benefit relevant to their own challenges.

2. *Nonbiased endorsements*: A great advantage of case studies is their peer-to-peer influence and "show me" versus "tell me." By having an outside party endorse your offering, you can avoid coming off as self-serving. Moreover, target audiences are more likely to empathize with someone in their own shoes.

3. *Word-of-mouth sharing*: Many would argue that the greatest way to improve word-of-mouth marketing is to amplify the voices of your customers. And case studies appeal to a basic human instinct to tell a story and give advice. So by sharing their success stories, you are essentially empowering your case study subjects to sway the decisions of your target audience.

4. *Mid-funnel response*: Case studies supply insight into how a problem was solved, thereby making it useful for the consideration stage of the buying decision cycle. But more importantly, case studies can be crucial at the zero moment of truth (ZMOT). This is time when the prospect is about to purchase and merely wants final reinforcement through peer reviews, buyer's guides, and customer success stories. According to Weber Shandwick, the average buyer consults 11 consumer reviews on the path to purchase.[12]

5. *Fine-tuned collateral*: Rather than packing repurposed articles, brochures, and data sheets into a customer application folder, sales personnel can handpick success stories from a library of cases that most resemble the prospect's pain points and interests. This further adds an element of variety and personalization to the sales collateral.

6. *Expertise*: As the archive of case studies grows, you have more opportunity to showcase your expertise and where you excel. Only now, you have the backing of outside endorsements.

7. *Easily repurposed*: A typical case study runs around 1,500–2,000 words, making it easily repurposed for e-Books, podcasts, best practice guide, and blogs.

8. *Build partnerships with evangelists*: Several case study writers highlight the success they have had forging better relationships with those willing to produce a case study. To begin, the discovery of willing subjects often reveals your true evangelists. If conducted more as a journalistic piece than an endorsement, the case subject themselves could gain from the publicity.

Blogs

Blogs are essentially websites that are regularly updated and displayed in reverse-chronological order (e.g., most recent updates are displayed first). The content is broken down into posts and published simultaneously to many sites (syndicated) using an RSS feed that alerts subscribers when new content is posted. Each post hosts a comment section where readers are encouraged to provide feedback or engage in a discussion.

As a predominantly top-funnel asset, they provide marketers with great opportunities to showcase their expertise and build trust one small chunk at a time. And as blogging expert, Jeff Bullas, states "blogging gives the introvert a voice." Limited effort and personality strain is required to get on this stage. Any reader advice or helpful tips can be offered in the language of your own voice but in an unintimidating format resembling that of a Word document.

For many firms, a corporate blog is the centerpiece of their content-marketing strategy. Blogs can be readily shared on almost any social platform. And they often serve as an aggregator of all other content in the form of downloads, links, embeds, and recordings. This not only provides a central repository for all of your media elements but also contributes to search results. But more than an aggregator of searchable content, blogs also function as the center of *conversation* as well. Because of the audience

feedback and ability to host new topics, blogs provide an excellent opportunity to trigger discussion while gauging audience sentiment.

An examination of the most popular types of blogs will reveal the following 12 archetypes. Since its early beginnings, the *how-to's* continue to dominate the archetypes especially if they offer detailed information not easy to find elsewhere. These blogs normally average around 1,500 words and incorporate short video clips to reinforce visual learning. These how-to blogs could be more readily scheduled than other blog types as its tips are not tied to external events. Others like *industry news, ratings,* and *reports* often require a significant time lapse between releases.

Among the key benefits of blogs over alternative communications methods are the following:

1. *Ease of publishing and updating*: Blogs are hosted on very user-friendly platforms, like WordPress, Blogger, and many other free sites, so that almost anyone can set up and maintain their posts. Even the process for embedding, linking, and moderating comments has reached the point where little, if any, web master support is required. And in contrast to that required for editing video content, updating blog posts is not more difficult than crafting an e-mail.

2. *Easily scannable*: Unlike podcasts, webinars, and videos, a quick scan of a blog post can let a viewer know if the content is relevant. And by skimming text, parts of the blog could be skipped. This is more challenging in audio and video where rewinds and bouncing across content leads to more time consumed in reaching relevant points.

3. *Easily found*: Blogs can be syndicated through blog directory services and subscribed through RSS. This makes blog content more readily discovered while saving viewers time in search since they are alerted of any updates. The ability to optimize blog text around key phrases makes it highly discoverable by search engines as well. Google's Panda, Penguin, and Hummingbird algorithms place a premium on continually refreshed content.

4. *Easily linked*: Blogs are more oriented to the topics of interest to your audience, thereby attracting far more inbound links to its postings than can be expected for a more self-serving website landing page. And with the ability to easily cross-link postings, bloggers can

interconnect a series of related posts. This further boosts the search engine performance.

5. *Top of the funnel* (ToFu): Blogs are a great way to establish connection with target audiences early in their buying stage. Because they are less resource intensive than mid-funnel content, they can be more regularly published.

6. *Owned content*: With the exception of blogs hosted on LinkedIn, Tumblr, and other social-networking platforms, most are hosted on domains owned by the blogger. This limits the risk of unexpected and undesired changes made by platform suppliers. A good practice when establishing your blog domain is to ensure you have your name in the URL and not that of the software platform supplier (e.g., blog.yourcompany.com vs blog.wordpress.com). Otherwise you are merely building traffic for the platform provider.

7. *Conversation with targets*: Unlike a web landing page that hosts comments, blogs are designed to facilitate conversations with its audiences. In the process, this often helps build communities as responders feel connected to each other. It also provides greater opportunities for the blogger to identify, monitor, and connect with target audiences.

8. *Word-of-mouth spread*: More than news articles and subscribed content, blogs can have the most *viral* impact on a content-marketing strategy. Messages are highly portable, making them ideal for sharing across any device and across any platform. And with word of mouth being twice as effective as traditional marketing in terms of more lasting results and new customer acquisitions, blogs offer a great opportunity to improve the bottom line.[13]

9. *Trail of trustworthiness*: In his book, *Youtility*, Jay Baer discusses the use of bricks and feathers in content planning.[14] Blogs serve as feathers, or a lighter content that allows readers to check you out before digesting a 45-sminute webinar.

Small businesses, in particular, benefit from blogging as the cost and time consumed to host a blog is far less than most content-marketing alternatives. And since each post serves as a continually refreshed website page, websites with blogs have 434 percent more indexed pages in which

to attract the attention of search engines. Other notable statistics especially encouraging to small businesses are the following:[15]

- Small businesses with blogs generate 126 percent more leads.
- About 81 percent of U.S. consumers trust advice from blogs.
- About 37 percent of marketers believe blogs are the most important type of content marketing.

However, with an estimated 400 million blogs registered globally, the
challenge to small businesses in particular is syndicating, socially sharing,
and advertising their blog posts in an ever-growing noisy blogosphere.
Chapter 3 discusses in more detail how to amplify your blog exposure.
This section describes what it takes to ensure that your blogs are *tuned* to
target audiences, *focused* on attraction, and backed by consistent *quality*.

e-Books

> *"The eBook has become the current standard for the long-form content*
> *package. A lot of companies are moving away from the verbose white*
> *paper to the sleeker, more appealing eBook.*
>   — Joe Pulizzi, author of Epic Content Marketing

Marketing at the top and MoFu often involves the use of e-Books. And
unlike their more technical cousin, white papers, these 6–50 page PDF
documents are well suited for infotainment. Because they are usually
graphics heavy, e-Books provide a great avenue for businesses to communicate complex information in a fun and interesting way. This is especially
important at a time when audiences are seeking ways to be entertained or
inspired when they consume content.

In the process of infotaining, you have an even greater way to show
your expertise than what can be done in a short blog post. For those new
to content, e-Books offer an easy way to launch in-depth content. Free
downloaded graphics and page assembly templates, for example, are offered by companies like Hubspot. Once developed, the document can
then be easily saved as a PDF file where it can be stored on your own
computer site or via a hosting service like Google Drive or SlideShare. As

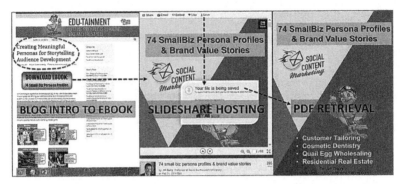

Figure 1.4 Downloading Process for an eBook from Blog to SlideShare

demonstrated in Figure 1.4, an e-Book can garner SlideShare traffic while being hosted as a blog download.

Among the key benefits of e-Books over alternative communications methods are the following:

1. *More in-depth content*: e-Books offer more in-depth perspectives than what can be offered in a blog post. Blogs are normally consumed for more immediate needs. Consequently, you run the risk of losing your audience with a very in-depth post that is too long to digest at the time. e-Books, on the other hand, normally follow a blog or an e-mail introduction to the content. These intros allow a preview of its usefulness while permitting an easy way to download and archive the e-Book until it could be read at a more convenient time.

2. *Searchability*: Search engines love longer content. In fact, according to Jeff Bullas, a world-renowned content-marketing strategist, the average content length for a web page in the top 10 results for most searched keywords is 2,000 words or more.[16] Although not one of the best for SEO optimization, PDFs are nevertheless well scanned by search engines.

3. *Thought leadership*: e-Books provide ample opportunity for you to demonstrate your expertise by solving complex problems more completely than you can expect from blog posts. Over time, a series of e-Books can become an excellent training resource that adds to your thought leadership.

4. *Test trialing content*: Unlike a printed book, e-Books can be dissected and released as your individual topics are completed. This further allows for an exploration of what really fascinates your audience before devoting too many resources.

5. *Opt-in for growing e-mail lists*: By providing far more value than a brief blog post, e-Books have a greater opportunity to enlist opt-ins for e-mail. With a registration form, some information can be collected about the subscriber. In addition, the downloads are easily tracked thereby making them ideal for lead qualification.

6. *Broad EPUB audience*: Converting your e-Book to an EPUB-style format can make it available on a Kindle, Nook, or iPad. The fact that e-Book sales grew from $68 million in 2008 to over $3 billion today attests to the popularity of readers enjoying this format.

7. *Portability*: Available on any smart device, e-Books are always within reach.

8. *Interactivity*: e-Books are able to accommodate tweetable quotes, graphics, and links for a rich content experience.

9. *Speed of release*: As an alternative to traditional publishing, e-Books offer a much quicker route to production while providing instant attachment through e-mail.

Some of the more popular applications of e-Books include its use in playbooks or guidelines for mastering a task. Others applications include the compilation of procedures, expert insights, or case studies that collectively provide a comprehensive insight into solving problems.

For e-Books to be effective, they need to follow the same rules applied to blogging including the use of imagery, small blocks of text, and short titles that will pique your audiences' curiosity. In addition, e-Books that reference key influencers in the content have been shown to greatly boost their circulation while adding credibility.

Overall, e-Books offer a great way to advance your engagement with target audiences. And when matched with a preceding trail of blog posts, it not only remains one of the better methods for validating your expertise, it offer sufficient enough value for your readers to download a registration form. From there, Chapters 4 and 5 will explain how the captured e-mail can jump-start the process of converting leads to customers.

e-Newsletters

e-Newsletters remain the third highest content-marketing tactic used by B2B and B2C marketers. Despite its once tarnished image in the early days of e-mail blasting, this content remains useful to audience seeking the following:

- updated trend information and other relevant business news;
- helpful tips on trade-related or other reader challenges;
- educational digests on new concepts or helpful how-to's;
- curated clips of periodic newsworthy topics;
- links for related resources; and
- ratings and reviews.

Its real value over blogs and e-Books is the timeliness of topics where updates are regularly expected. So when deciding whether you should use e-mail newsletters in your content strategy, you should first consider the nature of topics that lend themselves to habitual communication with your target audience.

Managed properly, e-Newsletters offer a valid means of regularly interacting with your target on a variety of updatable newsworthy items. Some candidate topics include updates on industry trade shows, periodic forecasts, industry news, expert tips, and product or service reviews. And by targeting the information based on a subscribed audience of readers, information could be tailored to the local and other specialized interests of your readers. This is more of a challenge for e-Books and blogs that lack a subscription mechanism.

e-Newsletters also have an advantage of providing a content change-up while still staying focused on a targeted audience. Notice how this was done for a real-estate accounting firm in a quarterly newsletter aimed at property managers in South Florida. Among the topics covered in the issue were the following:

- New tri-county property management positions posted on LinkedIn
- An interview with the continental group on COA and HOA collection challenges
- New property developments in Palm Beach County
- Review of the top rated residential property management software
- Preview of this year's South Florida PM-EXPO

Much of this information was repurposed from blogs and a review already in progress but with a more humanized approach. This human side was accomplished by using a recognized community expert and by posting local community photos. This coincides with the results of a study by the Nielsen Norman Group whose findings suggest that "readers become emotionally attached to e-Newsletters and look forward to receiving them, provided they are timely and informative."[17]

e-Newsletters that share behind-the-scenes insights and community goodwill activities can also strike an emotional chord with audiences beyond what can be expected from e-Books, webinars, or podcasts. And by making these insights local and exclusive to subscribed members, audiences feel more intimately engaged with your firm while associating your brand with corporate citizenry.

Authoritative Reports

Another form of content that could greatly benefit your target audience is *white papers* and *market reports*. Unlike the more entertaining style of an e-Book, however, this content has a more technical tone. Their purpose is to convey survey or study results from research.

The benefit to readers, especially in B2B settings, is having documented evidence to back the study claims. This adds credibility to your thought leadership while allowing your readers to leverage your findings as support for their own positions. Buyers, in particular, use white papers and market reports to justify their choices. e-Books and infographics in this case may not be taken seriously enough.

Slideware

Almost every successful content marketing has found a way to leverage their blogs and e-Books into slide decks that allow them to host webinars or live presentations. What many may not realize, however, is the tremendous social power behind slide sharing. Readers enjoy the page-by-page flips of predominantly visual content that have always been the preference among business professionals too busy to read a lot of words. Be even more importantly, the booming success of SlideShare has convinced many firms to publicly host their content.

Referred to by Forbes as the quite giant of content marketing, Slide-Share remains the world's largest content sharing platform. Slideshare's special ties to LinkedIn allow you to seamlessly expose your slide decks or e-Books in your LinkedIn profile (Figure 1.5) as a way to boost your thought leadership. Because it provides social proof by way of views, comments, and downloads, those viewing your LinkedIn profile can ascertain your popularity as well.

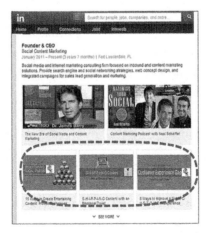

Figure 1.5 Embedding Slideware on Your LinkedIn Profile

To create an effective presentation useful to your audience, the slides should be highly graphic. The fewer the words, the better. Once developed, the slides get uploaded from a PDF format into your SlideShare account channel where over 60 million visitors per month can like, comment, download, and easily share your content.

Branded Content Tools and Apps

Perhaps the most promising form of educational content that audiences find useful is when content solves problems in real time. Known as branded content tools, these apps offer self-help assistance or gather information from prospects for use in customized assessments. Discussed widely in Chapter 12, brands and small businesses are discovering how these apps can help solve immediate problems like removing stains or fixing a drain.

On the less urgent end of the spectrum, many branded content tools are used in analysis support where user data can feed an ROI calculator or product configurator on their smart phones as your audience gets close to making a decision. This offers great potential to marketers when addressing mid-funnel and bottom-funnel opportunities for sales conversion.

Creating a Content-Marketing Landscape to Map Your Format Requirements

Now comes the grueling research part of understanding what content best resonates with your audience. By knowing content objective (instruction, insights, or decision making) and the format preferences (webinars, podcasts, blogs, e-Books, etc.), you are well on your way to discovering how your content will be useful.

What remains is an examination or content popularity in your industry as well as the resource demands to produce each type of content. Shown in Figure 1.6 is an example of a content landscape to consider when examining your most feasible media tactics. To help tailor what content is applicable to your industry, the table also shows the popularity of each type across resources to publish regularly updated content.

		Content Marketing Usage*			**Content Delivery Formats**	Instruction — Evergreen				Business Insights							Decision Aids (Evaluation through Purchase)							
						How-to Tips	Tutorials & eLearning	Demos	Checklists	Topics & Trends	News	Market Intelligence	Expert Insights	Resource Lists	Forums	Media Events	Ratings	Guides & Reviews	Previews	Example Usage	Evidence	Trial Support	Templates	FAQs
		Consistency Requirement	B2B	Technology MKtg	B2C																			
Audio/Video	Podcasts (Very High)		40%	29%	19%	Expert Interviews	✓				✓		✓	✓		✓								✓
						Panel Discussion & Debates								✓										✓
						Video Podcast	✓	✓	✓		✓	✓		✓		✓	✓								✓
						On-Air Call-In Stories															✓	✓		
	Live Action Explainer Videos (Low)		88%	86%	72%	Step-by-Step Instruction	✓	✓	✓													✓		
						Showcasing															✓	✓		
						On-Location, Trailers and Shows								✓		✓								
						Customer Reviews															✓			
						Behind-the-Scenes/Documentary											✓							
						Conference, Seminars & Workshops	✓							✓								✓		✓
						Roundtables & Interviews	✓				✓	✓		✓	✓							✓		✓
						Vine Stop Motions	✓																	
						Stats Video						✓	✓											
						Virtual Tours				✓														
	Animated Videos					Screencasts	✓	✓	✓		✓	✓		✓	✓					✓	✓			
						Whiteboard Animation	✓	✓													✓			
						Motion Graphics	✓		✓				✓								✓			
	Virtual Seminars (Med)		79%	80%	30%	Webinars				✓														
						Webcasts				✓				✓	✓									
						Hangouts on Air		✓	✓	✓	✓	✓	✓	✓	✓									
						Teleseminars				✓				✓	✓									
	Customer Success Stories (Low)		82%	86%	41%	Case Histories													✓	✓	✓			
						Video Case Studies													✓	✓				
						Testimonials															✓			
Text	Blogs (High)		79%	88%	80%	Text-based Posts	✓				✓	✓	✓	✓	✓	✓		✓	✓	✓	✓	✓		✓
						Microblogs (Twitter, SMS, Tumblr)							✓			✓								
						Micro-Videos (e.g, Vines, Pheeds)		✓												✓				
						Video, Audio & Photo Blogs	✓		✓		✓	✓	✓	✓		✓	✓	✓	✓	✓	✓	✓		✓
	eBooks (Med)		38%	45%	23%	PDFs & Readers	✓		✓															
						Playbooks								✓										
						Audio Books	✓		✓															
	eNewsletters (High)		86%	84%	76%	Content-rich Newsletters	✓				✓	✓	✓	✓	✓		✓	✓	✓					✓
						Digests	✓					✓	✓		✓									
		(Med)	41%	22%	30%	Digital Magazines	✓				✓	✓	✓			✓		✓					
	Articles (Med)		80%	78%	70%	Directories & Syndications	✓					✓			✓	✓	✓						
						News Releases						✓			✓									
						Editorial Microsites	✓					✓												
	Reports (Med)		71%	65%	30%	White Papers							✓	✓							✓			
						Research and Surveys						✓		✓							✓			
						Fact Sheets								✓										✓
Imagery	Slideware/Presentations (Low)		67%	64%	40%	Slide Decks	✓				✓	✓				✓	✓			✓		✓		✓
						Galleries													✓	✓	✓			
						Animated Presentations	✓	✓																
						Infographics	✓				✓	✓							✓	✓				
	Interactive Tools & FREEmiums	(Med)	38%	40%	37%	Branded Content Tools																	✓	✓
		(Med)	28%	30%	39%	Self-Help Apps					✓	✓						✓	✓	✓			
		(Med)	38%	36%	46%	Mobile Content	✓		✓	✓	✓							✓	✓	✓			

*Source: Content Marketing Institute/MarketingProfs (B2B, B2C, Technology Marketers)

Figure 1.6 Content Landscape for Preparing Media Tactics

Situational Triggers for Timely Placements

High on the list of many content-marketing plans is the timely sequencing of content across a target audience's buying cycle. At the ToFu, content marketers have an opportunity to encounter audiences right at the time they recognize a pain point. Known as situational triggers, these moments provide timely opportunities to post blogs and other ToFu content.

Figure 1.7 Situational Triggers for Cosmetic Dentistry

Consider the case of a cosmetic dentist shown in Figure 1.7. Many dentists wait for signs of aging teeth as the moment to present their message. Others see the value of encountering prospects the moment they detect hair loss, discover new wrinkles, or experience aging ailments.

Using this moment as a situational trigger, their content could be developed on the subject of antiaging, which features smile makeovers as one of the antiaging remedies. This assumes that the content is not perceived as self-serving (about teeth) or biased (about the dentist).

Continuing the analysis across other targeted personas, moments of encounter could then be identified for audiences planning to walk down the aisle, perform on stage, or mingle in high-society circles. When timed to reach the audience as they experience these early *awareness* pressures, the content can then create an opportunity to influence the *consideration* and *evaluation* phases of the audience's decision making as well.

Transparent Content to Create Early Trust

Talk about things no one wants to discuss.
— Marcus Sheridan, founder, The Sales Lion

Now that your content is seen as timely, relevant, useful, and synchronized, the next objective is to demonstrate your *transparency*. This means revealing your insights on sensitive business issues like your price, your problems, and who does the best job—all the issues marketers dread discussing. Why would we reveal what we were taught should always be held close to the vest? Because it addresses your target audience's biggest questions. Your contributions not only save them time, but you also relieve them of the most aggravating part of their search process.

No one understands this more than swimming pool installer River Pools and Spas that went from near bankruptcy to one of the largest in-ground pool construction companies in the country. Their turnaround came by educating their target audiences on what matters most to them. The owner, Marcus Sheridan, blogged his way to success. And he blogged about issues few companies want to discuss.

River Pools and Spas understood the power of solving lingering problems. Marcus Sheridan essentially took information from his website FAQs and translated them into useful content. But rather than having prospects dig out the data from reviews and competitive sites, they proactively met their audiences in the early research phases with donated content. Today, some prospects download nearly 100 pages of this content before committing to a contract. And they did this by being *transparent*. The company blogs on subjects we were told to put off until later in the buying stage. For Marcus Sheridan, this meant preempting his target audience's biggest pain points with answers to the following:

- What does a fiber glass pool cost?
- Who are the best suppliers?
- What are some of the shortcomings in pool life and installation?

To his pleasure, no one else seemed willing to address these issues for fear of competitive exploitation or the risk of creating a premature expectation with the prospect.

Like Marcus, a common practice followed by leading bloggers is to actually survey their customers on what they are most anxious about when considering a solution the blogger can address. Others examine the FAQs logged over time from their field sales force or customer support teams. Regardless of the mechanism, the closer the question relates to sensitive pricing and problems, the greater the opportunity you have to demonstrate transparency.

Knowing that sales and profits will come later, River Pools and Spas first proved themselves as a worthy member of their prospects' attention. And by risking exploitation from divulging free and competitively sensitive information, the firm started a trail of trustworthiness. The gesture of helpfulness, in essence, opened the doors for prospects to determine if the firm's contributions are useful and relevant to their passions or business challenges.

Engaging Content for Attentive Learning

As this chapter deals with educating our audiences, we only need to consider the level of attention deficit pervading our society. To keep students engaged, we have to:

1. adapt to their learning and communication styles;
2. keep them involved; and
3. entertain them as much as possible.

The same applies to readers, listeners, and viewers of our content. If we expect to stand out from the growing noise of content marketing, we need to engage them.

Selecting Content Communication Modes that Resonate with Target Audience

The first stage of the defining engaging content involves the selection of a communication mode most suitable to a target audience's learning style. Does the audience prefer to listen, read, or view? And if a visual context rules the day, are they better served with graphics, photos, animations, slides, or videos?

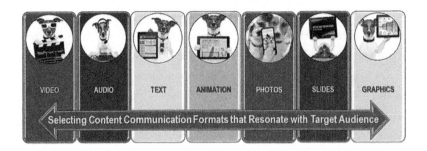

Viewing Content

It goes without saying that a picture is worth a thousand words. In fact, we process visuals 60,000 times faster than text. Perhaps the most widely discussed topic in social content circles over the past year has been visual storytelling, a subject covered in Chapter 3. But visuals also play a key role in instruction and information. The rapid rise of slide decks, infographics, and photo galleries is testimony to how brands and small businesses are embracing this short-form *imagery* format by audiences overwhelmed with text.

But if a picture is worth a thousand words, then a video is worth a million. In fact, according to Dr. James McQuivey of Forrester Research, one minute of video is worth 1.8 million words. As the top format for content marketing, videos especially pique the interest of your target audience while establishing an emotional connection. And with 78 percent of the world adult population watching at least one video a week, it is not surprising that videos have moved front and center in most content-marketing strategies.[18]

What has fueled the growth of video is a combination of its growing popularity and effectiveness in driving internet traffic. According to The Hazlett Group, Cisco, and Imedia Connection, consumer video traffic will reach 55, 69, and 90 percent, respectively, of all global Internet traffic in the very near term.[19] To fully grasp the enormity of this popularity, consider that over 6 billion hours of video are now watched on YouTube every month by an estimated 1.15 billion people. Without a doubt, video content has become the most crucial component for most content-marketing strategies.

Like most content distributed through social media, videos are useful in storytelling and education. The former, a subject covered in Chapter 3, represents a new generation of connection based on entertaining and inspiring audiences. And according to experts, this application clearly has more potential in terms of engagement and emotional connection. However, the use of video for instruction and information has arguably more impact on helping target audiences make an informed buying decision.

Listening to Content

Next to video, audio has the next highest impact on humanizing content. Its preference over video has much to do with its "on the go" accessibility and suitability for multitaskers. And whether it's used for audio books, podcasting, slidecasting, streaming radio talk shows, or online conference recordings, audio represents the only practical way for "mobile-equipped" audiences to consume content while exercising, commuting, waiting in line, or working at their desk.

As almost all new-generation cars equip passengers with plug-in smartphone podcasting (e.g., Apple CarPlay, Stitcher, and TuneIn), audiences will become more accustomed to selecting their own audio content on demand. The advantage to content marketers is that audio provides one of the best ways to build credibility and authority.

When released consistently, audio content builds a high level of intimacy with subscribed audiences without having to incur the higher costs of radio broadcasting and most online video productions. Quality sound can now be produced for less than $200 for a microphone and software. And the ease of social sharing on MP3s and audio platforms rivals that of YouTube videos.

Of course, a downside to audio is the fact that they are linear, meaning that you cannot skim them. And if the audio quality or conversational style of the host is not that of a radio broadcaster, audiences could quickly get turned off.

Reading Content

With the continual rise of microblogs, textual content will remain a preferred choice among those accustomed to short-form tweets, posts, and text messaging. Add to this the accelerating growth in native advertising content, and a strong case can be developed for textual content surviving the onslaught of social video, visual storytelling, and infographics.

Textual formats still have the advantage of quick release times, quick loading times, and low-budget development. Despite the hype surrounding video search results, more opportunities are given to textual blogs and articles to score precisely on targeted key words. Finally, text has the advantage of self-paced scrutiny, skimming, and repurposing.

Getting Audience Involvement

One way to keep our audiences engaged in our content is to get them involved. Consider content that asks us how to resolve a debate, solve a riddle, or offer an opinion. Aren't you at least curious to know whether you have the correct answer?

Research demonstrates that audiences are often entertained by a cognitive challenge or through conclusion curiosity. Although not as powerful as humor or performance entertainment, this technique is often the preferred choice of content marketers seeking to engage their audiences under a reasonable budget.

Among the most popular types of participation that perform the best on engagement are the following:

- completing the message;
- resolving the problem; and
- following a script.

Common to each method is a way to attract us with a mental motivation to finish the exercise. If successful, we can applaud our wits and talents at mastering the task. In the process, content marketers get us to ponder over the concept or follow the steps of mastery.

In so doing, they lay the trail that pulls us through their entire message. That is why this technique scores high on engagement. But content marketers face a tough challenge in their attempts to direct our cognitive efforts on a meaningful and well-understood brand message.

Consider the wave of eye tests and other mind games flooding our LinkedIn updates. Our attention to these games is evidenced by the

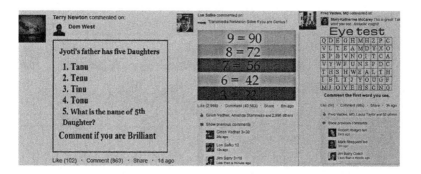

inordinately high amount of comments as readers attempt the math or to solve the puzzle. But unless the game leads to a brand story or educational content, the game merely serves as a marketing gimmick.

One way to keep your audiences involved in your content is to fuel a debate. By leaving your blogs open ended (i.e., letting you audience decide for themselves vs you providing an answer), you can encourage readers to engage deeper into the content. This can often be accomplished with polls embedded in the blog that ask readers to cast a vote. In the process of stimulating a debate, the content marketer has an opportunity to keep the audience engaged in the content.

Making Content Entertaining

Without a doubt, the move toward entertaining content in B2B as well as B2C environments represents the most dramatic shift to how we market in a growing sea of content. Chapter 3 covers in more detail how the use of humor, astonishment, concept imagery, heartfelt moments, performances, and storytelling is critical to build an emotional connection that supersedes any content engagement at the cognitive level.

Deliverable Content for Audience Convenience

Much like the pressure felt by universities customizing their courseware for classroom, online and hybrid formats, content marketers are challenged with adapting all of their content to fit the social platform and device preferences of their targeted audiences.

Black = Major Gray = Minor		Instruction				Information				Entertainment				Inspiration			
Platform	Use*	Post	Image	Video	Link	Post	Image	Video	Link	Post	Image	Video	Link	Post	Image	Video	Link
Facebook	94%																
Twitter/Vine	83%																
LinkedIn	71%																
YouTube	57%																
Blogging	55%																
Google+	54%																
Pinterest	47%																
Instagram	28%																

* Percent of marketers using the social media platform (Social Media Examiner, 2014)

Figure 1.8 Compatibility of Content with Most Popular Platforms

Chapter 9 discusses the need to embrace omni-channels especially in a growing population of mobile platforms that cannot accommodate many of the content formats used for desktop display. Chapter 8 also discusses the strong drive toward native advertising where content resembles surrounding advertising. Whether it's a sponsored post or short-form advertorial, this requires content to be repurposed as microcontent that seamlessly blends into someone else's news feed or feature article.

Perhaps the biggest challenge to content marketers is adapting the content to the tone, style, and audience expectations of all of the major social-media platforms. Each platform has a unique way to accept posts or links to your content. Moreover, some are more infotainment oriented, while others are more serious or instructional in nature. Shown in Figure 1.8 is an example of how the top platforms vary in their content expectations. This is a typical representation that does not apply to all industries.

Summary Model of Trusted Content for Education

In summary, for content to educate our target audiences, it has to be useful, trusted, and engaging. Shown in Figure 1.9 is a model of the relationships between each trust determinant to each other and the outcome variable *education*. Also shown are the content requirements to consider when developing your content-marketing strategy.

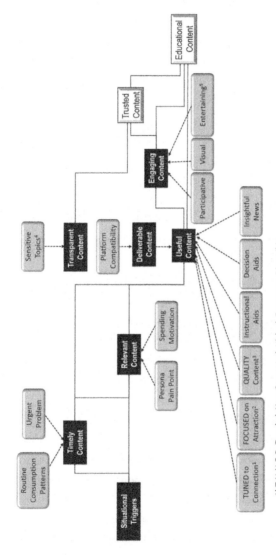

1) T-U-N-E-D: Trended, User Generated, Niched, Evergreen, Digestible
2) F-O-C-U-S-E-D: Frequent, Optimized, Cross-Platform, Unique, Shareable, Eye-Catching, Documented
3) Q-U-A-L-I-T-Y: Quick, Unbiased, Advisable, Lead Generative, Image Intensive, Talk-worthy, Your Voice
4) Discussions of price, supplier product problems, etc.
5) Chapter Two: Surprising, Humanized, Inspiring, Playful, Passionate, Told as a Story

Figure 1.9 *Summary Model of Trusted and Educational Content*

Notes

1. "If Your Content Marketing is for Everybody, It's for Nobody" by Joe Pulizzi of Content Marketing Institute (http://bit.ly/1nKb9R9).

2. About 97 million Americans drive to work alone in their car every day. The average commute is just over 26 minutes. Taken from "The Podcasting Facts: Why Audio Is an Untapped Content Marketing Opportunity" by Jennifer Tribe (bit.ly/1sL6i7r) and "Is Audio the Next Big Thing in Digital Marketing?" by CrazyEgg and Russ Henneberry (bit.ly/1wmYxmM).

3. Edison Research and Arbitron (http://bit.ly/1sL6i7r).

4. "Why Podcasting Should Be Part of Your Marketing Strategy" by Jo Hague (http://bit.ly/1lXdPe5).

5. Social Media Marketing World (http://dustn.tv/smmw14-keynote-michael-stelzner/).

6. Chris Brogan comment taken from "The Podcasting Facts: Why Audio Is an Untapped Content Marketing Opportunity" by Jennifer Tribe (bit.ly/1sL6i7r).

7. Marketing Week (http://bit.ly/1iDRZNC).

8. "What Makes a Link Worthy Post—Part 1" by the Moz Blog's Casey Henry (http://bit.ly/1sDsBfb) posted to Link Building (bit.ly/1uLoPvK).

9. "How the Smartest Companies Leverage Visual Social Media" contributed by David K. Williams to Forbes (http://onforb.es/1lcsFZI) as a reference to ROI Research Study (slidesha.re/1t70Vyo).

10. "Video Metadata Drives Engagement Rates as Much as 300 Percent, RAMP's CEO" in Beet. TV's interview with Tom Wilde, CEO of content optimization platform RAMP (http://bit.ly/1lozoom).

11. 2013 B2B Content-Marketing Report sponsored by Spiceworks and others (http://slidesha.re/1voYuV2).

12. "Consumer Reviewers Wield More Power than Professional Critics in Driving Purchase Decisions" taken from Weber Shandwick press release (http://bit.ly/1pHyhnp).

13. Melissa Barker, Donald Barker, Nicholas Bormann, and Krista Neher. *Social Media Marketing: A Strategic Approach*. South-Western Cengage Learning. 2013. p. 91.

14. Jay Baer. *Youtility*. New York: Portfolio/Penguin. 2013.

15. "The Blog Economy" Infographic by Social4Retail (http://bit .ly/1o4zVtP).

16. "20 Powerful Ideas for Creating and Marketing Your EBook" by Jeff Bullas (http://bit.ly/1zlzJOo).

17. "Email Newsletter Design to Increase Conversion and Loyalty" by Neilson Norman Group (http://bit.ly/1nccPnh).

18. "Online Video 2013" by Pew Research (http://bit.ly/UGUyDZ).

19. "The Why and How of Video for Content Marketing" reference to Cisco contributed by SEJ's Bernadette Coleman (http://bit .ly/Vm8X95); "5 Ways to Optimize Video for Search" by imedia Connection's Diane Buzzeo (http://bit.ly/1phJkDA); "Why Video Marketing Is Key in 2014" by the Hayzlett Group's Jeffrey Hayzlett (http://bit.ly/1lOzHrY).

CHAPTER 2

Escorting Prospects with Frame-of-Mind Connections

We see our customers as invited guests to a party, and we are the hosts. It's our job to make every important aspect of the customer experience a little bit better.

—Jeff Bezos, founder and CEO of Amazon.com

Now that our content has been planned to meet the format objectives and pain points of our targeted personas, it has to fit your prospect's frame of mind. If done correctly, we could let our content do our talking in a less intrusive way than how it has been done traditionally. This more permissive way of marketing especially suits today's B2B buyer who is estimated to be two-thirds to 80 percent of the way to a buying decision before they reach out to a sales person.

Historically, lead generation and nurturing was a process controlled by sales people that advanced prospects from leads to customers through business card sharing, ad follow-ups, trade show courting, and cold call interrupts. Each of these elements would steadily advance a customer from overall awareness to information gathering (criteria development), competitor evaluations, and ultimately to a purchase.

From today's fast-growing adoption of inbound sales, however, we can conclude that relationship building through highly useful content sharing offers a more promising customer connection than what can be expected from traditional cold call techniques. Sales and marketing personnel are now collectively leveraging their content, social networks, and social customer relationship marketing CRM systems to nurture sales leads.

This process begins with the content landscape guidelines laid out in Chapter 1. The next logical step, therefore, is to align the content to your target audience's buying stage as though you are escorting, not pulling, your prospects through the funnel. Using marketing automation systems, the right content can be served to your prospect based on your prospects downloading behaviors. More on this will be discussed in Chapter 11.

Shown on the right of Figure 2.1 is an example of how carefully crafted content shared across social-media channels can progress a target audience from a potential sales lead to a customer. In this case, the sequenced release of blogs, e-newsletters, webinars, case studies, and product reviews can be leveraged as a means of progressing leads and prospects to customers. The keys to advancing customers through these stages is to continually create trust with seller familiarity, sincere problem solving, and incentives for prospects to test drive your offerings.

Early in the process of engagement, for example, target audiences are best met with content that allows them instant education on something you can potentially fix or further edify. This top-of-the-funnel (ToFu) content should then educate or help the visitor to better understand what they came looking for when they searched for content like yours.

Most often, ToFu content includes content that educate audiences about your area of expertise (but without suggesting your offerings at this stage). These techniques set the stage for you to demonstrate your knowledge while creating an atmosphere of trust. At the same time, your prospect is provided a solution free of charge. Consequently, they may share your advice to others.

Should you elect to go this route, you are now on the hook to continue feeding your audience with relevant content. When successful, your prospect gets a complete view of how you regularly solve their problems. You not only gain trust, the prospect begins to rely on you as a source of expertise. For example, consider how a video blog dealing with your

Figure 2.1 Comparison of Outbound and Inbound Marketing

industry segment's business challenges can create overall awareness of your industry contributions.

A series of "how-to" videos, articles, and blog posts can then enlighten your prospect on TALK-worthy topics. Hopefully, at this stage, your prospects are delighted with *free* content that solves problems close to home. A challenge at this point, however, is to keep the prospect engaged while advancing their motivation from early interest to desire to outright action (e.g., pulling out their wallet).

Now imagine this progression taking place without your coming across as pushing your agenda. At the same time, you want your prospect to advance from a "general awareness of a problem you can solve" to "what should they consider" to "why you are distinctly favorable."

In subsequent middle-of-the-funnel (MoFu) phases (information search and evaluation of alternatives), you can begin discussing your brand as some trust has been earned. Consider using techniques like reviews, case studies, and webinars where prospects can gather information that allows them a thorough and objective vendor evaluation. What you gain at this stage with helpful content is a customer that has developed a sentiment of allegiance toward your contributions. A challenge at this point, however, is to develop more content that invites the customer to test drive your offerings perhaps through an online (YouTube) demo, a webinar, or a free trial. More on this will be discussed in Chapter 13.

Shown in Figure 2.2 is an example of a quarterly content plan developed for the real-estate accounting firm discussed earlier. The content sequence addresses its property management audience using the landscape table shown in Figure 1.6 as a foundation for selecting its overall content selections. Keep in mind, however, that a company's content progression through its respective buyer journey differs widely across industries. This particular example is representative of professional services.

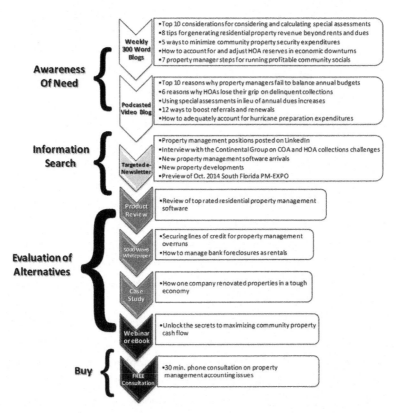

Figure 2.2 Example of Quarterly Content Progression Through Buyer Stage for Accountant Selling to Property Managers

CHAPTER 3

S-H-I-P-P-I-N-G Content with an Emotional Twist

Anyone who tries to make a distinction between education and entertainment doesn't know the first thing about either.
—Herbert Marshall McLuhan, philosopher
of communication theory

Now that content trails have been developed and sequenced in line with your audience's frame of mind, we need to dress it up for an emotional connection primarily through the use of storytelling, humor, and inspiration. With content that is timely, useful, and relevant, audiences begin to know us. And as we show evidence of transparency and empathy, we begin to earn their trust as well. But to really engage our audiences, we need to get them to *like* us.

i-P-L-E-A-S-E with Likeable Content

In his popular book, *Likeable Social Media*, Dave Kerpen describes how you can delight your customers with likeable content and social engagement. Consider his concepts as having to i-P-L-E-A-S-E with likeable content. If your blog, for example, can *inspire* others to share their own stories, audiences will undoubtedly grow to like you. The same holds for content that exudes your *passion*. But even the most enthusiastic piece will fall flat if your audience senses you are not interested in them. It is important that your content invites input. Drafting content that shows you *listen* and *empathize* with your audience will drive "likes" and "shares."

A great way to set the stage for likeable content is to get personal with your audience. Use language and share stories that reflect your own *values*. And do it in an *authentic* manner. Successful bloggers know that the days of PR-vetted speech have been long replaced with a voice that reflects a real person.

Wheel of Emotional Content Attributes

At the heart of any likeable social marketer is their heavy use of content that strikes an emotional chord. Content that evokes "high-arousal emotions" is more likely to go viral than is educational content. Consequently, marketers are capitalizing on emotional techniques to boost visibility and engagement even if the path of connection involves education.

Authors in the field of content marketing refer to this stage of strategy development either as amplifying, electrifying, or igniting content. Let's first start by calling it what it is: we are *shipping* our content through online channels. The reason for emotionalizing this content on its way for delivery is to get it ready for a surprise discovery or something that moves our audiences. Once opened, it needs to get your audience excited enough to digest it, share it, remember it, and, most of all, create one more sentimental attachment to you or your brand.

Scores of blogs and articles have covered the subject of emotional content. While some have justified a set of emotional stimuli from psychological studies, we seem to be left with a mixed bag of psychological stimuli, voice characteristics, and media formats as a framework for studying viral content. Add to that the myriad of expedited practitioner pieces on "6 ways to. . ., 7 emotions for. . ., etc.," and you can see why content marketers lack a cohesive set of meaningful emotional drivers.

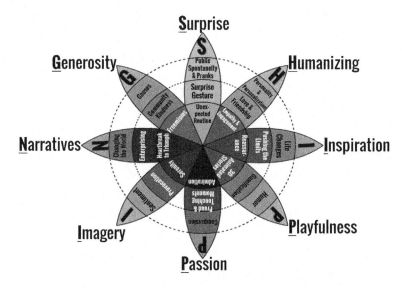

Figure 3.1 S-H-I-P-P-I-N-G Content with an Emotional Twist

There is, however, a convergence developing between theories of emotional drivers and what is implied from viral video statistics. For example, content marketers and researchers seem to agree that emotions associated with viral content have the following attributes:

1. They are either *personal*, *visual*, or *inspiring* in nature.
2. They get our audiences to *know*, *like*, and *trust* us.
3. They often entertain our audiences with *humor*, *games*, or *stories*.
4. They can reflect positive or negative conditions (e.g., joy vs fear).

Sorting out these characteristics for completeness and category distinction, an evaluation of viral content leads us to eight primary attributes of emotional content as displayed in Figure 3.1.

Surprising Audiences with Spontaneity, Pranks, and Bold Change

In almost all cases, content that goes viral has an element of surprise to trigger attention. By itself, however, surprise does not qualify as an emotion stimulus, but when combined with fear, sadness, anger, disgust, or joy, it accounts for nearly every case of emotional content.

This "element of surprise" often happens as an unexpected twist revealed toward the end of a content piece. In perhaps its most effective setting, the element of surprise is cast in a monotonous public setting that challenges crowd routines with a "let loose" spontaneity.

Dozens of flash mob videos garnered millions of views when cast in unsuspected public settings including malls, train stations, airports, public squares, and universities. Consider how effective T-Mobile's was in stirring hundreds of folks at London's Liverpool Street Station (http://bit .ly/1uB3NWf). The unsuspected breakout of dancers presents a strong case for public spontaneity as an audience engager. By adding this *element of surprise* to the dancing euphoria, the video garnered over 4 million views.

In similar manner, Banco Sabadell (http://bit.ly/1oCPP1H) surprised a huge outdoor audience with well-orchestrated music. Beginning with a small number of professional musicians, the audience was overwhelmed by an eventual full orchestra accompanied by a music choir. In less than two years following its release on YouTube, the video surpassed 50 million views.

Besides flash mobs, firms have capitalized on surprising crowds with augmented reality. British digital agency Appshaker stirred up a crowd at a UK mall for National Geographic Channel. The passerby's were invited to interact with wild animals and other fictional characters on a big screen (http://bit.ly/1y8aXm1).

Pepsi Max took this one step further in a public prank also created by augmented reality (http://bit.ly/1ryubdX). Crowds, in this case, were shown aliens and heart-stopping scenes through cameras disguised in bus shelters. And much like other crowd-disturbing entertainment, the video went viral. In a similar vein, a coffee shop in New York startled the wits out of unsuspecting customers witnessing a telekinetic tantrum (http:// bit.ly/WKPwrc). The video amassed over 55 million views in less than 6 months. This combination of surprise and fear attests to the impact that negative emotions can also have on viral content.

Besides spontaneous public disruptions, another element of surprise involves an unexpected change of routine. In a daring move to challenge the mundane airline-safety instructions we all dread, Virgin Atlantic surprised their patrons with an entertaining approach to the subject.

Passengers were likely startled to see such an unorthodox approach to conveying serious safety issues. But the performance of the same video on YouTube demonstrates its high favorability. Since its release, Delta (http://bit.ly/1nPkrhl), Philippine Airlines (http://bit.ly/1tkJECa), Southwest (http://bit.ly/1rLZ3uN), and others have followed suit.

But not all of these unexpected routines require exorbitant budgets. Melbourne Railways took a chance with their light-hearted approach to safety. Their "Dumb Ways to Die" video (http://bit.ly/1tUVBvT) not only reached 100M views and 100K thousand likes, the public service announcement was produced using low-budget animation and amateur tunes. Like Virgin Atlantic and other airlines, Metro clearly demonstrates that audiences need stimulation. And one way to accomplish this is through the element of surprise.

Humanizing Brands with Personality, Empathy, and Behind the Scenes

Humanizing brands is nothing new, but it wasn't as important back when brands controlled their own perceptions. With social media transferring control to consumers, however, open and honest conversations have taken over vetted speeches. And content marketers are quickly grasping that, without personality, brands will die on the vine. But brand personality requires more than a distinctive, humanized voice.

First, the values represented by the brand have to resonate with the target audience across every piece of content. If done effectively, a brand's personality often reaches a sweet spot usually in one of five dimensions:

1. excitement (Disney's *it's a small world*)
2. sincerity (Dove's *real beauty sketches*)
3. ruggedness (Red Bull's *give you wings*)
4. competence (Chipotle's *food with integrity*)
5. sophistication (Grey Goose's *fly beyond*).

GE shows its personality through its technology. They consistently show how their technology changes the lives of those that depend on it. From stories of a Japanese doctor jet skiing across islands with GE's medical equipment to Scottish islanders that harness the power of their tide-driven undersea turbines, GE's personality is cast as a caring and innovative provider of life-altering technologies.

Secondly, the voice has to be consistent across the enterprise. Here is where the rubber meets the road. A firm's personality has to be as consistently described and enforced enterprisewide as Apple's *making people's lives easier* or Virgin Atlantic's *vibrant, loose and fun image*. Undoubtedly, it helps if the voice is a reflection of the founder's personality and vision as in the case of Apple's Steve Jobs and Virgin's Richard Branson.

In addition to sporting a personality, brand humanizing requires us to drop the *corporate speak*. In his book, *There Is No B2B Or B2C: It's Human to Human #H2H*, Bryan Kramer builds a compelling case that much of what we read is riddled with messaging that is too complicated and overly thought out. Instead, he argues in his *5 Basic Rules for Speaking Human* that content should "market to the heart, and sell to the head." This means getting to the point in as few words as possible. It also means putting yourself in your customer's shoes when crafting communications.

A great example of this *empathy* toward customers can be seen in TSB Bank's Story of the Reverend Henry Duncan (http://bit.ly/1pz18V1), a man whose radical creation of a trustee savings bank resonated with ordinary hardworking folks. The stark contrast of Duncan and today's global investment firm resembles that of George Bailey and Henry Potter in "It's a Wonderful Life." In so doing TSB humanizes their brand. Another example of empathy is displayed by Ram Trucks (http://bit.ly/1qdPdNW). Their story of how God made a farmer on the eighth day is done as a tribute to the hard work ethic and unique attributes of a farmer. The video generated over 17M views and 55K likes.

Finally, emotional connections can be made through content when the audience is invited to play a role or belong to a community. Access to *behind-the-scenes* content, in particular, is a great way to build a sense of togetherness. J. Crew's "Color Crazy" video reached over a million views after introducing audiences to their down-to-earth and even quirky team.

By allowing users to help shape a brand through their crowd-sourced inputs or their own content, firms enable audiences to earn bragging rights. Microsoft can attest to this audience role back when Windows 7 was introduced. Their infamous "I'm a PC and Windows 7 was my idea" campaign created an emotional attachment to a brand not well known for humanizing.

Inspiring Audiences to Overcome, Shoot High, or Make a Difference

Much like entertaining content, inspirational messaging transcends the best of informative and instructional content. Did you ever notice how many tweets, posts, pins, videos, or other news feed updates are intended to lift our spirits or encourage us to pursue a better self? In general, most content of this type relates to

1. overcoming obstacles,
2. feeling spiritually lifted and grateful,
3. aspiring for better self endeavors,
4. pursuing dreams,
5. discovering talents and gifts, and
6. Eureka moments.

Among the ways that inspiring themes lead to viral content is through messages of hope and encouragement. This is often done by allowing us to live vicariously through the lives of those experiencing far greater misfortune.

In "My Last Days, Meet Zach Sobiech," I asked my students why they felt inspired from a video leading to Zach's final hours. Most claimed it gave them a sense of closure with their own issues. Others implied it made them feel grateful and more willing to take chances in life. This may explain why Pfizer's "More than Medication" (http://bit.ly/1l8Pxe2) performed so well. A boy deals with his emotions of a dying child by revealing his building graffiti that encourages her to be brave.

Other forms of inspiration include the many *no pain, no gain* moments of truth used primarily in sports content. Brands often capitalize on this technique to tap into our resilience and resolve. Perhaps no one does this better than Richard Simmons, whose promotion of weight loss programs over the past 35 years claims to have helped humanity lose over 12 million pounds. In Nike's "Find Your Greatness" campaign (http://bit.ly/UyMmFp), the centerpiece of content features an over-weight 12 year old, Nathan, toughing out a grueling and lonely jog. The campaign is not only meant to inspire everyday athletes, but it also supports their motivational hub for athletes looking to "share their progress and success through social channels."

Another way that inspiring content taps into our deepest emotions is through reassurance. Dove does this very effectively in their "Real Beauty Sketches (http://bit.ly/1qdUNzZ)." The tear-jerking video reached over 60M views in less than a year as women realized they are their worst beauty critics. Backed by a statistic that only 4 percent of women worldwide consider themselves beautiful, Dove creates an especially strong emotional bond in their commitment to "create a world where beauty is a source of confidence, not anxiety."

Finally, inspiration aimed at pushing our aspirations can work well in audience reach and engagement when backed by personalities we admire. From Eureka moments of newly recognized talents to first attempts at fighting depression, inspirational content can create perhaps the most lasting emotional connection with your audiences.

Entertaining Audiences with Humor, Games, and Animated Stories

Another way to spark emotional connections from content is through playfulness. Audiences are stimulated by games, animations, and humor. Humorous videos, in particular, offer perhaps the greatest opportunity to create an emotional connection with audiences. We only need to look at the vast knowledge gained from thousands of commercials recast on YouTube. My own study of over 3,000 commercials recast on YouTube found that over 95 percent of those social videos reaching over 50,000 views were playful in some way. And two-thirds of these involved some sort of humor. [1]

A challenge to brands and small businesses, however, is breaking the mold of the traditionally serious content used in their industries. But consider how serious businesses like insurance are now convinced that humor trumps almost every type of video content. Geico, AFLAC, Allstate, Progressive, and State Farm have all taken this route after years of reluctance to poke fun of serious subjects. Add to this entertainment form the growing popularity of videos, and you can understand why recast commercials have become highly strategic elements in many content-marketing strategies. To understand humor and how it's applied, the scholarly literature points to three theories, whose various combinations lead to 10 types of humor listed later. In general, we tend to laugh when we

1. see something out of sorts (incongruity theory),
2. enjoy others' misfortunes (superiority theory), and
3. release ourselves from inhibitions (relief theory).

Humor Using Comic Wit

Stemming from the incongruity theory, comic wit remains the most popular humor technique used to attract and engage audiences. Consisting of exaggeration, irony, surprise twists, and perceptual discords, this cognitive form of humor makes us laugh at the unexpected.

Exaggeration

As shown in Figure 3.2, *exaggeration*, in particular, is the number one attention getter among all humor techniques used in viral YouTube videos. The use of exaggeration dates back centuries as a comic device and popular figure of speech known as hyperbole. Consistent with the theory of incongruity, it suggests laughter results from seeing things out of sorts.

Most of us laugh when we witness over-the-top demos or exaggerated stories. Perhaps the most famous of viral videos in this area is the case of Blendtec. The founder, Tom Dickson, produced a series of videos that grossly exaggerating how iPads, golf balls, and even a garden rake could blend in his blenders (http://bit.ly/1k62WbE). After 186 videos, Blendtec's retail sales increased 700 percent, while its YouTube site

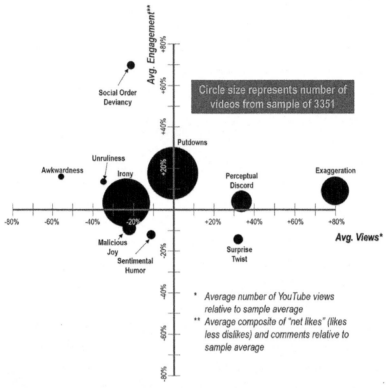

Figure 3.2 Performance Results of Social Videos Using Humor

enlisted 200,000+ subscribers and surpassed 200 million views. There over the top demos were featured on the *The Today Show*, *The History Channel*, *The Tonight Show*, and *The Wall Street Journal*.

An effective technique used in exaggeration taps into our emotional response to overreactive behaviors. In this case, we laugh at how others take such extremes to make their point. Forceful demonstrations, for example, are often loaded with intensity so that we can appreciate the peculiar nature of others. In a similar vein, some of the top viral videos show scenes of extreme naiveté or protectionism where we shamefully find ourselves or close ones exhibiting these same fanatic behaviors. The laughter in this case has much to do with pointing out our own quirks as overprotective Dads, star-struck admirers, or wired up Type A's.

Finally, many brands and small companies have capitalized on the visual side of exaggeration. Seeing the visual anomaly, our brains often ask: "can that really be true?" Some of the most popular comic devices used in this form of wit include the display of supernatural performances, motion distortion, exaggerated body reactions, and incredible allure.

The key to using this humor technique, however, is making it evident that the object of exaggeration is beyond the realms of possibility. For example, Aaron Rodgers throwing an 80 yard pass would amaze us, but LeBron James making a full court buzzer beater from the top of the stands would make us laugh.

The popularity of exaggeration as an entertainment device can be attributed to the following:

1. It rarely offends any particular audience.
2. It can be easily grasped visually, emotionally, or cognitively.
3. It can be easily produced in low-budget settings (e.g., BlendTec's 200M+ view channel success was achieved with a purported budget <$10K).

Perceptual Discord

Like exaggeration, perceptual discords represent a form of comic wit. But instead of showing extremes, they show us something out of touch. Stemming from the theory of incongruity, this concept entertains us by contrasting what we see with what is routinely expected. Mentally, we are asking ourselves: "Did I see that correctly?"

This perceptual discord can be realized in the form of visual anomalies like impersonations, eccentric behaviors, or bizarre substitutions. In each case, we detect a mismatch with common perceptions. In the case of odd behaviors, we often laugh at the innocence of children or animals acting as adult humans. Witnessing the character contrast, our laughter is created by a harmless cognitive shift where we often imagine an underdog putting others in their place.

Throughout the last decade, this concept has been played out with overperformances. Consider the babies in E-Trade and Evian that pose as adults. Several viral videos also feature animals going the extra mile to motivate themselves or their masters. A great example is the highly popular Nolan Cheddar video where a mouse driven by "Eye of the Tiger" musters up the energy to escape its trap (http://bit.ly/1s2NsFl).

Another technique used in perceptual discords relates to our visualizing objects or scenes taken out of context. Some of the top viral videos show unconventional routines or unusual settings surrounding the highlighted activity. In other cases, the viral videos make us laugh when we imagine a human depiction of abstract concepts or literal interpretation of idioms. EDS did this well in their portrayal of cowboys literally herding cats (http://bit.ly/1m2HW0y). Geico uses this technique regularly. One skit, in particular, exemplifies how "words really can hurt you" (http://bit.ly/1oy09YL) by showing a cowboy running into a large sign of letters spelling "The End." In each of these cases, the attempt at humor is based on audience detection of a mismatch with what their minds see as a common practice.

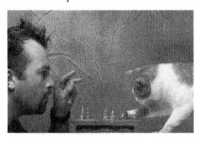

A concept similar to misrepresentation involves the substitution of animals or objects with a bizarre alternative. One popular technique includes anthropomorphism, where human attributes are ascribed to abstractions. Allstate used this form of humor to depict the concept of "mayhem" through the careless habits of an unruly actor who exemplified the dire consequences of poor insurance coverage.

Some viral YouTube videos portray scenes of animal substitutes such as that found in squirrels substituted for running bulls. Like sound imitations, these bizarre substitutes allow our imaginations to vicariously live through the substitute actor.

Finally, one comic device used in perceptual discord relates to nonsense. As a cognitive exercise, this form of humor makes us logically see something off kilter. Humor in this case arises out of our confusion with the relevance or choices made by the actor. Upon witnessing their naiveté or imbecile nature, we then laugh at blaming the confusion on the actor's ineptness or empty dialogues.

Surprise Twist

Surprise twists cause us to laugh as we witness or experience a change in course. Stemming from the theory of incongruity, this concept entertains us through a distracting segue. Mentally, we are asking ourselves: "Where did this come from?"

This surprise twist can be realized in the form of visual anomalies (e.g., sudden appearances, changes, or revelations) or conceptual incongruities (e.g., storyline twists or unexpected responses). In each case, we detect a mismatch with what we expect to occur next. Think of this as stopping in our tracks when a scene or statement suggests that something is off track. Research suggests that we laugh when our minds anticipate a certain outcome, only to be tricked at the end with a wrong or an uneventful answer.

This concept is not new. Years ago, Wendy's conducted a comical test taste of their hamburgers. In their famous 1989 commercial featuring a trucker, the participant was asked to choose from a delicious-looking hamburger A or a nasty-looking hamburger B. The trucker unexpectedly picked hamburger B. This unexpected twist would be followed with comments like: ". . .I'm a trucker, I could be eating this baby in Shaky Town and still tasting it in Salt Lake. . ."

Plot trickery works well here. A very successful method of stealing your attention is for the producer to take you down a subliminal storyline that ends in an unexpected twist. That is, just when you are drifting off to a predictable plot, the story takes an interesting turn. Geico did this well for years. By showing realistic scenes of a judicial court sentence, for example, the audience waiting for a verdict was surprised to hear the judge announcing his saving money on car insurance. This unanticipated change in events also works well in stories of twisted fate as well as in fantasies where the dreamer wakes up to a lackluster reality.

Snickers capitalized on these techniques in their transforming of cranky actors (e.g., Betty White, Roseanne Barr, Aretha Franklyn, Don

Rickles, and Joe Pesci) into younger folks ready to return to action after eating a Snickers bar. In these cases, the transformation itself serves as an unexpected twist that suggests we have been duped.

A related concept to this transformational surprise is visual surprise. In this case, we are introduced to the sudden arrival of a new character (e.g., alien creature) or an unexpected object. Advertisers like Dodge and Volvic use these techniques in their displays of wishful thinking. Finally, brands like Nationwide shock their audiences with a surprise ugly substitute as when the fantasized Fabio turns into a wrinkled old man (http://bit.ly/1s7agDY).

Irony

Irony, much like that of any perceptual discord, is characterized by a contrast, between expectations and reality. It makes us laugh by showing the opposite or undesired intentions of someone's actions. Mentally, we are saying to ourselves: "...I did not see that coming..." Irony can be realized in the form of visual anomalies (e.g., unusual pairing, wrong personas and temperaments, and hypocritical behaviors) or conceptual incongruities (e.g., wild coincidences, misunderstandings, or something scripted out of place). In each case, we detect a mismatch with what we expect to see.

Visual irony, or the use of two or more images that don't belong together, especially works well in content marketing. An unusual pairing of well-known characters or scenes, for example, makes us laugh at the imagined conflict. These inevitable battles were played out well in the 1970s show "The Odd Couple." The series featured a neurotic neat freak pitted against an untidy, cigar chomping gambler. Audiences, in this case, laughed at the how the two mismatched friends could possibly share an apartment following their divorces.

Other examples of visual irony include the casting of humans as animals or cyborgs as humans. In both cases, the irony is enjoyed as we witness the acting out of a creation mismatch. Similarly, an oxymoron like the living dead, friendly adversaries, or a screaming mime creates laughter as we envision the inherent conflict.

Another successful way to get laughter from irony is through the display of temperament anomalies. A common way to display this anomaly is with the mellowing of cantankerous personalities like the volatile John McEnroe or Bobby Knight. This can also be accomplished through the juxtaposing of characters in contradicting or aberrant ways. This has been done with examples of a mother and daughter fiercely arguing over each other's kind attributes as well as a beautiful woman admiring a man's unattractive habits.

A third technique used in irony involves the miscasting of character roles or intentions. This is often accomplished through the display of mistaken identities, adult acting children, or childish acting adults. This mismatch of personas can also create laughter when we see the least likely character to play a certain role. We often see this enacted in the form of unlikely hero figures.

Finally, we often laugh over situational irony in which actions have an effect that is contrary to what was expected. This often happens in the case of a coincidental backlash, where the odds of such an unexpected scene spoiler are infinitely low. Other cases of situational irony include the undesired outcomes resulting from misunderstandings or the scripting of behaviors in a misplaced or rhetorical setting. We sometimes see this displayed in videos through unorthodox routines, such as when employees let loose in an office setting.

Humor Using Putdowns, Malicious Joy, and Awkwardness

Yes, America still appreciates a good blonde or bubba joke. According to the theory of superiority, we often experience sudden glory when dethroning others for their bungled behaviors, stupidity, macho moments gone bad, or society satires. T-Mobile capitalized on this form of humor in their royal wedding spoof that surpassed 30M views. Using a host of royal look-alikes, they parted a shot at haughty royal etiquette with playful irreverence (http://bit.ly/1koY95o).

Putdowns

The use of mockery capitalizes on our emotional reaction to watching others experience a well-deserved putdown. Stemming from the theory of superiority, we often experience sudden glory when dethroning others or elevating ourselves at the expense of others' peculiarities. Of the viral videos featuring putdowns, most include mocked peculiarities, lofty conquests, society satires, or stereotyping.

The use of mockery dates back centuries as audiences watched imbeciles and maladroits parade on stage. Baby boomers likely recall the inept Deputy Barney Fife of Mayberry, who was oblivious to his idiosyncrasies and quirky nature. Seeing himself as a high-standing citizen, we often laughed hysterically at his gullibility and delusions of grandeur. This putdown is often felt through background mockery as well. Geico capitalized on this with their mockery of a poor farmer who spelled misspelled cow as c-o-w-e-i-e-i-o (http://bit.ly/1tzCLgy).

A second technique used in putdowns taps into our desire to dethrone the self-righteous, the popular, the pretentious, and the hypermasculine. Some of the top viral videos show scenes of humbled haughtiness featuring those we despise or compete against. A common technique is to use some form of outwitting that literally shames the victim or proves our superiority over them. Miller Lite is notorious for their macho moments gone bad (http://bit.ly/1rMDBm8). We can't help but laugh at the pretentious Joe Cool revealed for his inner femininity.

A number of top viral videos feature the sudden glory we feel when our society is mocked. Known as satire, we often relish the opportunity to poke fun of other cultures seen as pretentious or smug. This is often played out by exaggerating the cultural nuances or language peculiarities of audiences targeted by our sarcasm. Similarly, we poke fun of celebrated life styles with parodies of popular shows, sports events, or military operations. This is often done through witty dialogues (e.g., cheeky barbs) where the intent of the sarcasm is to mock a targeted society.

Like satires, the use of mimicry and impersonations work well as putdowns. One of the most popular ways of doing this is through the stereotyping of blondes or provincial men. The latter is often portrayed as an idiot or someone hypnotized under the spell of seduction.

Care has to be taken in the use of putdowns as an attempt to entertain audiences. Although they resonate well in Western cultures like the United States, it has limited appeal in Asia, Latin America, the Middle East, and Southern Europe. Putdowns can run counter to their relational and group-oriented values.

Malicious Joy

Malicious joy, or *schadenfreude*, refers to the pleasure we derive from seeing others fail or suffer misfortune. Also rooted in the theory of superiority, this feeling of sudden glory can occur when we witness bungled behaviors, unanticipated spoilers, unfortunate happenstances, deserved repercussions, or the acts of cretins.

A common approach for entertaining audiences with malicious joy is to poke fun of someone notorious for their clumsy or incompetent behaviors. The 1950's sitcom, "I Love Lucy," reached the highest popularity of any show at its time based on the bungling behaviors of Lucy. The naïve and accident-prone housewife had a knack for getting herself and her husband into trouble whenever she tried to make a name for herself.

Several viral YouTube videos are based on characters that are prone to accidents or saying the wrong thing. This is often displayed through the eyes of someone drunk or oblivious to their surroundings. Men, in particular, are often portrayed for their bungled behaviors resulting from their one-track minds. Consider how we laugh when women make futile attempts to seduce their husbands when engrossed in their games or jobs. We are likely laughing at the husband's obsessions and oblivion as well as the wife's futile attempts to get their attention.

Another successful way to get laughter from malicious joy is through the portrayal of spoilers. For example, many of us laugh when witnessing the spoiling of romance. Just when the mood is set, attempts at seduction are foiled by some unexpected event. A number of viral videos show similar results in views and engagement when a storyline ends with unexpected damage, injuries, or danger. This cause of laughter taps more into our emotional senses where a feeling of superiority is felt over those whose peace or excitement is snatched away.

A third technique used in malicious joy relates to bad luck. Shamefully, many of us laugh when others get dealt a bad hand. Who doesn't enjoy watching someone knocked down a notch when an unwise choice is based on attempts at heroism or chivalry. The same type of thrill emerges from bad timing such as when someone interrupts our concentration at the worst time or when the next person in line wins the grand prize.

Viral video results also attest to our delight in the misfortune of those exhibiting naïveté or simply keeping their eye off the ball. Especially when foolish mistakes result in catastrophic consequences, we often laugh hysterically at choices we know we are capable of committing ourselves.

But perhaps even more than bad luck or unexpected spoiler is the laughter resulting from well-deserved retaliation. This often happens when the actions of a featured villain backfire. In a similar vein, we laugh at paybacks against someone we despise or who is unveiled of their devious intentions. Doritos did this very well in their commercial of a baby snatching the bag of chips from an annoying older sibling who incessantly teased the toddler (http://bit.ly/WPH61O). The payback results in our own feeling of sudden glory that we experience when living vicariously through the underdog.

On the lighter side, some sponsors use innocent repercussions to highlight the misfortunes of someone overzealous or careless. Lending Tree took this route in their depiction of Stanley Johnson, who shamefully reveals that his lavish lifestyle has put him in debt to his eyeballs (http://bit.ly/1n7zgWw). Although not as deserving as the villainous victim of a backfire, we still relish the thought of witnessing the aftermath of someone short cutting their path to success.

Finally, an effective use of malicious joy relates to the casting of cretins whose low-class demeanor elevates our own status. For centuries, comedies of derelicts, the grotesque, and the deformed have aroused fits of laughter from audiences. A number of sponsors have obtained high scores in views and engagement from the portrayal of people seen as physically deformed (e.g., 700 lb. sumo wrestler).

Similar results, however, can be achieved when portraying folks as mentally subnormal. Both Geico (http://bit.ly/1u49isx) and FedEx (http://bit.ly/1oRuth3) capitalized on cretin sneering with their casting of Neanderthals in modern settings. Vonage chose a similar tactic by casting airheads and derelicts in both their "People do Stupid Things" and "Chief Generosity Officer" campaigns.

Awkwardness

Why we laugh at awkward moments has much to do with the pleasure derived from seeing others fail or suffer misfortune. Also rooted in the theory of superiority, this disparaging form of humor leads to a feeling of sudden glory when we displace our own histories of embarrassing moments onto others. Among the types of humor that capitalize on awkwardness are remorseful regrets, uncomfortable settings, exercising humility, and revealed secrets.

One way to enjoy others' misfortunes is through the depiction of embarrassing situations where victims are left speechless. Consider how we laugh at those experiencing fear and remorse after they realize they are in a "no win" situation. Geico did this by showing Abe Lincoln faced with a tough predicament of being honest or offending his wife (http://bit.ly/1xG20LJ).

In the sitcom, *Everybody Loves Raymond*, Robert and Ray Barone often found themselves in a sticky situation. Both were prone to engaging their mouths before their brains as regretful statements and actions put them in the dog house. We laughed, for example, when Ray was forced to choose between ingratiating his wife or his dominating mother.

The laughter in these cases typically results from the remorse felt by the victim from their regretful actions or statements. By displacing our own recollection of these embarrassments onto others, we are in effect saying: "I am glad this did not happen to me." Arguably, this laughter increases the more a victim is caught off guard or left with an unsolvable quandary.

Another successful way to get laughter from awkwardness is through scenes of discomfort that arise when someone gets too intimate or reveals too much information. A number of commercials feature the discomfort that men in particular feel when other guys get too close or expose their creepy behaviors. Doritos capitalized on this with their ad featuring a man licking another man's fingers. A similar sense of misfortune is realized when a young boy faces the dreaded kiss of an assertive girl or when a father is pressed to answer "where do babies come from?" We are likely reliving our own experiences of the fear that results from being put on a spot.

This same displaced embarrassment can also arise when we witness others having to explain themselves after exposing their vulnerabilities. In this case, we are laughing at the relief from not being the one who has to exercise humility. Southwest uses this technique in their "Wanna Get Away" campaigns. The story-line features characters often put on the spot publicly to explain their mistakes. This technique especially works well when featuring men inadvertently exposing their feminine or child sides. The feeling of shame can also result when quiet words are broadcast publicly or when surrounding audiences get the wrong impression from seemingly perverted behaviors.

Another method used to create awkward moments involves the exposure of someone's embarrassing intentions. This often includes the unraveling of a character's foiled deceptions when caught red handed. This exposure may reveal a man's true colors or his inappropriate glances at another woman. In this case, we are likely laughing at their behavioral hypocrisy as well as their misfortune of having a poor disguise.

Humor Using Unruliness and Social-Order Deviancy

The relief theory of humor explains why we laugh when letting loose of our inhibitions. Several videos exceeded 10 million views when accompanied by unruly behaviors or the violation of sacred taboos. IKEA, in particular, is known for their edgy content that makes us laugh when parents act out (http://bit.ly/UDOqvG).

Unruliness

Some have taken the route of depicting explosive behavior from intimidating icons in their approach to this style of humor. Consider how Snicker's Mr. T, Nike's Clay Matthews, and Reebock's "Terry Tate Office Linebacker" videos reached millions of views as these icons disrupt peaceful settings.

The relief theory contends that laughter is created when we release tension or nervous energy such as when we unleash our suppressed desires. Consequently, we love watching others act out uncontrollably or violate some social order. In effect, we are likely enjoying the observation of others acting out our own inhibitions through hysteria, impulsive outbursts, displaced irritation, or exercising improprieties.

A popular technique for entertaining audiences with humor is to show people unleashing their anxiety through uncontrollable screaming and yelling. In the 1950s, the popular sitcom, *The Honeymooners*, featured a bellowing, short-tempered Ralph Kramden who would easily spin out of control. Audiences laughed at his infamous "BANG, ZOOM! Straight to the Moon!" The relief theory would attribute these fits of laughter to our own desires to let out steam. Other examples of hysteria in viral YouTube videos include scenes of angry bosses losing their control or folks experiencing nervous breakdowns. Similarly, many of the popular sports-related commercials show scenes of fanatics going over the edge to support their teams.

Another successful way to get laughter from unruliness is through scenes of impulsive outbursts. Some viral YouTube videos reached views in the millions as audiences witnessed forceful demonstrations, body explosions, or outright belligerence. The tension relief can be explained as an innate desire we may all have to act out our aggression.

A third technique used in unruliness involves our desire to express deep irritation. This is often accomplished by having us share the irritation and the subsequent desire to fiercely lash out at others' facing annoying habits. Consider the Geico's viral video where an annoying pig continually utters "Wee! Wee! Wee!" or the vexatious camel in their hump day video who repeatedly asks "Guess What Day It Is?" Our own laughter comes from the expression of irritation shown on the faces of those annoyed. This can also be accomplished by showing scenes of those irritated by incessant talkers. In effect, we are sharing the desires of the irritated actors to berate or strike the annoying subjects.

Finally, another common way to release suppressed desires is to display scenes of wishful naughtiness. Who doesn't want to disobey society rules on stature, proper behavior, or appropriate demeanor? Consider how audiences laugh when Mr. T acts out on our behalf or when Harley Davidson attracts the recalcitrant with their acts of rebellion. Besides aggression and disobedience, these improprieties often include such forbidden behaviors as invasive peeking.

Social-Order Deviancy

The most engaging form of humor in viral videos involves social-order deviancy or those behaviors that challenge society rules and expectations. Many of us love watching others unleash their innate desire to break the law, enter forbidden territory, or simply act out our inhibitions. Most of the viral videos featuring this form of humor involve society irreverence, taboos, offensive behaviors, or unleashed mania.

A popular technique for entertaining audiences with social-order deviancy is to poke fun of pompous society folks. In the 1960's sitcom, "The Beverly Hillbillies," Jed Clampett and his poor backwoods family transplanted to Beverly Hills, California, after striking oil on their land. In the series, audiences laugh hysterically as the rags to riches family unknowingly mocks the pos-

turing of high society by retaining their hillbilly lifestyle in a luxurious Hollywood house. Being exploited by rich bankers, the Clampetts often come out ahead with their provincial wisdom. In effect, they put high society in their place.

Several viral YouTube videos are based on high-society satires, rule breaking, and undermining authority. Common to all is the release of tension we experience by unloading on someone's statutes. Witness how this works when we outwit the censorship imposed by honorable judges, pious clergymen, or smug professors.

Another successful way to get laughter from social-order deviancy is through the depiction of forbidden society behaviors. Many of us laugh when witnessing the spoiling of sacred rituals. Who doesn't love watching others break taboos? This likely results from sharing their pressures in having to sustain a devout life. A similar thrill arises when we strip off clothing, break office rules, or slap a smug antagonist. Whether it's vicariously acting out naughty behaviors or simply fighting back, we feel liberated from society rules.

A third technique used in social-order deviancy involves offensive behaviors. Here again, we enjoy watching others mock society. In this case, the mockery is through tactless behaviors. This could include bad manners or disgusting personal habits. A common technique used in this humor is to highlight reactions to poor hygiene such as from foot odor, perspiration, or flatulence. As the perfect target of our tactless behavior, this especially works well when exposing the offense to those sensitive to protocol or classy surroundings.

Other categories of social-order deviancy involve letting loose with craziness. One of the oldest forms of humor involve the depiction of mad scientists. In effect, we are laughing at the disorder associated with an esteemed profession much like we laugh at disruptive behavior in public places. In many viral videos, for example, you can attribute the humor to disruptions created from screaming and destroying property in serene surroundings.

Finally, the witnessing of women swooning over men in insane frenzies has been a highly successful humor technique over the years. In 1995, Diet Coke featured an office of ladies running to windows to get a glimpse of a sexy construction worker (http://bit.ly/1rNpyN4). Axe took this concept a step further in a video that garnered over 50M views by featuring hoards of bikini-clad jungle women closing in on their prey. In this case, the hunted was a man freshly deodorized with Axe (http://bit.ly/1pu7J5M).

Sentimental Humor Based on Innocence, Anxiety Relief, and Melodrama

Sentimental humor taps into our emotions through an arousal-safety mechanism. For example, in the first stage or arousal safety, emotions are aroused with sentimentality, empathy, or some form of negative anxiety. As the story-line develops, we then see this heightened arousal state as safe, cute, or inconsequential. This shift from high arousal to relief is what creates laughter.

A way to imagine this type of humor is to consider how we laugh. Comic wit, for example, is normally expressed as "Ah Hah." Laughter from disparaging humor (e.g., putdowns) is normally expressed as "Ha, Ha."

Sentimental humor would be expressed as "Ahhh." This could happen when we witness someone escaping danger as well as when we experience a child doing something cute.

Among the types of humor that capitalize on this arousal-safety mechanism are those involving false alarms, melodrama, or child innocence. Children, for example, can easily arouse our emotions with their youthful discoveries and mimicry of adulthood. The laughter tends to result when we see them successfully overcome their struggles to get through complicated situations. These story-lines usually start with a sentimental attachment or an empathetic feeling toward the child. We then laugh when we see how their first battles with courage, romance, or independence conclude with a happy ending.

In some situations, we may be laughing at how their trials prove more fruitful than our own. This may be the reason why we love scenes of children reflecting our own inner self. No character perhaps aroused us more with child innocence than Shirley Temple. The child prodigy started her film career at the age of 3. With her innocent coquetry, she was known for her advice to clergymen and other adults that often had profound implications.

Several viral YouTube videos are based on child innocence where the laughter results from children topping their adult counterparts as well as from our vicariously living through their incorruptibility. Doritos no doubt enjoyed great success with their commercial featuring a feisty 5 year old warning his mother's suitor to mind his manners (http://bit.ly/1s8p0mX).

AT&T's campaign (http://bit.ly/1nYls6x) reached millions of viewers across its episodes of "It's Not Complicated." Taking a lesson from Shirley Temple, they capitalized on kids answering oddly, sweetly, and hilariously to questions like "What's better: Bigger or smaller? Faster or slower? More or less?"

Another successful way to get laughter from sentimental humor is through the relief of fear and anxiety. For example, just when we expect some disturbing outcome, a story-line then shows the fears to be baseless. The arousal-safety mechanism in this case starts with a buildup of suspense. As the fearful sensation rouses within us, we then experience a physiological shift as the anxiety fizzles into something inconsequential.

This swing in emotional response is what produces laughter. Dirt Devil did this with a viral video featuring what appears to be an exorcism (http://bit.ly/1k9RATV). The hair-raising drama leads us to a convulsing, demon-possessed woman plastered to the ceiling. But just when our fears our aroused, we are relieved to find a neighbor upstairs creating the gravity pull with her vacuum cleaner.

Sentimental humor can also be created through melodrama. Consider how we laugh when we experience someone's over theatrical behaviors. For example, a story-line may start with someone's passionate reaction to a mundane situation. But as we begin to process their intensity with our own empathetic reflections, we then find the cause of their melodrama to be unfounded.

In effect, this arousal-safety mechanism takes us from our own passionate empathy to a feeling of relief from a false alarm. Laughter then results from the arousal-safety shift. Similarly, we might laugh as we conclude the melodramatic actor is rather pathetic.

Another method used in sentimental humor derives from the exposure of inner secrets such as when we witness someone passing in and out of dreams. A fantasy, for example, could arouse our emotions. We then laugh from a shift in these emotions as we are made aware of the false state. This arousal-safety mechanism could also work when an innocent scene turns out to have sexual overtones. In essence, we are likely laughing at the tension relief we experience from keeping our inner desires secret.

Finally, inner secrets can produce laughter when we observe and hear a contradicting inner voice. In this case, we are likely experiencing an emotional shift when the imagined inner voice allows us to safely escape from a hostile or an awkward situation.

Shown in Figure 3.3 is a summary of the comic devices used in humorous content supported by the incongruity theory, superiority theory, and relief theory.

Theory of Incongruity	39 Miscast Temperament	80 Beauty Conquered Male	120 Extreme Screaming
EXAGGERATION	40 Soft Tough Guy	**MALICIOUS JOY**	**Impulsive Outbursts**
CONCEPTUAL DISCORD	41 Unlikely Friendliness	**Bungling Behaviors**	121 Belligerance
Exaggerated Outcomes	42 Unusually Considerate	81 Accident Prone	122 Forceful Demonstration
1 Exaggerated Results	**Ironic Persona**	82 Futile Attempts	123 Spontaneous Performance
2 Exaggerated Response	43 Adult Acting Child	83 Innocently Offensive	124 Body Explosion
3 Exaggerated Nightmare Reactions	44 Childish Adult	84 Toxic Stupor	**Displaced Irritation**
4 Exaggerated Stories	45 Miscast Role	**Unanticipated Spoiler**	125 Annoying Natures
Understatement	46 Mistaken Identity	85 Unexpected Danger	126 Incessant Talker
5 Unrattled by Danger	47 Unlikely Hero	86 Unexpected Injury	127 Ending the Annoyance
6 Exaggerated Simplicity	**Situational Irony**	87 Unexpected Damage	128 Annoying Repetitions
7 Exaggerated Concealment	48 Anachronisms	88 Spoiled Romance	**Exercising Improprieties**
8 Profound Grasp of the Obvious	49 Coincidental Backlash	**Unfortunate Happenstance**	129 Invasive Peeking
VISUAL ANOMALIES	50 Miscommunications	89 Bad Timing	130 Disorderly Pop Culture Lexicons
Exaggerated Qualities	51 Misplaced Routine	90 Bad Idea	131 Recalcitrance
9 Exaggerated Body Reactions	52 Misunderstood Intentions	91 Lost Opportunity	132 Unsightly Exposure
10 Supernatural Performance	**SURPRISE TWIST**	92 Unforeseen Consequences	**SOCIAL ORDER DEVIANCY**
11 Incredible Allure	**Conceptual Surprises**	**Deserved Repercussions**	**Society Irreverence**
12 Speed & Scale Distortion	53 Wrong Answer	93 Paybacks	133 High Society Satires
ABERRANT BEHAVIORS	54 Uneventful Conclusion	94 Backfires	134 Outwitting the Honorable
Overreactions	55 Absurd Chain Reaction	95 Hangovers	135 Rule Breaking
13 Taking Extreme Measures	**Plot Trickery**	96 Overextended	136 Undermining Authority
14 Awestruck	56 Storyline Twist	**Cretins**	**Forbidden Behaviors**
15 Over Intense	57 Fantasy Turned Reality	97 Cavemen	137 Taboos & Sacred Barriers
16 Over Heroic	58 Twist of Fate	98 Grotesque & Deformed	138 Exercising Professional Liberties
PERCEPTIONAL DISCORD	**Transformation**	99 Derelicts	139 Exhibitionism
Odd Behaviors	59 Age Transformation	100 Gross Incompetence	140 Face Slapping
17 Performing/ Talking Babies	60 Magic	**AWKWARDNESS**	**Offensive Behaviors**
18 Animal Willpower	61 Body Switch	**Remorseful Regrets**	141 Odor Offensive
19 Multiple Personalities	**Visual Surprise**	101 Tough Predicaments	142 Repulsive Behaviors
20 Foolishness	62 Surprise Revelation	102 Regretful Actions	143 Unrefined Behaviors
Misrepresented Context	63 Creature Appearance	103 Regretful Statements	144 Bleeped Language
21 Illustrated Idioms	64 Wishful Thinking	104 Caught Off Guard	**Unleashed Mania**
22 Humanized Depiction	**Superiority Theory**	**Uncomfortable Settings**	145 Mad Science
23 Unusual Setting	**PUTDOWNS**	105 Uncomfortable Male Bonding	146 Sadomasochism
24 Unconventional Routine	**Mocked Peculiarities**	106 Uncomfortable Intimacy	147 Public Disturbance
Bizarre Substitutions	65 Background Mockery	107 Uncomfortable Conversation	148 Swooning Women
25 Object Replacement	66 Illusory Superiority	108 Creepiness	**SENTIMENTAL HUMOR**
26 Sound Imitations	67 Maladroitness	**Exercising Humility**	**Child Innocence**
27 Animal Substitution	68 Quirkiness	109 Wrong Impression	149 Youthful Discoveries
28 Anthropomorphism	**Lofty Conquest**	110 Exposed Privacy	150 Inner Child
Nonsense	69 Outwitting	111 Public Embarrassment	151 Child Mimicry of Adulthood
29 Dim-witted	70 Macho Gone Sour	112 Unveiled Feminine Side	**Fear & Anxiety Relief**
30 Baffling Dialog	71 Arrogant Knockdowns	**Revealed Secrets**	152 Narrow Escape
31 Irrelevance	72 Unfair Advantage	113 Captured Glances	153 Fear of What's to Come
32 Confusing Response	**Society Satire**	114 Revealed Deceptions	154 Barely Escaped Detection
IRONY	73 Exaggerated Cultural Nuance	115 Exposed True Colors	**Melodrama**
Visual Irony	74 Parodies	116 Revealed Fantasies	155 Histrionic Behaviors
33 Cyborgs Acting as Humans	75 Language Peculiarities	**Relief Theory**	156 Melancholic Behaviors
34 Humans Acting as Animals	76 Cheeky Barbs	**UNRULINESS**	157 Fervent Behaviors
35 Hypocritical Behaviors	**Stereotyping**	**Hysteria**	**Inner Secrets**
36 Oxymorons	77 Blondes & Bubbas	117 Angry Yelling	158 Dream Exploits
37 Unusual Pairing	78 Stereotyped Professions	118 Nervous Breakdown	159 Suggestive Sexual Allusion
Ironic Temperament	79 Celebrity Impersonation	119 Sports Fanatical	160 Contradicting Inner Voice
38 Callous Turned Kind			

Figure 3.3 Comic Devices Used in Viral Video Content

Playful Content through Gamification

Playful content can also be created through gamification, or the use of game thinking in nongame contexts to solve problems and engage audiences. According to Gartner, more than 70 percent of the world's top 2,000 companies are expected to deploy at least one gamified application by the end of this year. Foursquare, in particular, brought attention to this concept with their rewarded badges. Since then, rewards have extended to everyday activities like ordering food or watching movies.

Much of the gamification is being used for motivation. In a recent blog post, Lee Odden points out that

> . . .*People are relying on this technology for feedback and motivation. Examples: Alarm clock app that donates money to charity every time you hit the snooze button. Nike Plus app notifies your social networks that you're going for a run; and when anyone likes your update, the app plays applause. Or Gym Shamer, which posts when you don't go to the gym. . ."*
>
> —Lee Odden, TopRank

So far, the concept shows promise in stimulating audience engagement especially when So So far, the concept shows promise in stimulating audience engagement especially when applied to tasks we normally dread (e.g., managing e-mail overload, fitness, diet, and medical checking). A growing trend is to create fun out of safety issues. Besides the Virgin Atlantic and Metro Trains examples cited earlier, Volkswagon created a fun initiative that encourages folks not to speed (http://bit.ly/1lh13nB).

Playful Content through 3D Animation and Immersive Experiences

Another growing trend in playfulness is the use of 3D animated stories. Especially when applied to holiday fun, this use of mini-movies has worked well for LEGO® and Coca Cola. But John Lewis took it to a new level in their viral Christmas advert "The Bear & The Hare (http://bit.ly/1m2QFA6)." Reaching nearly 13 million views, the storied content extends to their website with behind the scenes content and other entertaining features.

Caterpillar entered the foray of fun with their "Build for It" (http://bit.ly/WQgHkG) branding campaign. The viral video shows the lighter side of the heavy machinery company by using their equipment to play a game of Jenga with 600 lb. blocks.

Finally, brands are now sponsoring content that allows a more immersive experience. In Pepsi's "Now Is What You Make It" interactive video (http://bit.ly/UEkCPy), they allow fans to create their own experience by selecting additional interactive content as the video progresses.

Facebook's $2B acquisition of Oculus Rift suggests that an even more immersive experience for content consumers may be in the making. The 3D head-mounted display could potentially take virtual reality gaming experiences to a new level of content interaction.

Stirring Passions with Solidarity and Performances

In 1975, an unknown actor and film producer shocked the world with a $225 million film that later produced five more successful sequels. In the film, a kind-hearted debt collector named Rocky Balboa overcomes all odds as a prize fighter. To this date, the infamous "Gonna Fly Now" song is used by many to fuel their passions.

Emotions are often aroused when our favorite teams are competing or when we show allegiance to our country. This sense of pride and solidarity transcends beyond almost every other form of emotional connection when it is felt personally. With 12 million views, Coca Cola's "America Is Beautiful" video (http://bit.ly/1qOhOhS) along with Budweiser's 911 tribute (http://bit.ly/1oaxbNW) are great examples of how content can go viral when it taps into sentiments of allegiance. These tributes to our heritage can foster a community bond that runs deep and lasts long. Consider how New Zealand mustered up team spirit while reaching millions with their "Haka War Dance" (http://bit.ly/UGdMJr) and "This Is Not a Jersey."

But passionate feelings are not restricted to heartfelt moments. Content is often staged in performances that feature musicals, performing arts, drama, or moments of awe. My own study of viral videos showed how theater, choreographic beats, mini-drama, and musical interludes impact audience engagement through emotional connections.

Heightened Emotions with Imagery

Few would debate that smart businesses are incorporating more visuals into their content plans. The rapid rise of visual social media through Pinterest, Facebook/Instagram, Tumblr, Vine, Snapchat, and Vine are testimony to the appeal that imagery has over textual content. An estimated 90 percent of information transmitted in the brain is visual. This gives our content far greater opportunities to stand out from content noise.

Imagery, in particular, is unique in its evoking feelings of serenity, provocation, or deep sentiments. And when extended to videos, they take on multisensory aspects that often have a compounding effect on emotional arousal.

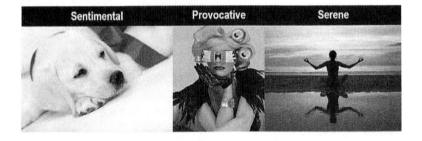

Using Narratives to Shape Stories of Quest and Rebirth

...When you tell a great story, people connect with you emotionally and want to get to know you. You become likeable...

—Dave Kerpan

Perhaps the greatest attention given to emotionalizing content by brands has been in the crafting of compelling brand stories. Storytelling is undoubtedly living up to its hype as a competitive advantage in the growing clutter of content overload. It creates a lasting emotional bond with fans by permitting a brand's personality to shine through the eyes of the audience. And by connecting emotionally, stories are more easily remembered and shared than value propositions. When a narrative reflects both the values of the brand and the targeted audience, storytelling can help brands distinguish themselves in an overwhelming sea of content.

Although seven types of plots are mentioned among storytelling researchers and practitioners, most viral videos featured over the past year include stories on the following:

- changing the world (e.g., Upside: Anything Is Possible),
- enterprising quests (e.g., Johnnie Walker—The Man Who Walked Around the World), and
- heartbreak to triumph endeavors (e.g., Duracell: Trust Your Power).

In their heartfelt series of raising Olympians, P&G's "Thank You Mom—Pick Them Back Up" (http://bit.ly/1kb2d94) reached over 20 million views as it captured the gut-wrenching trials of young athletes determined to succeed.

Creating Narratives with H-E-A-R-T-F-E-L-T Impacts

. . . For years, she fashioned herself as a fast tracking, glamorous woman from Los Angeles. After 25 years of city life, the stage was set for a cosmopolitan lawyer to hob-knob in the country club settings of corporate America. One day when paying a visit to her childhood hometown in the American Midwest, Marlboro Man captured her glance. Soon after, she found herself in the arms of a cowboy who would be the father of her four children. Her black heels turned to tractor wheels as she rode into the sunset with a slow-talking, easy-going cattle rancher. . .

This prairie-tale romance led to Ree Drummond's story as "The Pioneer Woman," an award-winning American blogger and a No. 1 New York best-selling author. Now the wife of cowboy, Ladd Drummond, her story attracted 1.4 million Facebook Likes and a blog reaching over 30 million page views a month while earning millions of dollars annually from display advertising.

What fascinate Ree's readers are her stories of ranch life and home schooling that feature real country-life characters. Her persona epitomizes the sensibilities of country living and essentially implies that those

HEARTFELT
Impact

Humanized Voice

Entertaining Value

Audience Involved

Remembered

Told, not Sold

Felt

Experienced

Liked

To be Continued

dreaming of being lassoed by a cowboy should follow her story of city girl turned country gal.

Ree represents a style of storytelling where alter egos long for the freedom to escape their hectic lifestyle roots into a more sensible and care free world. Much like the "la dolce vita" persona of Vespa owners or the rebellious demeanor of Harley Hogs, "The Pioneer Woman" appeals to an audience longing to let loose of their complex and regimental lifestyles.

But what about B2B content? Is there really any place for storytelling? Consider the way hundreds of business schools and thousands of operations managers learned about the theory of constraints. This popular management philosophy was introduced by storyteller, Eliyahu Goldratt in his 1984 book titled "The Goal."

Can you ever imagine a college textbook that you could not put down? Eli's sale of over 3 million copies and a movie is testimony to the power of story when solving production problems. Written as a suspenseful piece of fiction, Eli hooks his reader into an episodic work of adventure juxtaposed with his marital life. The main character, Alex, has a mentor, Jonah, who helps him solve the company problems and his marital challenges.

Hardly a social-media prediction went by this past year that did not mention brand storytelling as among the top trends to watch in 2014. This followed a year of 30–60 second slice-of-life narratives as well as plotted story-lines. But more importantly, we are witnesses to the routine adoption of 2–5 minute brand stories captured in animated storylines and mini-films, many of which are garnering millions of views. This longer-form release captures the true essence of storytelling. Some great examples include the following:

- TSB: The Story (http://bit.ly/1pz18V1)
- Glenlivet's Brand Story (http://bit.ly/1lk89Yt)
- Chipotle's Back to the Start (http://bit.ly/1pw5Aqk)
- Chipotle's The Scarecrow (http://bit.ly/UG0U6e)

- Nikon Brand Story "The Day" (http://bit.ly/1kqFOF7)
- Jose Cuervo Tradicional—History in a Bottle (http://bit
.ly/1jITKru)
- Dove Real Beauty Sketches (http://bit.ly/1qdUNzZ)
- Google Chrome: Dear Sophie (http://bit.ly/1m6q1pT).

Brands are jumping on this bandwagon as a way to connect with their audiences on an emotional level—and for good reason. We are being bombarded with so much content that many brands see the emotional route as perhaps the only way to standout.

Storytelling provides an opportunity for brands to inspire audiences. By offering a persuasive narrative, equipped with a hero, a conflict, and eventual resolution of the conflict, audiences can become part of the storyline. If done right, stories hook audiences into an anticipation for upcoming episodes while creating a growing connection with the stories protagonist. Over time, the brand is seen as providing something meaningful to the audiences' own challenges.

This can be done without pitching product features or directing your audience on what to do. It's done by allowing the audience to live vicariously through your own story, which, according to Dave Kerpan, is the secret to making a brand likeable.

Without a compelling narrative to capture your brand's vision and personality, personalized messaging and entertainment merely offer moments of attention and engagement. To be remembered, however, audiences need repeated doses of emotional lift often brought about from ongoing episodes and a story-line that resonates with their own life challenges.

In the past few years, we have even seen the adoption of brand stories in multiepisode web productions like Chipotle's "Farmed and Dangerous," Sony Cracker's "Comedians in Cars Getting Coffee" shown during the Super Bowl, and the "Brotherhood Pilot" presented by Esquire TV and Chivas. The high performance success of these native advertisements shows early signs that branded entertainment may be a powerful vehicle to create brand stories.

Common to this long-form narrative is a musical journey into the brand's roots often leading to obstacles, a perseverance to overcome and a moral to the story (e.g., Chipotle's call to cultivate a better world).

But the growing trend toward brand stories is not just limited to mini-series productions and slice-of-life narratives recast on YouTube. The concept of using storytelling is now being applied to web design, podcasts, imagery, and even data. What's fueling its rapid adoption is the incredible content overload hitting social channels. We are now producing enough content to explain why 90 percent of the world's data ever produced were created in just the last two years.

Stories offer an option to distinguish brands and small businesses from the noise. By provoking feelings and emotions, stories stand a greater chance of reaching prospects at the awareness stage of their buying cycle. And by allowing audience's to easily visualize a brand's vision, stories have a better shot at conveying meaning to an audience's own pain points. Add to that the more lasting impact that visual storytelling has than factual-based messages, and you can see why stories resonate more in an age of information overload.

Brands are also recognizing in a bigger way how their unique personality can distinguish their content from that of their competition. Ample evidence shows that audiences seek connection with an authentic brand voice whose values resonate with their own. This emotional connection overrides even the most powerful of value propositions especially at a time where trust in messages is at an all-time low.

Finally, brands are seeing how they can strike an emotional chord with their target personas from the vast amount of big data characterizing their audiences. Today's marketer has sufficient profile and behavioral data to craft a brand story that truly resonates with their followers. Therefore, be prepared for the incessant "Once Upon a Time" approaches to content strategies as brands seek to distinguish themselves with a lasting emotional connection. Boardroom meetings may even occur around a campfire previewing their latest "Tale of Two Budgets."

Discovering H-E-A-R-T-F-E-L-T Emotions that Trigger Content Sharing

An examination of audience reach and engagement leads us to nine story techniques (spelling H-E-A-R-T-F-E-L-T) that show the most promise for connecting emotionally. And by connecting through emotions, research suggests that the brand benefits from the following:

- greater awareness;
- quicker grasp of the brand message;
- more lasting recall;
- more powerful brand association; and
- greater opportunity for sharing content.

Humanitarian Acts Tug at the Heart of All Souls

When acts are performed by a person to protect life or human dignity, it rarely goes unnoticed. Like the Parable of the Good Samaritan, stories of personal sacrifice touch us all in a deep way. And when they are based on random acts of kindness or involve personal risk, it summons the compassion in many that long to see fresh glimpses of a benevolent world.

Arguably, it's among the few story themes whose moral fits almost every culture. And because it follows a familiar story arc involving a hero, obstacles to overcome, and a favorable transformation, stories of humanity seem to have universal appeal.

HEARTFELT Emotions

*H*umanitarian Acts

*E*xhilaration

*A*stonishment

*R*ebelliousness

*T*enderheartedness

*F*eeling Savoy

*E*ncouragement

*L*egendary Sentiments

*T*riumphant

Some great stories of humanity involve brands that stepped up to resolve a food or water shortage. DuPont stirred the hearts of many in their film showing how their hybrid rice approach helped sustain rice production in Vietnam (http://bit.ly/1xMg8TN).

Similarly, Charity: Water's role in solving a water crisis gained notoriety through the world. The founder, Scott Harrison's "Water Changes Everything" story is featured in conferences around the world. The popularity of their videos is testimony to the strong emotions roused when we witness people surviving hardships (http://bit.ly/1xMgoCk).

Exhilaration Tops the List of Positive Emotions

A study of the emotions most likely to generate social video success rated "exhilaration" number one. From scenes of jubilation or ecstasy, this form of emotional connection typically lasts longer and gets shared further than any other form of entertainment. WestJet's Christmas Miracle (http://bit.ly/1AIfydZ) garnered over 200,000 "likes" that brought tears of jubilation to the 40M+ watching unsuspected passengers getting their Christmas wish. The real-time giving turned a fairly unknown airline into a fun and caring brand.

Others like Red Bull and GoPro went the euphoria route achieving similar engagement results with jumps from the sky that pounded the hearts of audiences sharing the exhilaration. On one notable jump, Felix Baumgartner (http://bit.ly/1AIxGEy) broke the speed of sound in a 24 mile jump out of a stratospheric balloon that stunned millions. Stories like this inspire us to reach beyond our limits.

Astonishment Dazzles Us with the Spectacular

Passions could be stirred as we marvel over the spectacular. Exceptional reach and engagement has been noted when audiences are spellbound.

Like Apple's "Think Different," the marvel is often centered on those we admire (http://bit.ly/1nQBZIL).

The fact that we are entertained with a "wow" factor should not be surprising. Magicians, athletes, and beautiful models have always fascinated us as we ponder the limits of beauty, imagination, and human potential. We delight in the spectacular as well as the painstaking skills required to dazzle us. Among the types of astonishment that are used in high-performing videos are extraordinary beauty, masterful craftsmanship, and the stretch of human potential.

Rebelliousness Let's Us Escape from Our Roots

A common story form used by brands today taps into our rebelliousness natures. Consider how this was done by "The Pioneer Woman" as a way to encourage other women to escape from their uneventful life styles. Others like the Mini Cooper appeal to those trying to standout as they make the case that "normal is not amazing."

In her book, *The Fortune Cookie Principle*, Bernadette Jiwa discusses the mystique of the Vespa and the joy of riding uninhibited with the wind in your hair. "To these people, the Vespa was a style statement that helped them to feel like they could escape their own working-class roots. (p. 105)." A similar technique involves an appeal to independent thinkers. This is done well by Virgin Atlantic as well as Nike in their Nike Girl Effect videos (http://bit.ly/1rXhsVA).

Tenderhearted Moments Bring Tears to the Eyes

One way to connect your audience through emotions is through tear-jerking stories. Google and BERNAS use these story techniques in very dramatic ways.

Some have taken the route of stirring emotions through compassionate pleas. Christina Aguilera made a plea for the hungry and homeless during her mission trip

to Rwanda with the World Food Program. In a similar vein, Hope for Paws (http://bit.ly/UEOEmv) used their footage of a homeless dog living in the streets as a plea for animal rescue. Both went viral as dramatic displays touched the hearts of thousands.

On a softer side, hearts are often moved from the display of puppy love or family connections. Hallmark has done this for years in their sentimental displays of family affection. Especially when reflecting on nostalgic moments or the impact made by those that passed, these emotional connections can significantly stir emotions (http://bit .ly/1uNpD98).

Feeling Savvy Fuels a Sudden Glory

Another way to provoke emotions with our brand stories is to poke fun of bureaucratic institutions. This often leads us to a feeling of "sudden glory" as we bask in the sunlight of our superior choices. Oftentimes, we revel in our removal of unnecessary middle men. Consider, for example, how Amazon makes an emotional connection with us by removing retailers who stand in the way of efficiency. Similarly, Nespresso, Warby Parker, Zappos, and Spanx all represent cases where audiences celebrate their "feeling savvy" from saving money.

One of the most viral of videos in this domain is the razor blade putdowns sponsored by Dollar Shave Club (http://bit.ly/1rTpr2G). One of their videos is approaching 20M views as an amateur acting host describes how their more sensible approach to purchasing razors avoids unnecessary overhead costs.

This "feeling savvy" story-line technique especially works well when aimed at the socially irresponsible or artificial foods. Brands like Bahen & Co. and Chobani tap into our desire for real natural ingredients. By reaching 3 million views on YouTube, Chobani's Bear Game Day video (http://bit.ly/1u7Ttkt) is a testimony to this storytelling effect on our emotions.

Encouragement Comes from Witnessing Turnarounds

Audiences love to witness a remarkable turnaround. Consider how popular Marcus Sheridan became after turning around a near bankrupt swimming pool company to a world-leading installer of fiber glass pools. His story resembles that of David and Clare Hieatt, who resurrected legendary jeans brand, Hiut Denim.

Other stories that stir emotions through encouragement are those involving life-altering choices. Weight Watchers and Splenda do this in their stories of living healthy or losing weight.

Legendary Sentiments Tap into Better Times

Other stories, like Volkswagen, tap into tenderhearted moments with their farewells to the good old days. These nostalgic connections often conjure up memories of our favorite moments while providing a fresh perspective on our values.

Following the saddened demise of Detroit's car business, Chrysler's YouTube video tribute to the Motorcity reached millions. Like other legendary stories, tributes like this arouse our emotions from a sense of pride and longing to revisit the past. The NFL and Budweiser often use these story techniques as a way to rekindle our ties with the past. Similarly, Microsoft's "Child of the 90s" Internet Explorer ad is a sentimental trip back to when Gen Y's appreciated a simpler, slower, and more affordable life. The fact that it reached over 50 million views attests to the power of stories reminiscent of better days.

Triumphant against All Odds Makes Us Thankful

Everyone loves the success story of an overachiever. And like any story of triumph, we pull for an underdog or a handicapped individual to overcome their obstacles. But we also experience a moment of truth when realizing our lives have been spared against all odds.

Chevy and the American Cancer Society celebrated survivors of cancer as well as those who support them on the road to recover. Their 2014 Super Bowl commercial reached 1.7 million views in just three weeks. Knowing this could happen to all of us, it is easy to live vicariously through the grateful hearts of the triumphant.

Using H-E-A-R-T-F-E-L-T Elements to Design Stories for Entrepreneurs

Few would debate the success that stories have on legendary brands. From Disney to Apple, Coca Cola, and Chipotle, we have seen the power of storytelling in providing emotional connections that supersede the best of any product facts and figures. But for entrepreneurs with limited budgets, the adoption of stories may seem foreign to their understanding of marketing campaigns and promoting value propositions. In this next section, we explore the elements of storytelling that entrepreneurs should consider in designing their own content strategies.

HEARTFELT
Elements

Heroes

Episodes

Affirmative Value

Relevance

Trusted Source

Familiar Arc

Emotional Connections

Language of Audience

Transformations

Common to stories cited in the brand and content-marketing field is a narrative that inspires audiences to consider a change in their behaviors. Although the emotions elicited by the best of brand stories vary widely, the elements of heartfelt storytelling are fairly consistent.

Heroes, Villains, Mentors, and Moral

Story characters have to permit a dramatic narrative. One way to make it relatable is to feature your audience as heroes cast against villains standing in their way of living a better life.

Chipotle's campaigns cast a scarecrow as a superhero that represents socially responsible and healthy eaters. The hero is up against greedy farmers seeking to exploit hormone-injected cows. In their fight against these villains, Buck Marshall of the Industrial Food Image Bureau invites us on his crusade against harmful farming practices.

As the protagonist in "Farmed and Dangerous," Buck exposes the criminality of farming with scenes of exploding cows. But like most great stories, he serves as a mentor guiding us through a "hero journey" toward "cultivating a better world." Without these roles, the story follower has little involvement in a promising outcome. This is why brand stories are better left with audiences driving their own conclusions than brands "telling" them what to do.

Episodes for Story Buildup

Weaving stories into content is much like casting a TV series over a season of episodes. Most TV narratives have an overarching theme played out in part by each episode. But much like each series episode, you can't convey an entire story in each piece of content you post.

Great stories adopt themes that are consistently applied to each episode. In Geico's caveman series, a theme of "easiness" was played out in the form of "disrespected cretins." Each episode featured one more bout of disrespect. The same episodic style should  apply to any microcontent (e.g., blogs, e-Books, etc.) covered under the banner of a brand story. An episode should stand on its own merits while supporting an overarching moral to or changed life experience from the entire story.

Affirmative Value for an Audience's Life Choices

Filmmaker Andrew Stanton attributes our love for stories to their affirmative value. He claims that an effective story is one where the audience sees the storylines and characters as similar to their own. This connection not only creates a bond of shared values, but it also validates the reader's own life choices.

More than just a checklist of buying criteria, stories we like should have real meaning to the point that it actually shapes an audience's perception of value. In effect, the story connects to an audience's own narrative. It is at this point that the storyteller has an opportunity to persuade the audience with its brand ideas.

Relevance to Audience Needs

But to truly understand an audience's own narrative, the story itself has to be relevant to something the audience needs. Without this, the story merely becomes an episode of entertainment. It's when a story makes sense to other people's lives that it pings their radar. This can often be done by relating with your audience how your company overcame a similar challenge facing the audience.

Consider how Apple's and Virgin's story of reaching beyond the norm resonates with independent thinkers who thrive on raising the bar. Much of the success in attracting their followers has to do with the founders' penchants for overcoming odds. Similarly, Ree Drummond likely attracted millions of women to her Pioneer Women blog that shared her desire to escape a hectic and complex urban life.

Trusted Source

A fundamental tenet of any great brand story relates to its influence on audiences to trust the storyteller. Creative brand strategist, Mark Di Somma, perhaps said it best:

> . . .The story has to come from a credible source – buyers need to know the storyteller can be trusted. Your story needs to be consistent with the receiver's understanding of you because the person telling the story is in a position of trust. They have control of the narrative. To me, this is the make or break of storytelling. If we don't believe the storyteller, we'll never believe the story. Southwest Airlines have been telling a wacky story about loving to fly for decades. They absolutely walk the talk. . .
>
> —Mark Di Somma

Familiar Story Arc and Brand Connection

At the heart of every great story is a narrative arc that includes a beginning, a middle, and an end. Normally obstacles are placed in the path of the hero so as to advance the story across episodes of adversity. Where entrepreneurs can especially capitalize on this story arc format is in their origin story. A number of high-performing videos included entrepreneurs who overcome adversity in their early stages of growth or during a turnaround.

The same portrayal of struggles can be harvested in customer stories that highlight the worries facing customers. In the case of product stories,

this adversity presents an opportunity for the brand storyteller to
bleed the pain of their audience.

Key to any effective brand
story is its tie to the brand message. Duracell's highly successful
video of NFL player Derrick Coleman's struggle with hearing tied
very well to the battery company's
"Trust Your Power" theme (http://bit.ly/UGxxR9). Views of the video are
approaching 25 million.

Finally, great stories require a meaningful purpose often translated
into a "moral of the story." Chipotle unfolded a story of greed and animal abuse in the context of farming for cheaper food. But in the end,
audiences are easily convinced that organic farming and sustainability
pays off.

Emotional Content to Inspire Action

What separates a business story from the facts and figures associated with
brand's product promises is its ability to tap into an audience's beliefs,
passions, sympathies, or sentiments. And evidence shows that this type of
connection has greater impact on both brand awareness and loyalty. But
the key to making this emotional connection is first recognizing that audiences want to connect with something important or of a higher purpose.
If a brand's story can accomplish this, audiences can be "inspired to act"
as opposed to "convincing them to act" from product or service claims.

Language of the Audience's Story

The right story has to be the audience's story. Common to the narratives
highlighted earlier is a storyline that speaks the language of the audience.
In effect, the story empathizes with the audience's situation to a point
where audiences see themselves in the story. A great example of this is
the "Story of Kate" offered by Sprint Small Business Solutions (http://bit
.ly/1tESpXT).

Transform Audiences into Wiser People

Like any story, an objective of a brand story is to shape audience decisions and change their behaviors through a series of episodes. An effective story arc essentially sets the stage for meeting an unmet desire of the audience with a product that transforms their lives.

To do this effectively, the hero must face numerous setbacks as their journey plays out. Story arcs typically advance the hero from a low point to the removal of obstacles in their path. If handled effectively, the hero gets transformed into a wiser creature as they triumphantly face adversity.

> . . .*The end of a narrative arc is the denouement. It shows what happens as a result of all the conflict that the characters have gone through*. . .
>
> —Author Jenna Blum, *The Author at Work*

Displaying Generosity in Contributions, Kindness, and Causes

One of the greatest methods agreed by most content marketers to stir emotions is through generosity. And this starts with generous contribution of content. Let's face it. Audiences love to be rewarded. It's a sign of our attention to them as well as their reward for spending time with our brands.

Consumers are quite accustomed to receiving free content. But more importantly, audiences delight in knowing they received a gift. The same applies to thoughtful gestures as when WestJet surprised their arriving passengers with Christmas presents (http://bit.ly/1AIfydZ). The video reached over 35 million views in less than 3 months as the previous unknown airline expressed an extreme act of goodwill.

Most recently, TrueMove H Thailand released this amazing commercial centered on their theme "Giving Is the Best Communication" (http://bit.ly/1ogtYfZ). The video brings many tears to eyes as a benevo-lent citizen is paid back in his time of need.

Finally, Duracell demonstrated their generosity through community kindness. In their "Moments of Warmth Powered by You" (http://bit .ly/1pwxq5E), they surprised patrons of a bus shelter with hand-powered heating. The gesture not only resulted in Duracell's video reaching 1 mil-lion views in only 2 weeks, their benevolence was especially appreciated by winter-worn Canada residents. And it resonates well with the Duracell brand message of being powered by a human connection: ". . .In Canada, we have cold winters, but we also have each other. . ."

Eight Ways to Create Emotional Content

With the alarming levels of content hitting the Internet, it is clear that content marketers must find a way to distinguish themselves by emotion-ally amplifying their content. This will likely shift the bulk of content formats from one of instruction and information to one of entertainment and inspiration as shown in Figure 3.4.

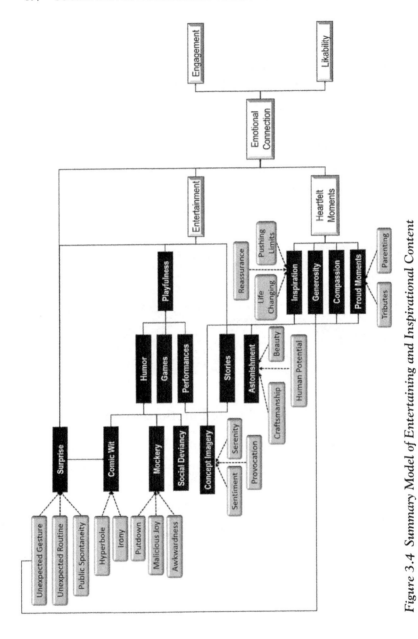

Figure 3.4 Summary Model of Entertaining and Inspirational Content

Note

1. "15 Ways to Create Entertaining Videos" by Jim Barry (slidesha
   .re/1t72EUi).

PART 2

Getting Audiences to R-A-I-S-E Your Brand

Now that your audiences have expressed interest in trusting, aligning with, liking, and knowing you, it's time to invoke their support in boosting your visibility. These next five chapters will describe how your target audiences could R-A-I-S-E your brand in the following way:

1. **R**ecognize you from quality content (Chapter 4)
2. **A**dvocate your brand through passionate employees (Chapter 5)
3. **I**nfluence your brand through industry thought leaders (Chapter 6)
4. **S**tamp your brand with reputable followers on social networks (Chapter 7)
5. **E**xpose your brand through syndication, search, and native advertising (Chapter 8).

CHAPTER 4

Earning Readership with Content Mastery

Don't focus on having great content. Focus on producing content that's great for your readers.

—Brian Clark, author at Copyblogger

In this era of infobesity, even the best of content goes unnoticed. Emotional content sparked by visual storytelling, entertainment, and inspirational messaging shows great promise in captivating audiences. But there are some basics to content mastery that have distinguished social-media pros that don't always elect to entertain and inspire. Many stay with an educational or informational objective. But common to most is a penchant for consistent quality, a focus on pain points, and great writing mechanics. In effect, they earn their readers through content that is:

- T-U-N-E-D (trended, user generated, niched, evergreen, digestible) for audience connection;
- F-O-C-U-S-E-D (frequent, optimized, cross-platform, unique, shareable, eye-catching, documented for SEO) on audience attraction; and
- Consistently created with high Q-U-A-L-I-T-Y (quick, unbiased, advisory, lead generating, image intensive, talk-worthy, your voice).

Making Your Content T-U-N-E-D
for Audience Connection

Getting your content T-U-N-E-D for audience connection implies that you are writing on burning issues relevant to your hypertargeted audience. It also means that the content is new and easy to digest since the average time to decide on content reading is under 10 seconds.

Trended Topics

So one of the first questions to ask when researching topics for your content is whether the topic is new and trending upward. To help in this effort, there are many tools you can use to gain insight about the latest Google and Twitter search queries. For example, I selected the domain name "blog.socialcontenmarketing.com" to host my blog based on what I found on Google Trends for search popularity as well as what Topsy revealed on the level of Twitter engagement for this term. Based on the results, it made sense to use the long-tailed term as a common thread throughout all of my posts.

But tuning your content to trends goes beyond a mere search for SEO queries. Another way to ensure high trending is to tie their posts

to current events. Just witness the many ways bloggers attempt to tie in Mother's Day or the Super Bowl into their blog post storylines.

User-Generated Questions

The second question to ask in tuning your content is whether the post is too focused on your own offerings instead of answering a user-generated question. One of the best ways to have your content resonate with an audience is to address an issue that keeps them up at night.

Another approach is to observe the questions that come up in discussion forums like those found in LinkedIn Groups. Ideally, you want to answer aggravating questions that cost your readers' time and money. This will further help in search results since questions on cost and aggravating pain points get searched very day.

Niched Audiences

Based on the exploding number of registered blogs, the route often taken by successful bloggers is to hypertarget their content with long-tailed topics. For example, to connect in today's overcrowded blogosphere, you have to offer more than advice on ladies footwear. You have to offer tips specific to elderly athletic women's footwear.

Ideally, every content post should be mapped to one of your target audience personas along the lines of the residential realtor example as shown in Figure 4.1. Starting with four targeted audiences identified by their spending motivations (sunbelt retreats, wealth management, life transition, and temporary accommodations), 16 personas were identified based on their unique habits and aspirations. This led to a clearer understanding of pain points that would not be recognized without dissecting the audience into distinct personas.

The mistake made by many is to assume you can write for everyone. But imagine the interest an ROI Maximizer persona would have in first purchase handholding or the interest a Mobile Crew persona would have in high-society acceptance. Targeting as niche an audience as possible allows realtors an opportunity to address a target audience's biggest pain point by tailoring everything to help only them. And by writing the

PAIN POINTS	Wealth Management				Sunbelt Retreats				Life Transitions				Temporary Accommodations			
	Career Starters	Upscalers	ROI Maximizers	Foreign Opportunists	Golf Enthusiasts	Equestrians	Swiss Family Robinsons	Snowbirds	Post-Distress Downscalers	Twilight Downscalers	New Beginnings	Job Transients	Off Campus Greeks	Mobile Crews	Weekend Warriors	Samaritans & Soldiers
Budget limited payments	√								√		√		√			
High society acceptance		√														
Proximity to golf courses					√											
Access to outdoor nature experience					√	√	√									
Acceptance into equestrian society lifestyle						√										
Horse stabling and ranch accommodations																
Family oriented residence						√					√					
First purchase handholding	√										√					
Future adaptable living conditions									√							
Future profit potential	√		√													
Minimal emotional loss									√	√						√
Minimal maintenance living										√				√	√	√
Off season snowbird rental property				√				√								
Prior home burden relief												√				
Quick move												√				
Retirement & family accommodations										√						
Season renting in tough economies				√												
Semi-permanent residence												√	√			
Reestablish themselves within their means									√							
Twilight year comforts										√						
Limited restrictions on lease obligations													√			
Year round temperate weather						√		√								
Active youth surroundings													√			
Favorable tax, currency & banking			√	√												
Overtime camaraderie														√	√	√
Work readiness in familiar surroundings														√	√	
Undervalued homes			√	√												
Affordable vacation home							√									
Wealth management	√	√														

Figure 4.1 Persona Pain Points Identified for Residential Realtor Bloggers

post as though it was solving a specific problem for a single person (i.e., single casting), readers will likely credit you with empathy, helpfulness, and expertise.

Evergreen

Once a content topic candidate is considered, it is important to ensure it doesn't date quickly. Known as evergreen content, some content posts can be written once and rerun in the future without it being rendered obsolete. This is why content on how-to's or foundational topics are more effective than news stories. Writing a piece on conservative politics, for example, could remain perpetually relevant. But a story on "Top Tea Party Members Likely to Shake Up the Republican Party" would not likely have any value two years from the post.

The timelessness of this content gives it a high search ranking and great potential for accumulating links over time. As a result, traffic to the site hosting your content will improve over time as the evergreen content continues to gain popularity with its target audiences.

Digestible

A final question to ask when tuning your content for audience connection relates to how easy it is to digest. Audiences like posts that are concise and to the point. This starts with putting aside your writing formalities and using a conversational tone. If you write like you speak, your content more often stays on topic.

Consider the use of visual components as much as possible provided that they are self-explanatory. As discussed earlier, visual components like infographics are mentally processed much quicker than text.

All this assumes that the reader caught the gist of your topic from a well-crafted title and an opening sentence question that sets the stage for what is to come. The headline itself has to let the reader know how the post will benefit them. Blogging pros will argue that the ideal headline is six words long, the ideal paragraph falls between 40 and 55 characters, and the ideal blog post takes about seven minutes to read, roughly equating to 1,600 words.[1]

Getting Content F-O-C-U-S-E-D
on Audience Attraction

Now that the content strategy and selected topics are tuned for the right audience connection, another critical exercise is to ensure that your content-writing efforts are focused on capturing the attention of your audience.

Frequent Postings

Content consistency is paramount. That is why it is important to blog at least twice a week especially when starting out. If there is nothing new for readers to see, they will quickly lose interest and see you as disengaged. But beyond the retention of repeat visitors, the frequency of posts impacts the number of new visitors to your site as well. Each new post, for example, adds to the number of indexed pages recognized by the search engines. Fresh content also signals to the search engines that your authority on the subject is backed by frequently updated information.

This not only improves the chances of target audiences simply *finding the content*, a study conducted by Hubspot revealed the following impacts on *lead generation*:[2]

- An average company will see a 45 percent growth in traffic when increasing total blog articles from 11–20 to 21–50 articles.
- Companies that increase blogging from 3–5 x/month to 6–8 x/month almost double their leads.

Optimized

According to Lee Odden, author of *Optimize*, "Blogs are one of the most powerful publishing platforms that integrates the best of SEO, content marketing and social media optimization" (p. 147).[3] As the centerpiece of content marketing, they serve as an aggregator of all your content while exploiting the power of its search potential and social outreach.

Search is greatly enhanced by its text-rich content and ability to attract links. But this requires attention to the following opportunities you have to boost search results.

1. Optimizing your blog domain URL, titles, and page construction descriptions around key phrases relevant to your target population and the benefits you provide.
2. Optimizing each *blog post* around keyword phrases you are targeting for persona pain points.

This last point refers to visible text opportunities as well as the hidden HTML text used in tagging and page construction. Each post provides an opportunity to exploit key phrases in the visible body of text where special attention should be given to the titles, headers, and the first paragraph of the post. In addition, bloggers have ample real estate in their HTML meta tags for describing their content through title descriptions, tags, anchor text, and image alt text.

The key is to tag and categorize everything but without overdoing the process. If the algorithms sense that you are engaged in keyword stuffing, you can get heavily penalized in search results. Instead, focus on simply being the best answer to what your target audience repeatedly asks. The latest of search algorithms (e.g., Hummingbird) will likely credit your content to a popular search query and reward you with high search results.

This also implies, however, that your content cannot be too short as it provides few opportunities to demonstrate your authority on the subject. So despite the pressure to keep blog posts short due to overcrowded content, blogging experts suggest that posts exceed 500 words for searchability as well as building thought leadership.

Cross-Platform

Blogs lend themselves well to hosting mid-of-funnel content often through registration pages, download links, and embedded presentations. For example, you can make an audio version of your blog post for an upcoming podcast show. This cross-promotion not only boosts the exposure of your other content (e.g., podcasts, webinars, videos, and apps), but it also allows a top-funnel to mid-funnel connection with your target audience.

The same applies in the outbound direction. You can make you posts social by abbreviated them for microblogs, newsletter digests, weekly roundups, social-media posts, or social-networking group discussions. A link to the more comprehensive blog post could then provide detailed information if needed.

In addition to cross-promoting, blog posts should be crafted with an intent to create multiple pieces of content often in the form of a blog series. Turning blogs posts into podcasts, slide decks, e-Books, or white papers are just a few of the many ways to repurpose your posts. This saves on resources while providing an avenue to mid-funnel content in the process. An additional blog post—remember this for search potential—can then be used as an introduction to the deeper content. As an example, see how this is done on my own blog for showcasing e-Books (http://bit .ly/1rz6dCu) and by the Content Marketing Institute for their podcast introductions (http://bit.ly/1m3x1Ye).

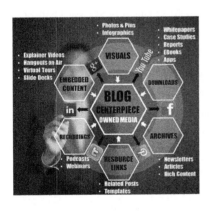

Unique

In order to deliver something of value to your target audience in your post, you need to offer something unique. If not, your audience will merely see you as a curator of others' ideas. A great way to start is to look for original content. This could include recently surveyed information or breaking news.

But as content-marketing experts will point out, unique content does not always have to be original. You can write about your unique strategies or experiences as well. Many bloggers, for example, merely provide a unique angle to widely discussed topics. If not their own, they invite experts to share their thoughts. Either way, by providing a unique perspective, you help your audience with interpretation and judgment.

I applied this to my own field when evaluating social-media books to read (http://bit.ly/1hrzk1G). There are plenty of practitioners who rate their top 10s; so I reviewed, rated, and ranked the top 25 social-media books from an *academic* perspective. As acknowledged by bestselling author, Jay Baer, the countdown offered something new to the social-media community.

Another approach to making your content unique is to play the role of the contrarian or devil's advocate. Readers then benefit from the counterpoints often giving you the credit for having a fresh perspective. And by building controversy into your argument, readers will often become more engaged as they feel compelled to share their own perspective.

Ironically, a fourth way to make your content unique is to back off on overaddressing audience needs and focus more on injecting your own passions as was described in the previous chapter. After all, it's how others respond to your ideas that count the most. Social-media author, Jay Acunzo, puts it this way: "If you *only* think about your audience, you'll likely start to sound exactly like all your competitors."[4] Ideally you want to blend you audience's interests with your own. This can best be accomplished with a personal story relevant to your audience.

Shareable

The key to making your content shareable is to first make your posts easy to share. Most content platforms allow you to accomplish this very easily

through plug-ins that include sharing across dozens of platforms. At minimum, your posts must reach where your target audiences hang out. This could include relevant LinkedIn groups, Google+ communities, and Twitter chats.

As described in Chapter 3, the more emotion felt from your post, the greater the opportunity to be shared. This could include the use of humor, heartfelt moments, feelings of astonishment, or inspirational stories. Another inducement to share is based on the passing of bragging rights. This is why articles on breaking news are key. Readers are often anxious to share what they believe to be an exclusive discovery.

To ensure your content is shareable with a relevant audience, it's important to syndicate it through an RSS feed or through the many blogging listing directories, social bookmarking sites, and news aggregators discussed more in Chapter 8. Finally, you can post the content outside your domain with the intent of creating a new audience. This can be done by featuring your posts as a guest blog on a high traffic site as well as posting on social networks like LinkedIn.

Eye-Catching Title

Without a doubt, headlines are the most important part of your post. And to craft one effectively, you have to pique your audience's curiosity. One way to do this is to distract them with a message that seems *out of sorts*. When asking my students what advertisement they remember on a highway sponsoring over 50 signs, they invariably recall two of them. One says "Your Wife Is Hot." Reading further, the sign says "You Better Fix Her Air Conditioning." The other says "We Buy Ugly." Both represent anomalies that capture our attention.

Asking a question—especially if it's provocative—can also pique your audience's attention. At minimum, curious readers may enjoy the insights from a contrary position like "Will Instagram Disappear"? Leading blogger, Jeff Bullas, often uses negative terms in his titles. His post on "The Top 15 Social Media Marketing Strategy Mistakes to Avoid" has amassed nearly 3K tweets.

Documented

As discussed earlier, the fast growth of video for content marketing has undoubtedly created the most powerful means of attracting and engaging target audiences. A challenge at this point, however, is to make the video searchable. One way to accomplish this is by transcribing the audio and posting the script along with the video. This will help the content get found by search engines. Once transcribed, the scripted version could be embellished with slides, diagrams, infographics, and photos to make it more appealing as a blog post.

The same could be accomplished for audio podcasts and conference presentations. Recordings can be spelled out into scripted versions with embedded slides and audio takes. This not only provides an additional opportunity to release another blog post, but it also captures the attention of search engines recognizing the embedded links potentially from high page-ranking sources as well as the keyword-rich text in the script. If permitted by the podcaster or presenter, the script could be optimized around additional search terms that further boost the page rank.

Creating Content with Consistent Q-U-A-L-I-T-Y

With your content now *tuned* to target audiences and *focused* on capturing their attention, a remaining step is to ensure your content is backed by consistent *quality*.

Quick and to the Point

As described earlier, the use of a conversational style and visuals makes a blog more scannable. But much can be done with writing structure to make it even quicker to digest. That is why expert bloggers spend considerable time on the first few sentences. This opening must spell out why the topic benefits your audience and what you plan to say.

The first point implies that the fewer points made the better. The concept works much like an ad. You have a limited number of seconds to convince your readers that the one pain point or passion they have will be well covered in your post. And there will be nothing else to distract them.

The second point means you have to "tell them what you are going to tell them". Then "tell them" in the body of your post. And then "tell them what you told them at the end of your post." Progression of the post should be quick and to the point if you want today's reader to stick around.

To accomplish this, leading bloggers like Ann Handley and C.C. Chapman offer the following advice:[5]

- Use bullets and lists to edit out unnecessary words.
- Make sentences and paragraphs short (<6 lines paragraph).
- Break up text with headings and subheadings.
- Highlight key points in quotes or bolded phrases.
- Use easy to read fonts.

Unbiased Content

What distinguishes true journalism from the average content post is the information-vetting process used to validate findings. Few would argue that traditional journalism is based on far more rigorous standards for source accuracy than what is found in the blogosphere. This does not imply you shouldn't express an opinion. But it does suggest that readers appreciate content that is *unbiased* and backed by either well-documented evidence or well-respected insights.

So for content to be considered high quality, the information offered in your post has to be accurate and reliable. Among the best ways to accomplish this is through empirically tested results or the insights offered by recognized experts in the field. This is why leading bloggers regularly post interviews with leading authorities often in the form of a playbook of insights from many experts.

Survey results from your own client sampling can also remove this biased perception especially if the sample is large, representative, and empirically tested with at least a reasonable methodology. This can be done without laying out the entire testing procedure in the base of the post. It merely requires a brief explanation or reference to the study background.

As an example, I released 15 blog posts on ways to create entertaining content from a study conducted on viral videos. Each post made reference to the study posted on SlideShare and included the following closing paragraph on the study background.

A total of 3351 high performing videos (> 50K views) were examined in this ranking of top YouTube videos. These viral videos included re-casted television commercials that were posted on YouTube as a social media video back channel. Statistics were then recorded on the number of likes, dislikes, comments and views, where an exploratory study was subsequently published with the Academy of Marketing Science and 2013 Cross-Cultural Research Conference.

Advisory

What often separates blogs from articles is the advisory nature of the latter. Blogs have to be either instructional, insightful, or helpful to decision making. Without advice from a credible source, we are merely adding to the information pile. If you are not convinced, just check out the popularity of blogs that begin with "5 Ways to . . ." or "7 Steps to . . ." Readers obviously have an expectation for following advice.

In addition to laying out an advisory trail, it helps to single out specific audience questions to answer. This is where comment trails on blogs and discussion forums serve as an excellent source of topics to consider in a blog post. Blogging pros will often pose questions to their audiences on Twitter, Facebook, or a LinkedIn Group like "What is you greatest challenge . . . ?" or "What question do you have regarding . . . ?" With large enough audience, the responses then serve as questions to answer in a blog post or newsletter.

By having a question-driven and advisory-driven style, your post may further benefit from readability. If the first sentence of the post starts with a question for your audience, a clear expectation of the post is made up front. Furthermore, should the post merely address answers to the question, readers will likely find the content more digestible and to the point.

Lead Generating

Blogs are used primarily as top-of-funnel content. This makes them ideal for capturing audience information at an early awareness stage. But much of that blog traffic may be wasted unless readers are encouraged to take immediate action after reading the content. This requires that your blog content host *lead generating* calls to action (CTA) such as the following:

1. *registering* for free webinars;
2. *downloading* white papers, case studies, reports, or e-Books;
3. *joining* live events;
4. *following* on Facebook, Twitter, or Pinterest;
5. *sharing* with friends;
6. *subscribing* to newsletters and blogs;
7. *offering* comments;
8. *posing* questions;
9. *requesting* demos or more information; and
10. *buying* through shopping carts.

These CTAs not only provide an avenue to maintain engagement, but they also help escort your prospects through the sales funnel (more on this in Chapter 4). A compelling CTA, for example, represents an opportunity for you to analyze data from the downloaded content or subscriptions and measure which topics had the greatest impact on conversion. And by encouraging your prospect to take the next step, you stay in the loop. This allows another opportunity to demonstrate your trustworthiness while keeping the prospect from researching elsewhere.

Image-Intensive Content

A clear drawback of predominantly textual content in a content post is its often overwhelming and impersonal appearance. Graphical and photo-based imagery not only require less mental processing; but, as described earlier, they also strike an emotional chord that even the best of written poetry cannot accomplish. Moreover, imagery allows you to mix up your content as a diversity tactic. Audiences often appreciate the change up.

It is no secret that images are the most shared media on the likes of Facebook. That in itself is testimony to its appeal as a content element. But the rise of photo-messaging apps (e.g., Snapchat), mobile photo-sharing services (e.g., Instagram), and visual discovery tools (e.g., Pinterest) attests to how dependent social-media users are on *viewing* something over *reading* something. Pinterest, in particular, has become one

of the leading drivers of traffic to websites. Your benefitting from this traffic, however, assumes that your blog post accommodates photos to be pinned. Besides photos, SlideShare decks can be embedded into your blog both as a site traffic builder and a preview of deeper content. Notice from this example on my own blog where an embedded slide gives you a preview of the content from SlideShare right on the blog. A downloaded e-Book, on the other hand, would not give you this built-in preview.

Talk-Worthy Content

For content to engage with your audience, they have to invite a dialogue. Some refer to this tactic as making your content REMARKable (by inviting remarks) or talk-worthy.

This may not be the same incentive they have to share or link to your content. Share-worthiness and link-worthiness have more to do with leveraging your bragging rights or backing your story. The intent of making your content *talk-worthy*, on the other hand, is to stimulate a conversation or invite feedback as a method to keep your readers involved.

Some of the most popular techniques for accomplishing this are to include open-ended posts that fuel a debate. Rather than solving the problem, you could engage in a series of points and counterpoints enlisting your reviewers to share their own thoughts. More reputable bloggers often engage their viewers for crowdsourcing (i.e., the process of gathering content by soliciting contributions from a large sample of followers). But even a simple request for feedback or response to a poll can often spur a dialogue.

Your Voice

One of the most common responses offered by content-marketing experts on tips for drawing in an audience is to be *authentic* and *enthusiastic*. This starts with writing about something you are passionate about and in a voice that best reflects your personality. As leading blogger, Michael Hyatt, points out, many bloggers attempt to be someone that they are not when building a blogging platform.[6] Instead, he prescribes one of three possibilities (authority, empathy, or transparency) to examine in defining your own authentic voice:

1. *The Sage*: This is a recognized expert in the field who can speak with *authority*.
2. *The Sherpa*: This is the trusted guide who has learned from their mistakes and who speaks with the voice of confidence and *empathy*.
3. *The Struggler*: This is a fellow traveler who merely shares their own successes and mistakes as they embark on their journey. They have the voice of *transparency* as they tell it like it is.

Once you determine your role as Sage, Sherpa, or Struggler, you have a clearer path as to how you want to solve your target audience's problems. The Sage may entertain an interview or FAQ format, while the Sherpa chooses a more talk-worthy approach where the two-way dialogue permits more shared experiences. The Struggler, on the other hand, may elect to be more visual in their approach so the reader gets a more intimate look at what works and what doesn't.

Regardless of the chosen role, upholding this authenticity requires that you stay consistent with the voice. Too often we read blogs written by someone with a low-key blogging tone only to hear a motivational speaker when they are interviewed in a podcast. By resorting to these pumped-up impersonations, you run the risk of tarnishing the connection your readers, listeners, or viewers may have had with your candor and personality.

Notes

1. "5 Steps to Get Followers to Amplify Your Best Content Marketing" by Content Marketing Institute's Dave Landry (http://bit .ly/1AUBQXa).
2. "12 Revealing Charts to Help You Benchmark Your Business Blogging Performance" by Hubspot's Pamela Vaughan.
3. Lee Odden. *Optimize*. New Jersey: Wiley. 2012. p. 147.
4. "Why 'Write for Your Audience' Has Become Dangerous Advice" by Jay Acunzo (bit.ly/1muU67j).
5. Ann Handley, and C.C. Chapman. *Content Rules*. New Jersey: Wiley. 2011. p. 148.
6. "5 Reasons You're Not Getting Traction with Your Platform" by Michael Hyatt, (bit.ly/1nAUNh9).

CHAPTER 5

Evangelizing with Employee A-D-V-O-C-A-T-E-S

By turning employees into trusted brand ambassadors, companies bring their strongest asset and their most vocal internal advocates in direct contact with their customer base.

—Ekaterina Walter, best-selling author

Much like the support given to ambassadors, brands are actively empowering employees to support their goals through social media. They are the most trusted and connected source to target audiences at a time when the growing demand for social media is stretching internal resources to their limits. And by tapping into the personal accounts of these employees, the reach of messaging can be greatly amplified.

In using these employees to scale their social-media efforts, companies are formalizing programs built around a social-media culture and tools for content sharing. They range from new hire onboarding exercises to comprehensive certificated programs. The rapid adoption of these programs is in part due to the growing popularity of software platforms that help identify, monitor, and mobilize these advocates.

Why Employee Advocacy Is So Critical

Companies are now seeing plenty of evidence on bottom line results from having employees champion their brands. A study by Northwestern University, for example, found a direct correlation between sales and the total number of people identified as brand advocates.[1] Supporting this finding, an IBM study demonstrated that traffic generated by their employee advocates converted seven times more frequently than that generated by other IBM sources.[2]

In effect, social media has created an expectation for trustworthy communications. Customers not only expect authentic and transparent communications, but they also know they can get this attention directly from front-line employees that they often see as peers. After all, most of us will trust experiences shared by family, friends, and colleagues over claims from a brand's logo or statements made by the CEO. And with employees knowing the most about a company, what better way to bridge brands with their customers than through employees. Consider the following nine reasons why employees serve as A-D-V-O-C-A-T-E-S.

Amplification of Personal Accounts

Brands and small businesses recognize how their companies can reap the benefits of each employee's sphere of social influence. By tapping into an employee's personal Twitter and Facebook accounts, for example, brands can often amplify their message an order of magnitude beyond what the brand can muster on its own. Consider the following typical case. A brand supported by 100 employees may be able to attract and sustain a fan community of 2,500 followers. But the 100 employees can potentially reach 25,000 followers if you consider the following:

- An estimated 70 percent of online American adults are on Facebook.
- An estimated 20 percent are on Twitter.
- The average Facebook user has over 300 friends.
- The average Twitter user has over 200 followers.

Delivery of Relevant Brand Experiences

Once acclimated to their role as advocate, employees are in a unique position to deliver relevant brand experiences. Starting with content, some programs supply employees with templates, photos, and graphics for brand correspondence. By mixing and matching the content elements for the employee's personal channels, the customer or prospect now sees something as more intimate and relevant to their channel experience. An Instagram shot of a brand experience from an employee's own account cannot only be amended with personal commentary, ; audiences will see the content as vetted by one of their own.

While helping NSU launch its social-media strategy for recruiting college-bound juniors and seniors in high school, I watched a clever dialogue take place between another university's employee and a prospect expressing her dismay over a bad experience. The employee elected to take a humorous route in a personal conversation that poked fun of their pending breakup. Not only did the series of tweets satisfy the prospect, but it also showed the university's light-hearted side. Consequently, the follow-up tweets suggested the prospect was back on board.

Oftentimes, this brand experience better fits the customer's frame of mind when it comes from an employee whose department is better suited to addressing customer issues. Imagine a legal representative whose profile on LinkedIn gave the customer a direct line connect—even off hours—in a conversation between two mothers. The legal representative would not have to pitch the brand experience. Their actions and demeanor would undoubtedly have a greater impact on lifetime customer value than the best of posted FAQ responses.

Voices for Real-Time Problem Solving

By launching an employee advocacy program, brands can engage their most vocal assets into direct contact with their customers at a time when target audiences are expecting near real-time responses. Responding to tweets in an hour has now become the norm. And just as front-line employees have become a brand's voice in the store, online employees have also become the expected point guards when customers reach out to them through their social-media channels.

While directing a team of customer service and sales professionals at BFGoodrich Aerospace, I found our customers to prefer proposals coming from customer service personnel troubleshooting their problems day after day. To them, these folks were the ones bailing them out of airplanes on the ground. The sales personnel, on the other hand, were seen by some as glad handers with little incentive to work through routine issues since most of them covered multiple accounts and rarely had an opportunity to engage outside of selling services.

Oversight of Ambassadors

A number of brands operate their brand ambassador programs described in Chapter 4 9 separate from employee advocacy programs. Mack Collier, however, offers a convincing argument for employees to spearhead brand advisory panels that work closely with customer advisory panels. An employee advocate, or brand liaison in this case, would ensure that feedback on brand performance and other insights are brought to the attention of brand managers.

By using employee advocates to oversee these roles, a brand is capitalizing on the perceived responsiveness of the advocate as well as their deeper insights into relevant issues. Furthermore, the presence of employees on panels ensures that the voice of the brand is heard and understood by brand management.

Content Creation

Depending on the conditions laid out in a company's social-media guidelines, many brands are permitting employee advocates to create their own content. Not only does this provide content closer to home for the customer, but it also permits a voice from someone they trust. Universities have stepped up to this with blogs hosted by faculty members in effect serving as advocates. Students, in this case, get a look at the real professor rather than hearing from the voice of admissions or enrollment who are further removed from the real classroom experience.

Employee created content is likely to be perceived as more relevant especially when crafted after FAQs addressed to their department. And by knowing that the company permitted content released by employees, the customer is likely to credit the piece as being more authentic and transparent.

Activism

Many employee advocates go out of their way to make their engagement visible and defend their brand when criticized. Known in some circles as proactivists, this special class of advocates enthusiastically let others know they stand behind their employer. A study by Weber Shandwick, in partnership with KRC Research, showed that activists typically represent over 20 percent of a workforce and are gaining in numbers and strength. One key to fueling their passion is to make brand storytelling easy to grasp. This will ensure that "employees are well informed and have something meaningful to say about their employers."[3]

Trusted Communication

Where a brand's vocal assets become especially powerful is when employees evangelize in their own natural habitat. As social-media dependency pressures us all to sound like real people, an expectation has developed not only in conversation tone but in content as well. Consumers now expect brands to be authentic and transparent in all of their communications. This means that their primary line of contact cannot be impersonated by legal vetted correspondence, CEOs with one-way messages, or those paid to pitch. The 2014 Edelman Trust Barometer, in fact, discovered that people are far more likely to trust a company's employees than its CEO especially on matters of engagement and integrity.[4]

Engagement

Once employee advocacy programs gain momentum among enthusiastic employees, a key challenge is to sustain their engagement. Successful brands often stimulate engagement by getting their employees involved in small campaigns. Employees, for example, could be rewarded for their involvement in hashtag-oriented campaigns where they share content on something theme specific.

As a smaller outreach, these opportunities allow for early customer feedback from advocates on how well the content is received. The exchange of general program thoughts and campaign questions can then build early confidence before expanding into broader initiatives like contests. In effect, each outreach opportunity provides a reason for leadership and advocates to stay engaged.

Research shows that advocates, like most employees, progress in their emotional journey from a fear of saying the wrong thing to feeling like they make a difference. Once this attitude is reached, solid leadership, content strategies, and governance can help build an outright desire in the employee to contribute to the brand's success.[5]

Scaling of Brand Relationships

By having employees act on a brand's behalf, companies can better scale their social-media marketing efforts. The sheer volume of customer correspondence on social media, coupled with the speed with which customers expect responses, makes the job of social-media marketing a daunting task. But by piloting employee advocacy programs, brands can judge what aspects of the program really payoff.

As content amplified through employee personal accounts starts to reveal tangible results, more advocates could be recruited from the existing staff of employees. This takes the burden off HR to hire social-media specialists while allowing valuable skill building for those seeking advanced career opportunities.

How to Lead an Employee Advocacy Program

Although employee advocacy programs vary in size and complexity, successful programs are normally characterized as activated from top leadership, driven by a social-media culture, and guided by well-documented objectives, policies, and performance metrics. And like most enterprise-wide team initiatives, success requires champions and a pilot program aimed at early adopters.

Training and governance has to extend beyond the mechanics of simply using advocacy platforms for content distribution to ways for

Creating Programs Conducive to Employee A-D-V-O-C-A-T-E-S

employees to extend the brand relationship and its overall story. And by measuring which people are the most active and successful sharers of content, brands can reward employee engagement while stimulating internal competition. In general, brands need to create a program conducive to A-D-V-O-C-A-T-E-S as shown.

Audits of Advocate Potential

Companies that adopt formal advocacy programs invariably get HR in the loop. Especially when equipped with Net Promoter Scores (NPS) and GlassDoor ratings, a brand can gauge the likelihood of a successful advocacy program by first taking the pulse of its employee satisfaction and loyalty. Human resources can assist by identifying the traits and availability of those predisposed to advocacy programs. Starting with the hiring of individuals, candidates are now being screened for their Klout scores and social-media acumen as an indication of their fit in advocacy programs.

Employee advocate programs like VoiceStorm and Zuberance can also help brands identify employees who are its best advocates. This identification is often based on social chatter that places employees in groups like detractors, advocates, and passives.

Susan Emerick, an employee advocacy expert, identified the following common characteristics to audit when seeking the best suited candidates as early adopters of a pilot advocacy programs.[6]

- Those whose technical or business topic expertise is strongly reflected by the brand's business priorities.
- Those comfortable with publishing, commenting, and collaborating in social-media environments.

- Those finding enjoyment in creating online relationships and enhancing their online professional networks.
- Those experienced in leveraging internal listening capabilities to build social graphs.
- Those with a track record of commitment to and evolving participation in achieving business objectives.

Documented Social-Media Policy

For employees to gain the confidence of a sustaining advocacy programs, brands must champion employee-friendly social-media policies so that employees know what they can and cannot do. These guidelines serve to inform employees about the full extent of their social-media outreach. In cases where employees are permitted to create content for the brand, the guidelines should ensure that any content adequately reflects the brand without unnecessarily restricting the author's voice or discouraging their participation.

A great example to consider is the guidelines used by a major brand. These guidelines were crowdsourced by their own employees[7]:

- know the business conduct guidelines;
- you are personally responsible for what you publish;
- identify yourself by name and role;
- disclaim if it's your personal opinion;
- respect copyrights;
- don't misuse the logo;
- don't disclose proprietary information;
- don't cite clients and partners without permission;
- respect your audience;
- be aware of your association with the company;
- respect others' opinions; and
- add value.

Value Understanding

A key challenge of many employee advocacy programs is letting participating employees understand the program benefits. Best practice companies like Dell, Zappos, and IBM know that this goes beyond their role in story dissemination. Employees need to know how programs benefit them personally.

Advocacy programs boost the marketability of employees by adding to their personal branding and thought leadership. Those companies that have social-media certificate programs or actively encourage participation through their corporate networking accounts validate the skills of those with aspiring career plans. And since numerous empirical studies show a strong positive relationship between employee satisfaction and customer satisfaction,[8] those appreciative of the benefits will likely project this attitude in their care of the customer.

Onboarding

Onboarding, or organizational socialization, plays a key role in preparing employees for advocacy programs. Among the key objectives established by many brands in the training of new hires and those new to advocacy is an in-depth orientation to the core values it espouses and the culture they want to nurture.

Zappos does this very well. They not only cultivate these values in their employee advocates, but they also surround them in an atmosphere where employees enjoy the work while feeling recognized and rewarded for their direct engagement with customers. Employees are given full autonomy to converse and exchange content freely on behalf of the brand to all of their prospects and customers. By screening hiring candidates based on perceived shared values, Zappos believes the employees will act responsibly in their use of social media.

Coaches

Especially in the early stages of advocate maturation, employees must know their backs are covered. This starts with having coaches nearby who guide them through thorny issues and baby steps. This not only helps the advocate overcome initial fear, the paired relationship provides helpful feedback to the coaching staff on recurring issues. A study by IBM, for example, found that success when going it alone was a paltry 9 percent. This compares to a 75 percent success rate when the employee advocate is paired with a coach.[9]

Activity Metrics

Like any successful initiative, employee advocacy programs need metrics defined upfront to gauge performance over time. This include amplification metrics like impressions, traffic, or followers; conversion metrics like leads generated, registration completions, and sign-ups; or marketing metrics like share of voice or sales. Important to employees is to know they are on track. And brands need to know what to tweak.

Tools and Platforms

Interviews with employees on what is critical to an advocacy program often points to the following success factors: content is located in one place where sharing can be done across multiple channels. This requires a platform that administers content for them while permitting bidirectional content sharing.

To facilitate the ongoing mobilization of employee advocate programs, software platforms are arriving in droves. Most like GaggleAMP, Triberr, and EveryoneSocial, Addvocate, DynamicSignal, SocialChorus, Expion, and PeopleLinx are designing their platforms to automate and simplify the process of content duration. In some cases, SEO value is often improved as employees contribute their own links through platform-advised anchor texting.

These platforms have dashboards for content research, progress reports, and report cards. For example, brands now have visibility into what content is shared, and by whom, as well as the clicks, engagement, and conversion information associated with each member of the advocacy program. And by sharing their leader boards, advocates are given an opportunity to compete and earn rewards.

Exciting and Encouraging Atmosphere

Early momentum in advocacy pilot projects can inject excitement in the atmosphere that is crucial to triggering the engagement process. As advocates read and share more content over time, for example, they become more engaged with the brand. In turn, this often increases the overall social activity of employees. The more social the employee, the higher the company ranks as a great place to work. Gallup, for example, demonstrated that companies with high employee engagement levels have nearly four times the earnings per share of their industry peers.10 Similarly, a study by Fortune, the Dachis Group, and Convince & Convert found, that 40 of the top companies to work for were also among the top companies ranked by a social-media business index.11

Much of this could be attributed to an atmosphere of excitement where employees feel rewarded for their engagement. In the case of Zappos, they are banking on employees discussing online how much they enjoy their work.12 In turn, they believe this will foster a tighter bond with their prospects and customers.

Social-Media Culture

As best stated by social-media expert Jay Baer, advocacy is born from culture and not from technology or marketing. Brands that create a culture encouraging social-media usage often find themselves in the enviable position of breeding true advocates. Add to this mindset the success of some more than others to jump-start high-performance teams, and you have an excellent remedy for success.

Some ways to reinforce this culture is through the reward systems and tools used to collaborate. Platforms that bring the internal communities together in their content delivery and conversation exchange represent an endorsement by senior leadership for employees to actively engage in social media (Figure 5.1). And when rewards are given in line

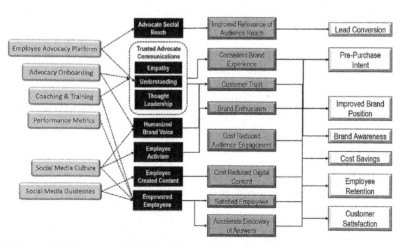

Figure 5.1 Summary Model of Evangelizing Employee Advocates

with their engagement, employees will feel even more encouraged to embrace the culture.

Notes

1. Chris Boudreaux and Susan F. Emerick. Most Powerful Brand on Earth: How to Transform Teams, Empower Employees, Integrate Partners, and Mobilize Customers to Beat the Competition in Digital and Social Media. New Jersey: Prentice Hall. 2013.
2. "Getting Started with an Employee Advocacy Program (Slide 10)" Social Media Today by Susan Emerick (http://slidesha .re/1pMO7Xe).
3. Kate Bullinger, Co-Lead, Global Employee Engagement & Change Management Weber Shandwick (http://bit.ly/1p4SwVx).
4. 2014 Edelman Trust Barometer Executive Summary (http://bit .ly/1uuSaNj).
5. Employee-Brand Relationship Model (http://bit.ly/1sdAfuF).
6. "Getting Started with an Employee Advocacy Program (Slide 14)" Social Media Today by Susan Emerick (http://slidesha .re/1pMO7Xe).
7. "7 Ingredients for Employee Social Advocacy" (Slide 10) by Jay Baer (http://slidesha.re/1tJ8NqT).
8. "Employee Satisfaction & Customer Satisfaction: Is There a Relationship?" by Caterina Bulgarella (http://bit.ly/1sbG5gf).
9. "7 Ingredients for Employee Social Advocacy" (Slide 26) by Jay Baer (http://slidesha.re/1tJ8NqT).
10. "Want to Find Brand Ambassadors? Start With Your Employees" by Forbes' contribution from Ekaterina Walter (http://onforb.es/ Yv0Ys3).
11. "Comparison of 100 Top Companies on Social Business and Corporate Culture" by Convince & Convert's Jay Baer (http://bit .ly/1qCDgVk).
12. "Want to Find Brand Ambassadors? Start with Your Employees" by Forbes' contribution from Ekaterina Walter (http://onforb.es/ Yv0Ys3).

CHAPTER 6

Enchant Influencers through O-U-T-R-E-A-C-H

If you can engage the influencer's passions, and work with them to craft a compelling logical appeal, then you can leverage the credibility of the influencer to actually sway hearts and minds.

—Tom Webster, Edison Research

Well-established brands and startups obviously face major challenges today in attempting to expose their content and engage their social communities. As the channels of content delivery get increasingly congested, few can break from the pack without the help of partners that can sway the sentiments of relevant audiences. This is where influencers come in. Finding, romancing, and collaborating with influencers are especially essential for entrepreneurs to jump-start their visibility.

Prior to the arrival of social media, influence marketing was done by courting a select few pundits or journalists that were rewarded for sponsoring a brand's message. But when the incentives disappeared, so did the loud speaker and the favorable brand attention. These folks are not the same as brand ambassadors or employee advocates. Influencers are motivated by their own objectives and not necessarily by a passion for our stories or a penchant for loyalty.

Where influencers go beyond advocates, however, is in their reach across a relevant audience. They have huge audiences that trust their opinions and let them shape conversations. And now with social media, companies need not focus on just a few influencers who may grow weary of a brand's messaging. Hundreds of them can be engaged online. Moreover, brands can now scale their outreach efforts to include influencers that focus on specific targeted audiences. With influence identifying tools described further, we can easily discover niche-oriented bloggers and podcasters that have an established relationship with a multitude of targeted personas.

To capitalize on the role that social-media channels have in permitting collaborations with influencers, an entire body of research and practitioner advice has been devoted to "influencing the influencer." Assumed in this courtship, however, is an entrepreneur with a reasonable amount of thought leadership themselves to qualify for the influencer's attention. Chapter 7 discusses this in more detail. But for now, let's focus on this booming field of influence marketing defined by Jay Baer as "engaging the people who have an audience, shape conversations, set trends, and impact how your brand is perceived."[1] For the sake of this discussion, influencers include bloggers, podcasters, industry analysts, business leaders, and other known authorities who command a large audience that is especially beneficial to entrepreneurs seeking to borrow their social capital. Not included are the influencers among consumers themselves that well-established brands often court in their promotion of new offerings.

Why Influencers Are So Critical

Shy of reaching influencers, entrepreneurs will likely find their content promotion efforts stall out. Even the best of compelling stories, hashtags, syndications, and search engine optimization described earlier will only go so far in organically growing audiences. With the help of influencers, however, firms can benefit from a quantum leap in both brand awareness and credibility. To demonstrate this, I conducted my own controlled experiment as a class exercise to show how a massive jump in my own thought leadership and followers required an influence outreach campaign. As described further, this campaign was necessary to inject new energy into my community that was not well motivated to share content and enlist new followers.

What makes influence marketing a hot topic in social-media circles is the combined effect of snowballing reach and trust. Often referred to as having significant reach, relevance, and resonance, influencers have social capital that lend extensive O-U-T-R-E-A-C-H to those that effectively court them. Consider the following eight ways they extend credibility to your brand while jump-starting your brand awareness among the consumers that count.

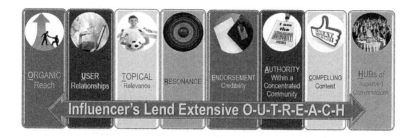

Organic Reach of Influencers

Influencers enjoy the unique position of having clout. This shows up in their ability to gain high search results as well as getting others to recognize their authority in certain circles. As described further, scoring from Klout, PeerIndex, and Kred earns them attention like the four stars of a general. Having Klout scores over 80 displayed on Twitter, for example, tells audiences that these folks command the attention of huge audiences that value their opinions.

If the content earns their attention to the point of their inviting you to guest blog, the blog post will likely have a far greater impact on your search engine results page (SERPs) than you can expect on your own. In some cases, it may even lead to a first-page entry. If not directly, exposure to your content could register high in SERPs from the Google+ posts of high influencers. Consider how this was done in Figure 6.1 following a piece I posted that caught the attention of some social-media influencers.

The post boosted the stature of these influencers to the point of their posting on Google+. Because of the many thousand members in their circles, their post earned top placement in SERPs for, at minimum, the

Figure 6.1 Organic Reach of Google+ Postings

tens of thousands in their Google+ circles. The reference to my blog post on a rising keyword phrase "social media influencers" contributed greatly to the over 5,000 page impressions from new visitors in just two weeks.

User–Community Relationships Enjoyed by Influencers

Besides their ability to extend your organic reach, influencers have relationships with their followers where trust has been earned over years of engagement. This typically follows their history of interacting on videos, podcasts, and blogs where opinions and stories carry a lot of weight. Moreover, they lead conversations that are approved and encouraged by their audiences. This is where going it alone can be very frustrating. The gestation period required by audiences to vet your content can take years. And if you expect to register a story message through multiple iterations of content pieces, piggybacking off the social capital of influencers becomes imperative.

Influencers in your industry can share stories of your brand to those who may never otherwise see your content. By collaborating with them, you can accelerate the delivery and sanctioning of your content with someone who is qualified to explain your story. And in the process, you have an opportunity to build your own thought leadership.

Topical Relevance of Influencer to a Focused Community

Many of the routes to grow your audience and expose your content organically further suffer from exposure to wasted eyeballs that could distract your lead generation efforts. Too often, entrepreneurs stake their efforts on SEO. As a result, marketing and sales can get flooded with unqualified leads. Search campaigns around keyword strategies could invite many readers whose background profiles are unknown or irrelevant to your targeted interests.

Influencers, on the other hand, can get your message across to people in their network that should have interest in your benefits given the influencer already addresses your niche. Just like moms like to talk to other moms and marathon runners like to talk to other runners, influencer audiences have already identified themselves as someone fascinated with specific topics of interest. The key to identifying the right influences is knowing what topics resonate the most with their niche audience. At minimum, traffic earned from the influencers podcast episodes or blog posts that are extendable to your brand should at least be more qualified as a potential lead. At best, the traffic includes those whose recommendations came from an influencer capable of swaying brand sentiment. In this case, the lead can be registered as a potential prospect.

Resonance

Perhaps even more important than *reach* and *relevance* is *resonance*. Brain Solis, a well-known authority on the subject, describes the three as the pillars of influence.[2] Reach is more a function of popularity and the goodwill earned across audiences. Relevance in this context implies the authority influencers have on a subject that is acknowledged by audiences who trust their expertise and have an affinity toward them on this subject matter. Resonance, on the other hand, relates to the ability influencers have on furthering discussions and sustaining engagement with these audiences. In effect, influencers with high resonance are able to echo your brand story to a relevant marketplace where the word of mouth can lead to audience actions.

Imagine, for example, that your content is compelling enough to gain the attention of targeted audiences. This may lead to their following you on Twitter or in Google+ circles. By itself, their following you only means you are potentially visible on their radar. But if your content registers well with the interests of your influencer's audiences, they may post or retweet your content. Now you have reached their audience feeds with a stamp of approval from someone they know, like, and trust.

Endorsement Credibility

Another important factor that contributes to the large following of influencers is their credibility in recommending brands to follow. An extensive survey conducted by Brian Solis and Vocus found that 51 percent of the respondents claimed they follow an influencer because of their opinion leadership. The same survey found that 40 percent follow the influencer because of their relationship with them.[3]

In many cases, the opinion expressed by these influencers can make or break your brand. Their expertise, coupled with the strong relationships they maintain with their audiences, makes them an especially reliable source for endorsements. Just like the impact NASCAR has on getting their audiences to buy their sponsored brands, the opinion of leading influences on social media can well become the consensus opinion of their audiences that ultimately sway sentiment toward a brand.

Influence Authority within a Concentrated Community

Besides their ability to provide visibility while shaping the perceptions audiences have of your brand, influencers can offer you insights into the way an industry can benefit from your brand. Given their regular interaction with widespread audiences, they are likely to be more aware of and capable of setting trends. Those that regularly host podcasts and collect numerous comments from their fans can especially provide insights into what your audience expects from your brand.

Since most successful influencers tend to hypertarget their audiences, they tend to have deep insights down to a psychographic niche. Overtime, they become authorities on what makes certain persona's tick. And when backed by trails of commentaries on their content, these influencers can crowdsource audience opinions that are very candid and insightful. This free research bodes well for brands otherwise faced with costly focus group research or constrained to profile data.

Quality Content with an Emotional Twist

The same survey conducted by Vocus and Brian Solis also found that 62 percent of the respondents follow an influencer because of the content they create. Because of their experience in crafting content useful and relevant to their audience, the writing skills of influencers are usually exceptional. Add to this the relational bond they have garnered from their unique perspective or likeable personality, and you can see why their content can be more compelling than what is published by brands.

Hub of Important Conversations

Finally, influencers have a better grasp of curating content around engaging conversations. What brands may attempt as a singular piece of content can often blend better in a topic hosted by an influencer that is framed better for discussion. Consider the many webinars hosted by brands that try to justify the worthiness of their topics. Influencers, on the other hand, start with trended topics that fascinate their audiences. They then use these conversations as a potential opportunity to sway sentiment toward your brand only if it lends credibility to the discussion. And because they have such a vested interest in audience engagement, they have earned a reputation for driving meaningful conversations.

How to Discover, Engage, and Romance Influencers

Courting the well-known authorities in your field requires a strategy beyond just brand exposure. Since the goal of influence marketing is to have others help you in sustainable engagement, as well as audience growth, entrepreneurs have to incentivize influencers to sway the brand sentiments of their audiences. These incentives could include exclusive information, new visibility, or compensation.

Key to a successful outreach campaign is the identification of the right influencers based on reach, resonance, and relevance. Once discovered, strategies are required to engage with the selected influencers to the point that they become advocates. This, in turn, requires a deep understanding of their own agendas so as to earn their accolades and harness their audiences.

Let's first start by dissecting what the pros do in finding, engaging, and collaborating with the right influencers. We will then continue with establishing goals and metrics required to measure and tweak outreach campaigns. Finally, steps will be examined for sustaining engagement with these influencers.

Identifying the Right Influencers

Influencers can be easily identified with the help of free tools like BuzzSumo, Traackr, Keyhole, and Little Bird. These tools provide a starting list of those who can exert influence on your topic through their wide and loyal audience. More importantly, they provide insights into the content that registers well with their audiences. From there, an evaluation of their popularity and a willingness to engage on your behalf can be made with free tools like Klout, PeerIndex, and Kred.

Notice how this was done in Table 6.1 for the case of social-media influencers. This list ranks the social capital of key individuals as indicative of their capacity to influence. The number of followers and fans can be used to determine their *reach*. Their *relevance* in the field of marketing is determined by their Kred scores for both influence and outreach. The latter has a maximum scale of 12 that measures the degree to which an influencer is generous in their engagements on a particular topic. Finally, *resonance,* an outcome of both relevance and reach, is measured by their Klout and PeerIndex scores. Collectively, these measures account for the social capital of certain individuals defined by the Word of Mouth Marketing Association (WOMMA) as having a "greater than average reach or impact through word of mouth in a relevant marketplace."

Table 6.1 Rating of Top Influencers in Social-Media Arenas

Influence Rank	Influencer	Reach (Followers in 000's) Composite Influence Index	Twitter	Google+	Relevance (Marketing) Kred (Influence)	Kred (Outreach)	Resonance Klout	PeerIndex	Influence Rank	Influencer	Reach (Followers in 000's) Composite Influence Index	Twitter	Google+	Relevance (Marketing) Kred (Influence)	Kred (Outreach)	Resonance Klout	PeerIndex
1	Gary Vaynerchuk	92	1090	2100	998	7	84	93	26	Michele Smorgon	86	41	10	978	8	78	83
2	Chris Brogan	92	292	130	998	8	85	91	27	Dave Morin	86	412	4	897	7	83	86
3	Guy Kawasaki	92	1420	6622	998	5	86	90	28	Michael Stelzner	86	84	27	984	6	79	81
4	Robert Scoble	91	414	5597	984	5	86	90	29	Michael Brito	86	116		980	7	78	82
5	Kim Garst	91	284	17	998	8	87	87	30	Zbynek Kysela	86	60	50	995	11	82	76
6	Brian Solis	91	230	67	998	6	85	89	31	Sarah Evans	86	104	34	975	5	79	81
7	Marsha Collier	91	94	21	994	8	87	87	32	Joe Pulizzi	85	56	8	990	7	78	79
8	Jessica Northey	91	589	1631	992	7	83	91	33	Geoff Livingston	85	20	13	988	8	78	79
9	Ann Tran	90	418	15	997	8	81	89	34	Pat Flynn	85	96	16	971	6	79	79
10	Darren Rowse	90	212	177	997	6	83	87	35	Erik Qualman	85	75	3	973	0	81	76
11	Jay Baer	89	130	30	998	7	82	86	36	Susan Gilbert	85	41	3	977	8	83	73
12	Michael Hyatt	89	229	0	986	5	82	86	37	Joel Comm	85	80	28	885	7	83	82
13	Jeremiah Owyang	88	154	69	995	6	79	86	38	David Armano	84	69	27	934	9	79	81
14	Beth Kanter	88	404	376	967	6	79	88	39	Gretchen Rubin	84	96		923	3	83	78
15	David Meerman Scott	88	110	19	986	6	82	83	40	Kerry Gorgone	84	14	4	976	8	79	76
16	Dave Kerpen	88	46	5	991	7	82	82	41	Shel Israel	84	29	15	926	6	80	79
17	Peter Shankman	88	164	3	988	5	80	84	42	Brian Halligan	84	40	2	964	5	80	75
18	Bryan Kramer	87	105	17	991	8	81	82	43	Chris Abraham	84	51	6	953	7	78	78
19	John Aguiar	87	141	37	989	7	78	85	44	Augie Ray	83	20		968	7	78	74
20	Scott Monty	87	106		982	6	79	82	45	Koka Sexton	83	39	0	968	6	79	72
21	Mitch Joel	87	63		989	5	81	81	46	Lewis Howes	83	100	26	948	0	78	75
22	Rich Simmonds	87	305	0	979	7	80	82	47	Gina Schreck	82	59	2	935	6	77	76
23	Lori Ruff	87	115	5	977	7	78	84	48	Douglas Karr	82	32	0	948	6	77	73
24	John Battelle	87	257	302	927	4	83	84	49	Andrea Vahl	81	12	6	961	6	78	69
25	Lee Odden	86	72	30	991	7	80	80	50	Linda Sherman Gordon	79	5	6	931	6	78	67

These complex algorithms for measuring various aspects of influence tap into an influencer's engagement on Twitter, LinkedIn, Google+, Facebook, YouTube, and even their blogging platforms. Although faulted for their machine-oriented approach to evaluating the many intangible effects an influencer has on its communities, these scoring tools have become the bastion of influence standards.

Developing Influence O-U-T-R-E-A-C-H

Enchanting influencers works much like the courtship process traditional marketers have with the media. Getting on their radar requires an understanding of their own agendas. And given their own risk in exposing someone unknown to their community, it helps to start with a reasonable amount of your own influence. This is where Klout scores surface again. Yes, we are being defined by a number. Just like explaining to a bank that a low credit score doesn't reflect your community giving and high grades as a parent, you have a lot more proving to do with a low Klout score.

Once you are on the radar of an influencer, it helps to let them know immediately how you can further their goodwill, grow their visibility, or boost their credentials. In effect, you want to enlist their efforts through O-U-T-R-E-A-C-H as demonstrated later.

Opportunities for Influencer Bonding

In conducting research on this subject, I am intrigued with the degree to which leaders in this field often publish posts to draw out other influencers. Knowing you belong to a club of elite members appeals to our innate desires to belong. Considering that a goal of many influencers is to book tours, get

meaningful book endorsements, or share panels with prestigious club members, one way to get their attention is to host events featuring their peers. Finding these venues could be as simple as hosting Google+ Hangouts on Air or podcasts. In these cases, it may not be as important to field a large audience as it is to allow influencers an opportunity to mingle.

Unique or Unannounced Content

Especially important to influencers is contributions of breaking or otherwise unannounced news. Giving influencers an exclusive look into recently discovered trends or hot topics gives them a venue for shaping conversations. The mere fact that many influencers are on the hook for regularly publishing blogs posts or podcast episodes makes your timely contributions all the more important.

Thought Leadership Platforms

Despite their already large followings, influencers are always seeking more visibility. As they develop new perspectives to lay the groundwork for book releases or a lecture circuit, they need platforms for boosting their thought leadership. By inviting their participation on panels or as expert commentary in playbooks, these influencers are given an opportunity to distinguish themselves.

Oftentimes, this visibility may be for test trialing new material. For example, some of the leaders I Skype into my classes will ask me to host new topics they are interested in spearheading. Before going live with large audiences, these smaller venues provide them an opportunity to practice their material while also gaining early audience reactions.

Recognition for Distinction

Every year, NSU hosts its Hall of Fame for Entrepreneurship. One year, a nominee publicly admitted that what he originally thought not to be a big deal was in fact a big deal. Influencers are influencers because they feed off crowd reaction. Even the most humble philanthropist treasures the opportunity to be recognized. But the recognition has to be genuine and from a source with high credibility in judging worthy candidates.

This is where entrepreneurs may feel challenged. Getting influencers to accept awards to the point of spending time on your brand may not be feasible. And simply handpicking awarded influencers from a good old boy network may not seem genuine. Lee Odden, an influencer expert, suggests that companies focus on new and upcoming influencers. They are not likely to be as sensitive to the prestige of award selection committees and will certainly appreciate the new limelight.

Easy Engagement to Start the Process

Oftentimes, the best way to earn influencer attention is through engagement on their turf. Influencers benefit from your commenting on their blogs or sharing their updates. And if you can interview them or capture the highlights of their presentations at events, they will likely notice your thoughtful contributions that go beyond pure fandom.

If asking them to cocreate content, it helps if you take the lead or make the process as painless as possible. For example, have them contribute microcontent that you later aggregate into a broader story or an opinion piece. In the other direction, by abstracting key points from their podcasts, blogs, or even books, you save them time creating shorter snippets to be later hosted in social-media posts or newsletters.

Authentication through Research

With so much competition among influencers to affirm their relative stature, you have an opportunity to potentially boost the perceived rankings of influencers with evidence supporting their unique claims. In particular, influencers often starve for empirical research of which they have little time or skill to conduct themselves. Especially if the study comes from a respected and objective source, research can often validate a position they take with their audiences. In addition, the study itself often provides a welcoming change of pace from the more editorial style of influencer conversations.

Common Interest Pursuits

As brand storytelling and social-media education went mainstream, I found many podcasters looking for fresh perspectives on the topic. This became a great opportunity for me to reach out to some influencers where we shared the same interests. Knowing they could share the podium with someone passionate about the subject, it made for an excellent tag team. By seeking those with common interests, the influencer is also relieved of having to find too many guests. Especially at times where a gap in scheduled content could lead to a bailed segment, a partner with common interests could be called upon on a regular basis.

Helping Influencer Causes

Ideally, your courtship process with an influencer should consider contributions to their causes. Giving them avenues to express their goodwill contributions could go a long way in posturing them as good corporate citizens. It could also complement their audience conversations or event promotions surrounding the cause. If connections could be made between your brand and a cause that resonates with the influencer's audience, you could help the influencer build off a recurring theme of social responsibility or community generosity.

Influencer Outreach Example for Entrepreneurs

As a class exercise in influencer outreach, I conducted my own campaign to boost visibility and credibility with the top social-media influencers. The intent of the outreach campaign was to

1. provide influencer value in the form of recognition and useful content for influencer followers;
2. get influencers to collaborate around a talk-worthy study; and
3. raise exposure to a future blog series.

Outreach Strategy

The strategy included the publishing of research related to the top influencers. Specifically, a study of social-media behaviors observed for the top social-media influencers concluded that these leaders are represented by four archetypes: educators, entertainers, charismatics, and coaches. The conclusions were posted on my blog (http://bit.ly/1q9B72F) and promoted on Twitter and LinkedIn.

The intent of the piece was to capture the attention of influencers as a way to reinvigorate my series on the top 25 social-media books. The series had stalled out as readers were either unaware of or disinterested in the choices from No. 20 to No. 25. As the book reviews approached the top 10, I wanted it to be noticed by all social-media influencers so as to raise my visibility and credibility as an academic influence. The blog featuring social-media archetypes was intended to raise these eyebrows through the chart shown in Figure 6.2.

SWOT Analysis

The following Strength, Weakness, Opportunity and Threat (SWOT) analysis was first conducted to see where I could best engage with influencers:

- *Strengths*: Academic credibility as a full-time professor teaching MBA courses in social-media marketing.

Figure 6.2 Study Chart Highlighted in Influencer Blog

- *Weaknesses*: Fairly recent start on social channels like Twitter and Google+ giving me limited reach, relevance, and resonance.
- *Opportunities*: Research backed by a solid methodology not likely to be conducted by leading practitioners in this field.
- *Threats*: Backlash from excluded influencers in the study as was the case after Forbes released their top 50 list of influencers (http://bit.ly/1uEfSHb).

Campaign Goals

Keeping all other blog activities constant, the traffic, shares, and engagement with the research were examined over the ensuing two weeks. Goals were established to ensure the campaign produced the following:

1. influencer boost in my social capital as measured by reach, relevance, and resonance;
2. positive brand sentiment expressed by these influencers;
3. engagement with these influencers on new content;
4. boost of personal Klout score to entice future followers; and
5. blog traffic growth to spur interest and further sharing.

Items 4 and 5 were included to ensure that opportunities for future influencer discussions were not thwarted by paltry traffic statistics and influence.

Boosting Social Capital

In order to measure the effectiveness of the first campaign goals, the following metrics were used to benchmark performance.

- *Reach*: Measured by the number of new influencer followers on Twitter, Google+, and LinkedIn.
- *Relevance*: Content relevant posts on Twitter, Google+, Facebook, LinkedIn updates, and blog comments.
- *Resonance*: The number of tweets, retweets, multitweet conversations, and twitter list placements by influencers.

Listed in Table 6.2 is a summary of results. From the response, it is clear that the content was compelling enough to attract many new influencers as well as share a favorable sentiment with their followers. What was not clear was their incentive to do both. For example, many followed but did not tweet or post the content to their followers. Others shared the content but did not follow. And of those that followed, only one placed

Table 6.2 Results of Influencer Outreach Campaign

Influence Rank	Influencer	Cinopez'z Influence Index	Twitter	Google+	Kred (Influence)	Kred (Outreach)	Klout	Peerindex	Cross-Influence Dialogue Campaign	Outreach Campaign	Twitter Followers	Google+ Circles	LinkedIn Connect	Google+ Posts	Pinterest Pins	LinkedIn Update	Blog Comments	Facebook Posts	Twitter Mentions	New Content Comments	Tweet/Retweet	Multi-Tweet Conversation	Twitter List Placement	Reach	Relevance	Resonance	Overall Target Potential
1	Gary Vaynerchuk	92	1090	2100	998	7	84	93																Low	Low	Low	Low
2	Chris Brogan	92	292	130	998	8	85	91																Low	Low	Low	Low
3	Guy Kawasaki	92	1420	6622	998	5	86	90																Low	Low	Low	Low
4	Robert Scoble	91	414	5597	984	5	86	90																Low	Low	Low	Low
5	Kim Garst	91	284	17	998	6	87	87	✓	✓		✓				✓		✓		✓	✓		Med	High	High	High
6	Brian Solis	91	230	67	998	6	85	89															Low	Low	Low	Low
7	Marsha Collier	91	94	21	994	8	87	87	✓	New New New		✓			✓		✓		✓	✓		High	High	High	High
8	Jessica Northey	91	589	1631	992	7	83	91		✓	✓				✓							Med	High	Low	Med
9	Ann Tran	90	418	15	997	8	81	89		✓												Med	Low	Low	Low
10	Darren Rowse	90	212	177	997	6	83	87			✓											Low	Low	Low	Low
11	Jay Baer	89	130	30	998	7	82	86			✓											Low	Low	Low	Low
12	Michael Hyatt	89	229	0	986	5	82	86														Low	Low	Low	Low
13	Jeremiah Owyang	88	154	69	995	6	79	86														Low	Low	Low	Low
14	Beth Kanter	88	404	376	967	6	79	88														Low	Low	Low	Low
15	David Meerman Scott	88	110	19	986	6	82	83			✓											Low	Low	Low	Low
16	Dave Kerpen	88	46	5	991	7	82	82		New		✓										Med	Low	Low	Low
17	Peter Shankman	88	164	3	988	5	80	84			✓											Low	Low	Low	Low
18	Bryan Kramer	87	105	17	991	8	81	82	✓	✓								✓				Med	Med	Low	Med
19	John Aguiar	87	141	37	989	7	78	85		✓	✓								✓			Med	Low	Med	Med
20	Scott Monty	87	106		982	6	79	84														Low	Low	Low	Low
21	Mitch Joel	87	63		989	5	81	81			✓											Low	Low	Low	Low
22	Rich Simmonds	87	305	0	979	7	80	82		New	New											Med	Low	Low	Low
23	Lori Ruff	87	115	5	977	7	78	84		✓	✓											Med	Low	Low	Low
24	John Battelle	87	257	302	927	4	83	84											✓			Low	Med	Low	Low
25	Lee Odden	86	72	30	991	7	80	80				✓	✓	✓								Low	High	Low	High
26	Michela Smorgon	86	41	10	978	8	78	83	✓	New New	✓				✓							High	High	Low	High
27	Dave Morin	86	412	4	897	7	83	88														Low	Low	Low	Low
28	Michael Stelzner	86	84	27	984	6	79	81				✓		✓		✓						Med	Med	Med	Med
29	Michael Brito	86	116		980	7	78	82		New		✓										Med	Low	Low	Low
30	Zbynek Kysela	86	60	50	995	11	82	76	✓	New New	✓	✓				✓	✓		✓	✓	✓	High	Med	High	High
31	Sarah Evans	86	104	34	975	5	79	81														Low	Low	Low	Low
32	Joe Pulizzi	85	56	8	990	7	78	79			✓											Low	Low	Low	Low
33	Geoff Livingston	85	29	13	988	8	78	79		New		✓										Med	Low	Low	Low
34	Pat Flynn	85	96	16	971	6	79	79														Low	Low	Low	Low
35	Erik Qualman	85	75	3	973	0	81	79														Low	Low	Low	Low
36	Susan Gilbert	85	41	3	977	8	83	73	✓	✓			✓									Med	Low	Low	Low
37	Joel Comm	85	80	28	865	7	83	82														Low	Low	Low	Low
38	David Armano	84	69	27	934	9	79	81		New		✓				✓						Low	Med	Low	High
39	Gretchen Rubin	84	96		923	3	83	78			✓											Low	Low	Low	Low
40	Kerry Gorgone	84	14	4	976	8	79	76		New	New						✓					Med	High	Low	Med
41	Shel Israel	84	29	15	926	6	80	79														Low	Low	Low	Low
42	Brian Halligan	84	48	2	964	5	80	75			✓											Low	Low	Low	Low
43	Chris Abraham	84	51	6	953	7	78	78														Low	Low	Low	Low
44	Augie Ray	83	20		968	7	78	74			✓											Low	Low	Low	Low
45	Koka Sexton	83	39	0	968	6	79	72	✓	New		✓					✓					Med	Med	Low	Med
46	Lewis Howes	83	100	26	948	0	78	75			✓											Low	Low	Low	Low
47	Gina Schreck	82	59	2	935	6	77	76	✓	New	New					✓	✓	✓		✓		Med	Med	Med	High
48	Douglas Karr	82	32	0	948	6	77	73			✓											Low	Low	Low	Low
49	Andrea Vahl	81	12	6	961	9	78	69	✓	✓						✓		✓	✓			Low	Med	Med	Med
50	Linda Sherman Gordon	79	5	6	931	6	76	67		New New		✓				✓		✓	✓	✓		Low	High	High	Med

Figure 6.3 Eample of Positive Brand Sentiment on Social Channels

me in a list of social-media experts. Without a placement in a Twitter list, any new tweets potentially get lost in the clutter of the influencer's feeds as many influencers follow thousands of others. Earning a listing or repeat connection with these folks would obviously require more quality content and meaningful engagement.

Where the outreach piece scored well was in response to the goal to boost engagement on new content as well as brand sentiment expressed by these influencers. Some examples of commentary that bodes well for my personal brand are shown in Figure 6.3.

Site Traffic, Personal Influence, and Social Proof

To measure the impact the outreach had on site traffic, social proof, and influence, all blogging and social engagement was held constant during the week following the influencer research posting. As seen in the results shown in Figure 6.4, the influence outreach clearly had an impact on accelerating visibility and attracting new followers. Klout scores improved 20 percent while the number of total shares reached over 2,500. Finally blog traffic boosted the overall Alexa traffic ranking from 2.1M to 635K from over 5,000 new visitor impressions (Figure 6.4).

Outreach Tactics

What made this outreach strategy work was relevant content that provided value to these influencers. Using the O-U-T-R-E-A-C-H tactics described earlier, consider how the campaign was able to borrow from the social capital possessed by these influencers to the point where seven influencers could be courted for future engagement (see far right column of Table 6.2).

The attraction of the blog post by several influencers was seeing their name validated in the context of an academic study on archetypes. But rather than overtly touting their initiation into an elite club, the study

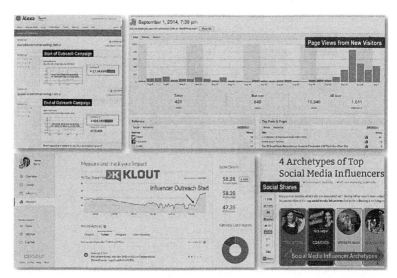

Figure 6.4 Results of Site Traffic, Personal Influence, and Social Proof

Figure 6.5 Engaging Google+ Post

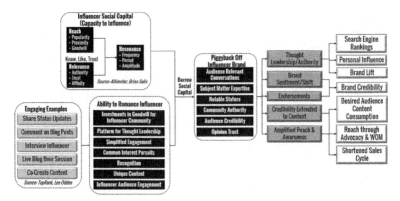

Figure 6.6 Summary Model of Influence Impact on Outcomes

provided a legitimate way for them to engage their audiences while boosting their credentials in the process.

Consider how this was done by Lee Odden who asked his audience what quadrant they fit in Figure 6.5. In the process of engaging them on a new topic, Lee validated his placement among the top thought leaders without drawing attention to himself ().

In summary, influence contributes to brand lift, reach and ultimately improved search engine results. Key to its success is your ability to romance the influencer as well as the influencer's social capital measured in reach, relevance and resonance. Shown in Figure 6.6 is a model of influence determinants and outcomes.

Notes

1. "Influencer Marketing, Rick Springfield, and a Bottle Opener that Opened Doors" by Convince& Convert's contribution from Barry Feldman (http://bit.ly/1BByACu).
2. "The Rise of Digital Influence and How to Measure It" by Brian Solis (http://bit.ly/1uyS7kE).
3. "What Makes an Influencer: a A Survey by Vocus and Brian Solis" Vocus White Paper (http://bit.ly/1AOU8t1).

CHAPTER 7

Enlist Followers with a S-T-A-M-P

Without an audience, all of our marketing—not just content marketing—is a tree falling in the forest that no one hears.

—Jeffrey Rohrs

There is perhaps no better example of "What comes first—the chicken or the egg?" than new users of social media building their proprietary audiences. What comes first—content or followers? Just like hosting a party of your friends can easily go sour if there is no conversation or activities, having a lot of social-media followers serves no purpose without content or engagement. At the other extreme, even the best of open houses hosted with great food, tours, and fun activities serves no purpose if you have no friends. The same applies to great content simply waiting to be exposed. Without a social-media audience, great content ends up in a library.

To recap, let's consider the resources at our disposal for spreading our stories. We have employees as a word-of-mouth advocates that could build our audience. And we have influencers that could lend us their huge audiences. We also have syndications and search engines described in Chapter 8 that will do their job exposing us to audiences interested in our topics. But how do we enlist new followers through our social-media channels that ultimately become a proprietary audience?

At a time when social networks are surprising us with poor organic feed results, brands are quickly discovering why they need their own audiences. Unless these audiences literally subscribe to our content, we have little control of messaging, targeting, and tracking the behaviors of our desired audiences. Content may go viral, but the ability to build relationships from it can only materialize if we capture their contact information for later conversations.

But in fairness to the social networks, these contact lists for e-mailing and texting messaging would remain small. After all, each fan, follower, and connection that touches your content has audiences in the hundreds on average. Consequently, when they provide an e-mail address—perhaps through some fan-welcoming incentive—your rolodex can fill up quickly. Ideally, we want to exploit social-networking channels for their reach and subscription incentives for proprietary audience development described further in Chapter 11.

Consider this as having to enlist followers with a S-T-A-M-P like the one shown later. Once we gain these followers, Chapter 10 will discuss how we keep them engaged. Chapter 11 will then explain how we escort them through the sales funnel.

Developing Strategies for Gaining New Followers

Enlisting followers on social media is no different than the steps we take to start and grow a club. We begin by tapping into our networks of hobbyists, faith followers, or school friends. We then let them know we

are worthy of leading the group based on our expertise. But to expand our pitch, we may have to advertise our club and count on local media to highlight its goodwill contributions and impact on the community. Finally, we get our club enthusiasts to sign-up.

Similarly, in social media, we start with our social networks and build a case for our running the community based on our thought leadership and profile strength. We then bank on Facebook, LinkedIn, and Twitter advertising to expand our reach while journalists, analysts, and others promote our press worthiness. Finally, we leverage this club membership stamp to start a dialogue with interested followers.

Building Social-Networking Strategies

A common perception of many brands and small businesses is to make their presence felt on every network. After all, customers now expect us to be where they are hanging out or have a customer service issue. But the level of attention need not be the same; for those with limited resources, being active on many social networks is like participating in all of your favorite community, hobby, and political clubs. You won't be effective.

Before diving into strategies to get more followers and fans, therefore, it behooves us to know if we are actively involved in the right networks. Experts in the field consistently suggest that you base your choice of primary network participation on the following:

1. the degree of importance placed on SEO, brand awareness, customer communication, or traffic referrals;
2. what your website traffic and other analytics suggest is your current source of traffic;
3. what fits the style and tone of content and engagement preferred by your audiences;
4. where your competition, influencers, and industry have a dominant presence; and
5. the overall reach, relevance, and resonance of the channel.

As discussed in the next chapter, marketers tend to use social media for one of three purposes: marketing their offerings, serving as a resource, or providing customer service. To that end, the choice of social network should be based on the degree to which the network suits these objectives. For example, some networks are well suited for one-on-one customer communications but do not provide the brand exposure or web traffic results for brands to effectively market their offerings.

The choice of network emphasis should at minimum consider the importance of the network in making content searchable, boosting brand awareness, creating an atmosphere for responsive customer service, and referring traffic to a website. CMO by Adobe provides an annual evaluation of eight networks based on their ability to address these marketing objectives. Shown in Figure 7.1 is their 2014 Social Landscape downloadable at http://cmo.cm/1yhcN4M.[1]

Once deciding on your network of emphasis, getting the **right** *followers* and *fans* requires insights into the peculiarities of the networks if you want to court a target audience qualifying as a sales prospect. The unique aspects of each network, as well as the approached taken to gain followers, is covered next. This is followed in ensuing sections on ways to make *connections* through thought leadership and enlist *subscribers* through proprietary audience strategy. Common to attracting all of these joiners are strategies that tailor incentives to attract their membership. The differences lie in the expectations of each joiner. Audience expert, Jeff Rohrs, for example, suggests that[2]

- followers (including connections) seek information;
- fans seek passion; and
- subscribers seek convenience.

Understanding and Attracting Followers on Twitter

Twitter provides instant, worldwide distribution of content. Covering everyone from television personalities to industry experts, it is heavily used for brand awareness, customer service, and driving web traffic. As of this

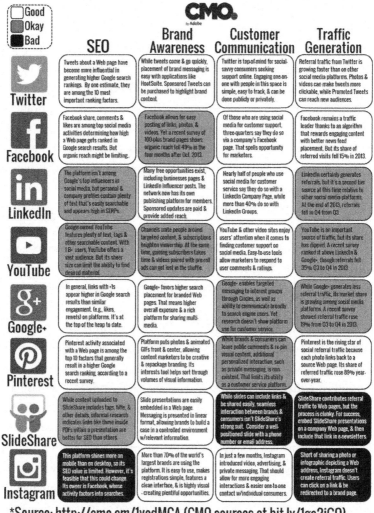

*Source: http://cmo.cm/1yedMCA (CMO sources at bit.ly/1go2jGO)

Figure 7.1 CMO's Guide to 2014 Social Landscape

writing, over 500 million tweets are sent per day by nearly 300 million monthly active users; the bulk (78 percent as of 4Q14) of which are on mobile.

Although Twitter is limited to only 140-character tweets, rich media can be accommodated through Vine and Twitter Cards. Besides adding photos and videos, the latter allows you to embed lead generation forms and capture e-mails for a more straightforward sales conversion process than can be expected when directing traffic to a landing page.

Collectively, these platform assets make Twitter ideal for reaching out and directly engaging with others. Because of its frequent and succinct way of providing useful information, the platform is conducive to building trails of trustworthy content mentioned earlier. The platform, along with LinkedIn, is arguably the best source for identifying yourself as an industry expert. Klout scores, for example, can be shown alongside each member's profile.

Twitter is also a great way to show the responsiveness and personality of your brand. As many companies elect to have their advocates represent their voice, brands become more likeable and human. This especially bodes well for those using Twitter as a customer service channel. Not only does the platform lends itself well to listening for brand sentiment, but it also provides a real-time channel for dealing with live customer issues. Other Others can then follow the brand's reaction to service as an indication of its responsiveness.

Finally, Twitter offers one of the easiest and fastest methods to build followers. Retweets of compelling content have an immediate impact on reaching new potential audiences. And when your tweets of new content include well-researched hashtags, your visibility can reach a new and relevant audience that regularly research content parked under these hashtags. Tools like HootSuite and TweetCaster alert readers in a custom feed when new content is published for a given hashtag. And tools like hashtags.org and hashtagify.me can help you research the right hashtags. Finally, the brevity of your social nametag, or Twitter handle (@JimBarryJr), makes the advertising of your brand more memorable. This greatly simplifies the ability of this platform to attract followers outside of its network.

Understanding and Attracting Fans on Facebook

Despite Millennials and Gen Z jumping ship from Facebook to Tumblr, Snapchat, Whisper, and other social platforms, the platform Facebook remains the ultimate in community sharing and engagement. With an estimated 1.3 billion monthly active users, of which 1 billion include mobile users, it is still the largest of social networks. What's more, nearly 800 million log in daily, making it the largest available audience served by any media in the world.

Where Facebook truly makes it mark is with a fan base seeking entertainment and highly personal engagement. It remains a platform of choice for discussing fun and trendy topics. And with its mobile photo-intensive style of engagement, fans can interact all day with just a few clicks on their smart devices. This entertaining and often inspirational style of engagement gives brands plenty of opportunity to share their stories and give their brand a personality.

Despite the constant surprises from Facebook on drastically changed feature and marketing models, Facebook offers some design advantages especially useful to B2C brands. Its custom interfacing allows a great deal of Facebook page versatility and consistency with brand messaging. Moreover, the overall effort required to build and maintain these pages can be scaled to the volume of content and fan engagement desired.

Known for its fan activation through "likes," brands recognize the growing visibility each fan represents as the average number of friends per fan continues to rise. According to Pew Research conducted in 2014, the average number of friends among adult users is 338 with a median of around 200 friends. As described in Figure 7.1, however, this rise in friends is offset by a rapid decline in organically reaching them in their news feeds.

Herein lies the problem with brands marketing on Facebook. Most marketers know the real battleground on Facebook is in the news feed; it's not on Facebook pages. Recent research shows that most Facebook users interact with page updates in their news feed rather than visiting Facebook pages. But now that the organic reach of pages is approaching less than 2 percent of their fans on average, brands have little choice but to "pay-to-play" for audience exposure. Why do this? There are 1.3 billion reasons why. Coupled with Facebook's superior ad network and strong mobile presence, it's a great way to scale your marketing efforts and globally reach a hypertargeted audience.

Gaining followers normally requires compelling content or an exciting brand story. Among the most popular ways to attract new fans is through contests or events hosted on Facebook. Described further in Chapter 10, the invite and event participation process is ideal for capturing new audiences. A photo contest, for instance, requires users to visit a custom tab on the brand's Facebook page in order to upload the photo and submit a contest entry. A registration opt-in then turns these audiences into subscribers. This is where a fan becomes far more valuable than just a follower.

But to entice them, fans need bigger incentives. Knowing they risk your invading their news feeds and misrepresenting your brand endorsements to their friends, they expect exclusive content, valuable coupons, or inside privileges with their membership. A common approach taken by many brands is to allow access to a series of video tutorials on their welcome page in exchange for their fan acceptance and contact information. A challenge with keeping fans on Facebook, however, is keeping them stimulated. Unless, fans are continually provided with sensationalized content, it's tough to keep their attention.

Once invited, fans on Facebook have perhaps the most comprehensive platform to have conversations with other fans while sharing picture, videos, and other content related to the brand. And with its acquisition of messaging WhatsApp, Facebook shows great promise in extending direct communications between fans and brands. Finally, Facebook's foray into virtual reality through Oculus Rift will help this platform address the growing demand for richer brand experiences on wearable devices.

Understanding and Attracting Connections on LinkedIn

With over 300 million members worldwide and 187 million monthly unique visitors, LinkedIn remains the world's largest professional network. In fact, an estimated one-third of world professionals are on LinkedIn. And their reliance on the network for B2B and overall professional correspondence continues to grow. Today, the average user spends 17 minutes monthly on this platform, and nearly 40 percent of its users check in daily.

What started out as a resume and Rolodex-oriented platform now rivals the best in community engagement. Like Facebook, it allows like-minded individuals to discuss topics of interest. Only LinkedIn relies on its 2.1 million

groups to do this. These groups are becoming increasingly targeted, making them useful in building thought leadership with a relevant audience.

The endorsement features provide a way to validate your expertise and credibility and examine the credentials of the endorser. As a result, it rivals Klout scores as a measure of influence. And now with its publishing features opened to almost all members, LinkedIn is providing its users with an opportunity to create and share content while adding it to their professional profile. Companies now have a venue for owned media residing right on the platform. This avoids the updating of abbreviated and networked restricted references to content while boosting the visibility of quality content across the entire network.

Unlike the reach of Twitter that restricts the visibility of your post to followers only (until retweeted), updates on LinkedIn could potentially reach those beyond your first degree of connections. And for some, LinkedIn now allows you to build an audience of followers beyond your network of connections. Although you cannot message directly with these followers at the present time, you can share photos, images, videos, and presentations across the community. Now members have the ability to follow other members that are not in their network while building their own group of followers.

What makes LinkedIn stand out is its low signal-to-noise ratio and ability to let others find you. Updates of your content have a far greater chance of being exposed to your target audiences than what you can expect on Twitter or Facebook. And with the groups moderating meaningful conversations around specific industry topics, B2B audiences have a venue for discussing key business challenges without the distraction of leisure oriented conversations.

The key to getting connections is the quality of your invite and profile. Having a great deal of common connections, endorsements from well-respected individuals and a powerful resume is a great start. But the invite itself could make the difference. By explaining how you can enhance their own network or referencing some meaningful Linked In dialogues you shared, the request will likely be taken more seriously.

To attract others to extend an invite to you, having a well-optimized profile is key. LinkedIn's own search engine provides professionals and brands an opportunity to showcase their expertise in the search bar. Listings under groups, companies, or individuals are ranked ordered much like that of other search engines. Key to achieving a high ranking is a profile well optimized around targeted terms as well as a large number of credible endorsements on skills associated with the term.

Understanding YouTube and Adding to Your Subscribers

With over 1 billion unique users per month, YouTube remains by far the most popular viewing site. And like Facebook and LinkedIn, content hosted on YouTube allows for community engagement in the form of likes, shares, and comments. But besides its popularity as a social network, it is also the second most popular search engine.

What was once a site reserved for video production experts is now used for content creation by almost every major brand. Today, more than 100 hours of video are uploaded to YouTube every minute as a result of the 6 billion hours of video watched every month and the ease with which even amateurs can host quality content.

The embedding of YouTube videos on other platforms including websites makes it especially valuable for video blogging, social-media posts, and LinkedIn profiles. And just like the tools permitted to edit or enhance videos, the process of embedding videos takes little effort and expertise. But what makes this platform especially popular is its seamless support across every mobile platform.

Where YouTube falls short as a social network is in its approach to earning subscriptions. Channels unite people around targeted content and not around the engagement of channels like Facebook. Brand stories, dialogues, and community events have to rely instead on other channels to coordinate conversations across the brand. Moreover, subscriptions take time as viewers normally need to see several iterations of content releases before electing to subscribe.

The key to earning subscriptions is to demonstrate value in future episodes or in customer service. The latter in particular has been embraced by brands that see "how-to" videos coupled with comments from viewers as a helpful way of demonstrating solutions to recurring issues.

Understanding Google+ and Adding to Your Circles

After Facebook, Google+ is the second most active social-networking site in the world. As of this writing, it has 359 million monthly users active in the *stream* where users see updates from those in their circles. As of this writing, Google+ remains a male-dominated network, with an estimated 70 percent of users being men. But most importantly, it's where social and search truly come together.

Given its similarity to Facebook in updates, engagement, and visual richness, a question often arises as to why someone wants to engage in one more network. A simple answer is "because it's Google." Google+ is not just a social network. It's a social layer on top of all Google properties. You are essentially seeing all of your peers in each experience on the Google platform that includes Gmail, YouTube, Android, Google Glass, Google Maps, and most importantly its search engine. In fact, the reason why *social* is now the new *SEO* has a lot to do with Google+. Your search results have much to do with social shares especially from those having a high page rank measured by their own sphere of Google+ influence.

But there are some significant differences between Facebook and Google+. Facebook is built more around communities where folks connect with others they already know. It's more about friends and family. Google+, on the other hand, is based more around activity- or interest-based networking. In this sense, Google+ is more like Twitter in that communities segregate and then group together under common interests. This provides a real benefit to brands that can now target their messages and market their offerings to those meeting a certain criteria.

What makes When used properly, Google+ has an unmatched advantage in search especially unique is its impact on search. But this takes more than a well-optimized profile; it takes an engaging platform, quality content, a +1 button on your web page, and a circle of influential followers. For example, research shows that receiving Google+1's is more important from an SEO perspective than the number of backlinks.[3] When someone of influence in your Circles hits the +1 button, for example, this authority can be transferred to your blog post in the form of a backlink. This is one reason having a few power influencers in your Circles is more valuable than having a lot of followers.

Besides its impact on search, a distinctive networking capability of Google+ includes its ability to host Hangouts, a capability especially appealing to the tech professions. You can connect up to 10 people in a Skype like video conference. These free video conferencing calls add a business-oriented dimension that keep professionals engaged in work-related matters. But as explained in Figure 7.1, Google+ has yet to capitalize on its YouTube assets or targeted messaging to interest groups (through circles) that make it a worthwhile platform for customer service.

Where this capability shows real promise is in its Hangouts on air (HOA) described in Chapter 1. HOA provides a unique medium for webcasting that can be recording for later retrieval. Moreover, by capitalizing on the video-editing features and public exposure of YouTube, Google allows these panel-oriented broadcasts to reach primetime levels of quality often rivaling that of talk shows.

Community building on Google+ amounts to adding folks to your circles where you can organize them into groups or lists for sharing. Like most other platforms, your followers see the content of your stream thereby making the choice to join you a matter of quality vs congestion. But since the overall signal-to-noise ratio remains relatively high on Google+, brands find the efforts to build circles worthwhile. Once the circle is created, specific private content can be displayed in the stream of that circle under a category designated by the user.

One way to gain new members in your circles is getting them to find your content by using the right hashtags or through search. For example, the longer a post exists, the longer it stays in the Google index. Consequently, the more folks search for and interact with the content over time, the higher it potentially places at the top of conversations and searches. More importantly, this content gestation allows brands to expose their entire storyline since the content lasts forever. Contrast this with Facebook fans whose interest often wanes over time; consequently, they have less opportunity to put the story pieces together. And brands have fewer opportunities to escort them through the sales funnel.

Joining the right Google+ Communities can also invite new members to your circles. Although you can join a broader audience and capitalize on more widespread dialogue through Google Communities, only those in your circles fall in the category of subscribers. You cannot e-mail those in your communities unless there are in your circles as well. Nevertheless, the more those in your communities see you as an influential leader of conversations of interest, the more likely they will follow and encourage others to follow you. Tools like CircleCount.com can help you identify the right communities. The key to getting these members to then join your circle is to first follow those that regularly engage and respond themselves. Then continually participate in their conversation as well as amplify their content. Like most networks, the more visual your content, and the more it is about your viewers, the more likely they are to follow.

Understanding and Attracting Followers on Pinterest

Pinterest is an aspirational social-media platform in that people use it to find things that they want. It now reaches over 70 million users, 40 million of which are monthly active, while accumulating 25 billion pins in just its first three years of existence. But despite its small size relative to the aforementioned networks, Pinterest drives more referral traffic than LinkedIn, YouTube, and Google+ combined. And according to Social-Media Examiner's Industry Report, 50 percent of marketers plan on increasing their Pinterest marketing.[4] Among the reasons for this growing demand is that Pinterest

1. caters to a visual audience;
2. is a female-dominated network more prone to spontaneous shopping;
3. lends itself to e-commerce; and
4. performs well in search.

As discussed in Chapters 1 and 3, the rapid migration toward visual content serves the higher population of visually oriented learners as well as the rapid adoption by brands of visual storytelling. And since visuals are at center stage, the average Pinterest user spends an average of 1 hour and 17 minutes per month on the site compared to 36 minutes on Twitter and 12 minutes on Facebook.

And with an estimated 80–83 percent of the network users being female, it's no surprise that Pinterest now accounts for about 41 percent of e-commerce traffic.[5] Women make or influence 85 percent of all purchasing decisions. They also account for 58 percent of all total online spending.[6]

But perhaps the most important reason why Pinterest has attracted the attention of most brands is its ability to drive sales. Despite its far smaller audience than Facebook and Google+, Pinterest accounts for more than 23 percent of all social-media-driven sales. Research also shows that an estimated 47 percent of online consumers in the United States have made a purchase based on Pinterest recommendations. Moreover, the average order placed by users of the platform is $179—compare that to $80 for Facebook and $69 for Twitter.[7]

Like many of the other networks, the key to growing and keeping audiences on Pinterest is to offer content that is useful, inspirational, insightful, or engaging. This obviously works better for brands that lend themselves to fun and aspirational themes. In fact, over 40 percent of pins are in the fashion, food, and home décor categories. But a surprising trend is the growing activity of brand categories outside of retail that have made headway with less than inspiring products.

These brands understand that success on Pinterest requires you to put your products in context. In essence, it has more to do with inspiring others with the lifestyles represented by their brand—not selling products. GE does this very well with their innovative design concepts or stories reflective of their culture. And like other successful brands on Pinterest, the company pins photos that inspire others to share their own experiences. Leading

Pinterest expert, Cynthia Sanchez, suggests that brands imagine audiences saying "how can I . . . someday I want to . . . my favorite . . . that's cool." If they can envision their boards responding in this way, Pinterest can then serve more as an aspirational platform than a digital catalog.

Creating an engaging audience on Pinterest can take many avenues but a typical strategy involves attracting followers, earning re-pins, and driving traffic to your website. Gaining followers is a bit more straightforward than the complex search-and-amplify strategies described earlier for Google+. Among the most popular ways to attract followers on Pinterest are the following:

1. *Partner with influential guest pinners*: By collaborating on group boards, you can invite other users to contribute pins to a cocurating board; their activity on your board shows up in both your followers' and the guest pinner's followers' feeds. If some of the contributors are super pinners, this could expose your pins to potentially huge audiences. Free services like PinGroupie can help you find these group boards that potentially attract influential pinners.

2. *User-relevant hashtags*: Using hashtags on pin descriptions that are trending will ensure that audiences find you and see the relevance of your pins to their interests.

3. *Contribute to others' boards*: Commenting thoughtfully, and without spamming, on other's pins will often result in a follow especially when the comments include names of others positively referenced or thanked in the comment. The same applies to tagging and liking. Together these contributions add to a spirit of relationship building.

4. *Use rich pins*: Rich pins allow you to add price and availability information. Pins with prices are known to get a third more likes. This further helps with subscription building as users will often gratefully accept e-mail notices of a product on sale.

5. *Pin and share a lot of images*: The more you share, the more other users will see your pins and its details, thereby encouraging them to view your page. Integrate your own content with the best of other people's content. This helps build your reputation as a thought leader and a tastemaker. Remember social media is a multidirectional conversation. This ultimately attracts more followers as Pinterest will

recommend your boards to those pinning the same image especially when you regularly pin images others enjoy.

6. *Add buttons and widgets*: Make sure your website is optimized for Pinterest sharing by including its buttons alongside your other social-

sharing options. In addition, you can boost your sharing pinning activity by adding a "pin this" button to your visuals. But most importantly, make sure your site includes high-quality pinnable visuals that could really dress up someone's boards. This way, Pinterest users can feel confident that your content complements their brand story. This should attract their followers' interest in the pin leading to your site. This same audience could then be encouraged to follow you on Pinterest as well.

7. *Host contest*: As described in the Chapter 8, Pinterest is well suited to hosting contests that could attract new followers.

Understanding and Attracting Followers on Instagram

Instagram is a mobile app for sharing photos and videos. As the Facebook-owned photo- and video-sharing service, it is the fastest growing and arguably the most consumed social-media platform. The average Instagram user spends over 4 hours a month taking, filtering, editing, and sharing photos. As of this writing, it has over 200 million monthly active users that have accounted for more than 20 billion photos uploaded to the service since its inception. More importantly, almost 60 percent of these users rely on the social network on a daily basis. This has led to nearly half of the top 100 brands on Instagram posting daily.

What makes Instagram stand out is its direct messaging and extraordinary engagement with users. According to Adweek, Instagram is achieving three times the engagement per post when compared to Facebook. Research by Forrester shows it gets 15 times more engagement than Twitter or Google+. Much of this is attributed to its visual-centric orientation where inspirational images and 15-second videos create a strong bond across a community of like-minded followers.

But keeping these followers takes more than simply uploading photos. Like most of the aforementioned networks, success on Instagram requires you to be highly conversational often by answering questions or participating in discussions. Some great ways to keep this engagement on Instagram is to

1. invite engagement through behind the scenes content or getting followers to guess something about your brand;
2. invite user-generated videos or images that show the goofy or creative sides of followers often in exchange for contest prizes;
3. dress up your photos using filters and text-based imagery. Apps like Wordswag are a great tool for adding text to your imagery;
4. maintain brand authenticity and trust by consistency portraying the same brand theme or tone; and
5. stay on top of your comments, tagging, geo-tagging, and sharing of other people's visuals and images.

Like Pinterest, the attraction of audiences on Instagram requires engaging with other's content. Although Pinterest is used more as an aspirational media that attracts shoppers in need of something, Instagram caters to a younger generation who likes to feature themselves and engage daily for fear of missing out. In fact, its notoriety includes the birth of the selfie.

As a mobile app, Instagram enjoys higher viewership than Pinterest. And because of Instagram Direct and Facebook's acquisition of WhatsApp, expect Facebook to exploit its direct messaging capability to allow for even more engaging interactions as well as one-to-one contacting for customer service. Pinterest, on the other hand, has no way to handle personal interaction like private messaging.

On the other hand, Pinterest Instagram lacks the sales conversion aspects of Pinterest. Direct links to a website are not possible at the moment, thereby making it problematic for e-commerce transactions. Consequently, Instagram serves more as a top-of-funnel brand builder or middle-of-funnel content source. The latter is made possible by the consumer endorsements represented when user's share or comment on photos. Sales conversion, however, requires continuous cross-promotion of Instagram with other channels like Twitter, Facebook, and e-mail.

Among the most popular approaches used by successful brands on Instagram to grow their followers are the following:

1. *Use hashtags*: Using hashtag tracking tools like Tagboard or Keyhole, your content can be better grouped along conversations and ideas, thereby making it easier for others to discover you. A study conducted by social-media scientist, Dan Zarrella, concluded that hashtags on Instagram can also create a sense of community and build brand loyalty.[8]

2. *Use analytics*: Instagram is supported by great analytics tools like Iconosquare or Websta that allow you to monitor who is engaging and what they like. But it also allows you to examine your competition for what their followers like or dislike. This becomes an excellent source for reaching out to potential followers of your own.

3. *Put the spotlight on your followers*: The more you use real content created by your current followers, the more they are motivated to draw out more followers for you.

4. *Create Instagram badges*: The top social-media influencer, Kim Garst, points out that "adding a badge to your Facebook, website, or blog that links to your Instagram will be sure to gain you more followers."[9]

5. *Regularly post and interact*: Like the other networks, Instagram audiences are built from liking and commenting on other's content on a regular basis. The same applies to sharing. The more you share compelling content from your followers, the more likely they will share your content in return. To ensure you are posting at the right times, tools like Schedugram will help you schedule updates during those peak periods when your potential followers are likely to engagement.

6. *Cross-promote*: Given its isolation away from your website, it's important to post your imagery and videos on other social channels as well. This raises your overall visibility while helping you gain new followers.

Understanding and Attracting Followers on SlideShare

SlideShare is the world's largest content-marketing platform owned by LinkedIn since 2012. What started out as a repository of presentation

slide decks has grown into a social-networking platform for serious professionals. Now enjoying
over 60 million unique visitors a
month, SlideShare is used to host
presentations, infographics, videos,
e-Books, white papers, and a variety of other PDF-formatted docu-

ments. And like the other mentioned networks, its suitability to image- and
video-based content in mobile-friendly formats addresses the growing demand for visual content on the go.

Where SlideShare stands out from other networks is in its ability to

1. climb high in SERPs;
2. seamlessly accommodate almost any type of content in a slide-to-
   slide format;
3. address the entire sales funnel;
4. facilitate lead generation;
5. serve as a content hub;
6. contribute to LinkedIn profiles and updates; and
7. develop relationships with audiences seeking research and education
   on a neutral platform.

Because of the large audience of users, search engine results from Slide-
Share presentations typically outweigh what can be accomplished from a
company's own website. And because it can accommodate so many other
platforms, it contributes greatly to building followers and boosting search
results. For example, SlideShare presentations can be embedded in blogs
and LinkedIn profiles that drive those followers to your SlideShare site
where they can often follow you there as well. In the reverse, YouTube
videos, webinar recordings, and e-Books can be hosted on SlideShare,
thereby encouraging your SlideShare followers to subscribe to your blog
or video channels.

However, where SlideShare has really made its mark is in lead generation. Major brands are now finding this platform to be the number 1 or
2 source of all their new leads. One reason for this is its broad applicability

across the sales funnel. Slides addressing "how-to's" and industry insights serve the top of the funnel. Embedded calls to action can then be used to earn subscribers as the platform introduces your e-Books, webinar recordings, and product reviews. Finally, price comparison sheets and other bottom-of-funnel content can lead to a qualified prospect or sale. And since SlideShare offers easy to fill lead generation forms, this whole process of lead nurturing can be well integrated into your CRM or marketing automation tools without having the user leave the platform.

Finally, much like the other platforms, gaining followers on SlideShare has much to do with your engagement with others' content through *comments* and *likes*. And to capture their attention, you need high-quality visuals preferably aimed at education or insightful research. Fortunately, there are many tools like Canva, slideidea, and Haiku Deck that can help dress up your content. And with a premium account, you have ample analytics to gauge your progress in producing quality content as well as in attracting the right influencers.

Developing Thought Leadership Strategies for Audience Development

So far, we have discussed how social networks, advocacy, and content can set the stage for you to discover and engage with prospective customers. But a fundamental premise here is that these viewers are fascinated with what you have to say. In effect, they see you as a thought leader or someone they *trust* as an *authority* on *relevant* topics early in their buying journey.

Gaining this trust means less talking about what you do and more discussion around why you do it. Consider the thought leadership Dove developed in their Real Beauty series. Rather than touting their expertise in soap, their stories of women's self-esteem made them more of an authority on intrinsic beauty. Results of their campaigns clearly show a lift in brand affinity and most likely led to stronger engagement and trust among a niche of women too hard on themselves.

Once you can identify the personas whose challenges resonate with your authority, social networking allows you to connect and communicate with them while shoring up your *thought leadership* stature in the process. But this takes more than a solid content strategy; it takes an understanding of your audience's key questions as well as your assertion of leadership in the right venues.

Understanding the Right Content Essentials

Becoming a thought leader is a long-term, layered process that begins with a trail of trustworthy content a reader is willing to try out. Over time, you may become recognized as an authority on relevant topics if you resonate with what's most important to your audiences. Depending on where your audience is in their buying journey, this authority is normally derived from audiences recognizing your visionary insights, new business models, or innovative solutions to business problems. These insights can come from benchmarking surveys, data analysis, or simply collections of perspectives from influencers.

What is important is for audiences to see you as consistently provide interesting, accurate, and helpful ideas. Here is where visuals like infographics play a key role. And the key to gaining a reputation for helpfulness is to make sure your content does not just reflect your unique perspective on a hot topic. It has to reflect your audience's agenda since your level of authority is greatly determined by how well you answer their most important questions. This can come from blog comments as well as social-media group discussions discussed further in Chapter 8.

But content itself is rarely sufficient enough for anyone to earn the respect and reputation for being a trusted subject matter expert. Thought leaders are known to engage regularly with their audiences to the point where their followers become advocates. They also have a sizeable capacity for conducting in-depth research as well as hosting venues that showcase your business expertise. Simply curating the best of influencer content may posture you as a respected editorialist, but it's not likely to posture you as an authority capable of shaping opinions or shifting industry paradigms.

Hosting Venues to Showcase Expertise

One way to assert your thought leadership is to host your own content or shows on topics relevant to your targeted audiences. And given that the primary purpose for developing thought leadership is to court prospects early in their buying stage, these venues should start small. Most of us have limited patience to digest middle-of-funnel content until a trail of bite-sized blogs or SlideShare presentations, for example, validates a perception of authority. From there, the following forums can be tapped as venues for building thought leadership:

1. hosting weekly podcasts, Google+ hangouts, webinars, or chats;
2. monitoring groups/communities on LinkedIn, Facebook, Google+, or industry forums;
3. organizing virtual speaking events; and
4. guest blogging for leading influencers.

By taking charge of these events and forums, your brand has a sustaining platform in which to regularly engage your audience. And by taking the initiative to lead, you will likely elevate your brand's perceived authority in the process. Moreover, you have far more opportunities to convey your brand story.

Developing Social Advertising Strategies for Audience Development

What may seem to run counter to the principle behind inbound marketing is the role of social advertising in boosting audience reach and engagement. Advertising in the social environment has been far better received by digital audiences than traditional display ads whose reputation for being intrusive has led to exceptionally low response rates. What makes social advertising unique is its highly targeted messaging to an audience that has already qualified themselves with their profile and engagement data.

With **active** monthly users of social networking now over 1 billion, it makes sense to attract their attention while on these channels. And now with Facebook, Twitter, and others forced to monetize their platforms, expect "pay-to-play" to be the only answer for capturing your audiences' attention in their news feeds. This may bode well for small businesses whose time table to reach organic results is far too short. In the past, Facebook required an extensive presence and engagement on their platform to qualify for top spots in a fan's news feeds. Over time, this exposure was dominated by big brands that had the staying power and resources to organically rise to the top. But with the cost of social ads often down to cents per click, small businesses can now afford to place a well-targeted ad that boosts their exposure among existing followers as well as reaches new followers of similar interests.

The popularity of these ads has reached the point to where it is dominating the media landscape. Shown in Figure 7.2 is a forecast of global ad revenues across social networks. The projected 28 percent compounded annual growth rate reflects the early success made by self-serve ad platforms offered by Facebook, Twitter, LinkedIn, Google+, Pinterest, Instagram, and others.

As demonstrated in Table 7.1, Facebook clearly has the lead on versatility, analytics, audience development, and opportunities for boosted engagement. Twitter's Promoted Accounts, Tweet, and Trends offer advantages in attracting new followers. And LinkedIn offers the best in hypertargeting. Newcomers Pinterest, Google+, and Instagram are still testing the viability of their platforms to the general public. Google+ has the distinct advantage of having the +Posts displayed across the entire Google Display Network. Instagram shows promise in providing a solid platform for both mobile and video ads. And Pinterest, like YouTube, has a bottom-of-funnel advantage with their Promoted Pins.

Figure 7.2 Social-Network Advertising (total revenues, $billions)

Table 7.1 Evaluation of Social-Network Self-Service Ad Platforms

The table classifies ad features by Platform and Capability, with a Description, and rates each against the following grouped criteria (columns): **New Followers** (New Target Audiences, Highly Targeted Audiences, Off-Property Followers, New Mobile Followers), **Engagement** (Shares/Likes/Comments, 2nd Screen/Social TV, Video), **Brand Lift** (Brand Awareness, Boost Brand Conversation, Ranking/Attention), **Content Marketing & Lead Generation** (Off-Property Content Offer, Scaled Distribution, Conversion Tracking, Opt-in Downloads, Landing Page Conversion, Traffic to Content/Website, Visual Content), and **Promotions** (Event Announcements, Location based Advertising, New Product Launch, Ebook/Webinar, Offers).

Platform	Capability	Feature	Description
Facebook (FB)	Ad Types	Promoted Post	Seen like organic post to fans unaware of post. Good for current fans. Recent, short duration. > target/bid options than boost post.
		Boost Post	Like promoted post, but simpler w/target interest/friends of fans liking page. Good for new & current audiences. Simple. Ltd. keywords/duration.
		Page Post Ad	Already published (right side or SERP) content. Helps page promo. Target demographics/interest/connections.
		Domain Ads	Seen on right hand rail. Takes you off FB property when clicking. Used for campaigns where conversion is outside FB.
		Dark Posts	Unpublished FB news feed posts that allows ad split test w/out inundating fans with testing/irrelevant messages.
	Targeting & Retargeting	Custom Audiences	Takes email lists and targets FB audiences via ID match.
		Web Custom Audience	Finds FB audiences from cookie placed on website visitor. Allows target of site visitor as fan or through FB ad.
		Lookalike Audience	Identifies audiences on FB w/similar attributes to custom audiences. Can be targeted through Power Editor.
		Nearby Friends	Allows FB data to pinpoint local targeted ads.
		Social TV Space	Partnering w/2nd Sync for sponsors to exploit TV dialog.
		FB Exchange Ntwk	Extends ad campaign beyond FB to other mobile apps.
	Analytics	Insights	Provides FB page performance info. Helps find demographic data about audience and how they discover/respond to posts.
		Conversion Tracking	Tracking pixel for ROI exam of post ad view actions.
Twitter	Ad Types	Promoted Tweets	PPC sponsored tweet in search/aud. feed from relevant followers/behaviors. Target wants/followers/interests.
		Promoted Trends	PPCs w/time, context- & event-sensitive trends along top trends. Shows search results for topic/sponsor's tweet. Boosts dialog on offer/event/launch.
		Promoted Accounts	PPC ad seen as "Who to Follow" for attracting followers & expand social proof based on who promoter follows.
	Targeting & Retargeting	Social TV Space	Partners BlueFin Labs, Mesagraph & Second Sync help sponsors exploit TV content conversation on Twitter.
		Mobile App Targeting	Allows mobile app advertisers to fine tune ad targeting based on app actions like install, purchase or sign-up.
		Target Interests	Promoted Tweet targeting from bio info matches of account/tweet optimized around target terms. Missing FB advanced target granularity.
	Analytics	Native Analytics Tool	Shows impressions, engagement, link clicks, RTs & replies.
LinkedIn	Ad Types	Sponsored Updates	Native ads for promoting content directly in news feeds.
		Display Advertising	Targeted image/text/video ads run on CPC/CPM/auctions. Sends visitor to site/FB page for Like. Helps group/co. pg ads.
		Sponsored InMail	Allows messaging to members' inboxes.
	Targeting	Profile Targeting	Allows companies to narrowly target audience including job, age, gender, co. size & industry.
YouTube	Ad Types	Display Advertising	Banners spanning all site areas except home page. Seen on right of feature video above video suggests.
		Overlay In-video Ads	Transparent overlay ads on lower video portion.
		In-stream Ads	Video ads inserted before/during/after main video.
Other	Google+	-Post Ads	Posts served throughout Google Display Ntwk. -Post ads & FB custom audience work together finding, tracking & marketing to greater audience.
	Pinterest	Promoted Pins	CPC for pins to appear in relevant search/category.
	Snapchat	Story Ads	Optionally viewed ads about company's "stories."
	Foursquare	Display Advertising	Targets users browsing web/apps with Turns ad exchange partners incl. FB Exchange.
	Instagram	Sponsored Photos	Sponsored photos/videos in newsfeed w/ad feedback.

Why Social Advertising is on the Rise

Social ads provide a unique way of conversing with ad viewers. Across all of the social-networking platforms offering ads is an engagement opportunity much like that offered by any post intended to reach audiences organically. Viewers can like, comment on, or share an ad. Without this boost in engagement, brands are at the mercy of news feed algorithms that are making it increasingly difficult to expose your content. As of this writing, for example, the opportunity for your content to reach the feed of your Facebook fans has dropped to under 3 percent. So even the best of engaging posts have practically no chance of reaching your audiences without a paid advertising boost.

What may have surprised many is the overall receptivity of audiences to social ads as they have become contextually relevant. The rich databases that support social-network targeting platforms can tailor an ad based on where you are; what interests you express in your profiles; where you have browsed; and what patterns of engagement you showed on a network. Although creepy to some, this big data insight can ensure that all of us see only relevant messaging.

Another key advantage of advertising in social networks is the many paths available to drive traffic to or promote something on your website. Ads are constructed to allow direct ordering right from the platform. In other cases, events and product launches are promoted through social ads so as to exploit the conversations surrounding the promotion. Similarly, social ads allow social networks to capitalize from web traffic. Facebook's web custom audiences, for example, will identify and match visitors of your website to a Facebook ID where that same visitor can be subsequently retargeted with an ad on Facebook.

Trends in Social Advertising

Because of the huge insights social networks have on what people are doing, their databases far surpass the intelligence gathered on most other media platforms. As a result, ad network exchanges now center on Facebook and Twitter data. Moreover, mobile has essentially become social. Both Facebook and Twitter now dominate the mobile landscape of ads as their user's access these networks more on mobile than on their desktop. And with these networks representing the bulk of their time spent when on mobile devices, it makes sense for mobile ads to be social in nature.

In recent years, these networks have tested out video, audience networks, and buying options similar to that offered by Google and other digital ad platforms. And as they compete with the larger digital ad platforms, their analytics offerings have extended to conversion tracking. Most are now embracing bid pricing and programmatic buys as well. Finally, Twitter's use of Vine and Facebook's use of Instagram videos have made the ad experience far more engaging than the traditional text, link, and photo options of the past.

Developing Media Coverage Strategies for Audience Development

In addition to the owned media and paid media strategies discussed so far, marketers have a number of earned media opportunities to grow their followers. One involves media relations, a field that has dramatically changed as a result of social media. Disappearing, for example, is the press release pitches to select reporters that PR folks employed as a tactic to get their product stories scooped up by the press. Instead, companies are communicating and collaborating with the media through social channels on subjects that are vetted for relevance.

Social-Media Changes to Media Relations Landscape

Among the major changes to this media relations landscape that impacts our content-marketing strategies are the following:

1. *PR-to-media communications through social channels*: Journalists, bloggers, and analysts often prefer communicating to PR representatives through Twitter and other social channels. A study by Cision, in fact, found that 25 percent of them now prefer this route over phone calls and e-mail.[10]
2. *Urgent demand for quality content*: The decline in traditional publications, shortened news cycles, instant broadcasting through social mobile technologies, and news migration to brand publishing puts all the more pressure on journalists to expand their horizons and broaden their networks for researching stories.
3. *Searchable content*: Newsworthy content can be readily discovered through search engines and social graphs, making it less required to pitch your content.
4. *Searchable journalism*: Numerous directories and story topic solicitors are available to help marketers find the right opportunities for parking their content.

5. *Scalable content to assemble news*: The transition from costly online news-room repositories to scalable content across video, photo, and text libraries simplifies the job of journalists having to decipher what is newsworthy.

With the changing landscape calling for more relevant and expedient content delivery, as well as relationship building through social media, marketers have an opportunity to exploit what was traditionally the domain of legacy PR firms. These large agencies would regularly court select journalists and analysts often in preparation for press releases or damage control. Today, this news would be pre-empted by social channels way too fast for traditional media to respond. Instead, media has moved online while masses of brand publishers, bloggers, and small business marketers smother the social channels with real-time news. Attention, therefore, goes to the first to disclose credible and relevant insights. This means that your name recognition on social-networking channels and content recognition in search trumps the best of PR agency pitches.

Building Media Relationship Strategies

Despite the change in landscape, many aspects of engagement between PR representatives and their media counterparts remain the same. Journalists still have to be courted, pitched, and helped. Social media has merely expedited the process and broadened the horizons for media relations. Finding the right match between a journalist seeking stories on newsworthy topics and a marketer whose content resonates with that topic becomes more natural in today's social settings. Prior to social media, PR agencies often exploited their personal relationships to force this connection.

Today, a number of directories and social networks have simplified this match-making discovery. Services like Muck Rack can help discover journalists by publication source and topic. Others like JournalistTweets curates tweets from journalists often as a way to sort them by industry topics. LinkedIn groups have been formed that huddle agencies, marketers, and media folks around common industry topics. Finally, services like Help a Reporter Out (HARO) will regularly solicit content on topics sought by journalists.

Once you discover the right journalist interested in your topics, you need to have the journalists discover you. The good news is that journalists and industry analysts are able to find you more than ever before as they comb through your photo galleries, executive bios, online press releases, webinars, case studies, and other content relevant to their story interests. This is where your company and personal profiles help. Make sure your Twitter profile, for example, reflects the topics for which you want journalists to recognize your areas of expertise.

Courting these journalists who now have you on their radar is much like that suggested earlier when courting influencers. Like influencers, journalists appreciate when you take the time to research their interests and respond to their own content. Simple responses to tweets and posts with thoughtful commentary could replace what the martini lunches accomplished on *Mad Men*. This further alleviates the need to pitch as the journalists will begin to follow you and potentially subscribe to your content. And unlike the "one-time" press release, your tweets could be posted more regularly and on a broader range of potentially relevant topics.

The key to staying on the radar of these journalists with your content is to make it easy to deal with you and your content. This is where social-sharing buttons, RSS feeds, and subscriptions help. But it is equally important to ensure your SEO strategy reflects the terms these journalists are likely to use in their own coverage of a breaking news item or themes they cover on a regular basis. In effect, your SEO efforts should extend to your entire online newsroom.

Once the connection is made and content is proposed, marketers have a great opportunity for publication if they see its value from the eyes of the journalist. With so many new faces arriving out of the social-media channels, journalists get inundated with irrelevant and overpromoted content often from unknown sources. Some steps taken by marketing pros to get their content at the top of the stack include the following:

1. *Understand their agenda*: Taking the time to understand a journalist's perspective and story angles can go a long way in capturing interest. This means making your content more about the bigger story surrounding your offerings or company announcement than the announcement itself.
2. *Simplify the delivery process*: Since content can be atomized across video, imagery, and text, organizing your newsroom into manageable assets can simplify the job of story assembly. Many journalists are turned off to the e-mail attachments that attempt to cover all

bases. A better approach is to abbreviate the story and show paths to embellishment on your social-media galleries or website newsrooms.

3. *Use executive bylines*: Allowing journalists access to your executives can go a long way especially when their quotes or commentary provide fresh insights.

4. *Make it understood*: Telling your story in rich media format like video invariably works better than the best of any textual content. Moreover, if the story is told in the form of a customer testimony, it will likely register more with a reporter seeking an intimate audience connection.

Developing Profile Strategies

One of the most effective ways to attract new followers is through your own social-media profiles. Cross-promoting your social-media presence across all of your assets increases the chances that new visitors will join you elsewhere. And much of this is dependent upon the quality, consistency, and personality of the brand displayed in each of your profiles.

Although social-networking platforms may differ widely in their audience appeal, the profiles of high-performing brands typically have the following characteristics in common:

1. profiles are highly visual;
2. follow buttons and links are prominently displayed on each profile for all other channels where the brand is a participant;
3. profiles are consistently optimized around key word phrases assigned by the brand for high search results;
4. personal profiles are used to augment the reach of company pages;
5. social handles and links are included in e-mail signatures, website pages, and offline collateral;
6. accolades, endorsements, and recommendations are captured in the professional networks;
7. profiles are written around benefits gained from the company's offerings; and
8. the design appearance of the profile theme is consistent across platforms while maintaining a form, fit, and function intended by each platform (Figure 7.3).

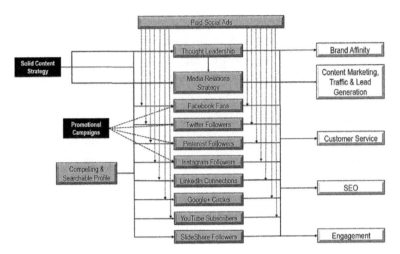

Figure 7.3 Summary Model of Enlisting Followers with a S-T-A-M-P

Notes

1. Table generated by and permission granted by CMO by Adobe.
2. Jeffery Rohrs. *Audience: Marketing in the Age of Subscribers, Fans & Followers.* New Jersey: Wiley. 2014.
3. Neal Schaffer. *Maximize Your Social.* New Jersey: Wiley. 2013. p. 96.
4. "2014 Social Media Marketing Industry Report" published by Social Media Examiner's Michael Stelzner (http://bit.ly/1uPwOKL).
5. "30 Reasons to Market Your Business on Pinterest in 2014" by NerdGraph Infographics (http://bit.ly/1yjTwzu).
6. "Pinterest: How You Can Rock This Social Media Platform" by Heidi Cohen (http://bit.ly/1o9KRpB).
7. "8 Ways to Get More Pinterest Followers" contributed by Pam Dyer to Pamorama (http://bit.ly/1u7YTiH).
8. "Instagram User Generated Content Rocks Marketing Results" by Heidi Cohen (http://bit.ly/1uNgdbz) and "New Data Shows the Importance of Hashtags on Instagram" by Dan Zarrella (http://bit.ly/1oaur0j).
9. "6 Ways to Instantly Blow Up Your Instagram" by Kim Garst (http://bit.ly/1mnaJ5U).
10. "The Social Media Pitch: What Do Journalists Prefer?" contributed to Cision by Lisa Denten (http://bit.ly/1qznSE7).

CHAPTER 8

Expose Content that Will R-U-N-L-A-P-S

Create content that reaches your audience's audience.

—Ann Handley, MarketingProfs

Now that our content is aimed at educating audiences around their pain points while making an emotional connection for a more trustworthy relationship, we are ready to expose it. Think of this next stage as running laps with your inflamed content in hand. A powerful storyline, comic surprise, or passionate plea may make the content standout. But unless it's widely circulated, any intended emotional connection will be lost.

Key to this exposure is the suitability of the content for SEO, syndicating, social sharing, posting, social-media promotion, and link building. To be searchable, the content has to incorporate a unified keyword strategy that merits exposure on the search engine results page (SERP). But for maximum gains, the content should exploit every avenue for syndication much like that employed in news casting. This means that the content often has to be rescaled and repurposed to suit the requirements of its destination platforms.

And if necessary to promote the content for exposure, marketers have many avenues for sponsoring content that mimic the posts of news feeds in which they appear. Otherwise known as native advertising, this branded content allows for promotional messaging to seamlessly blend into a social or news platform but without annoying audiences with the interrupting nature of traditional advertising.

Finally, the content itself has to resonate with viewers to the point where audiences become advocates willing to share and link to the content. This not only extends the reach of your published content, but it boosts its SERPs as well. Together the organic, syndicated, and social reach of your content work hand in hand, distributing your content while landing new subscribers. In essence, you want to R-U-N-L-A-P-S to expose your content.

RSS and Other Syndication for Publishing Platform Exposure

Syndication, or the publishing of content on another's website, is a great way to earn visibility for your content while boosting your credibility in the process. Provided that you are given credit for your author contributions, small businesses in particular can gain considerable visibility in having their content hosted on popular news sites often while earning backlinks in the process.

Of the many ways to syndicate your content, the most popular forms used by entrepreneurs are described and evaluated in Figure 8.1. In general, these content discovery and syndication sites include platforms for hosting:

1. really simple syndication (RSS) feeds;
2. community-voted social news;
3. social bookmarking;
4. social journalism;
5. blog and link directories;

Description	Criteria for Article Acceptance	Criteria for Display Dominance	Content Source	SEO Backlinks	Path to Content Visibility	Benefit	Drawbacks	Suitability	Popularity & Future
COMMUNITY VOTED SOCIAL NEWS Digg, Reddit, Newsvine	Users submit time sensitive news & links for others' approval				High social sharing from prominence	Voting public exposure + posting singular posts	Have to be active in news voting community		Offset by smart discovery engines & news aggregators
SOCIAL BOOKMARKING SITES Delicious, StumbleUpon, BizSugar	Stores relevant news/links w/shared tagging, user edits & web doc sharing				Content centered around individual interests	Smaller story traffic through bookmarking collaboration	Interest fit vs voting slows dissemination		Offset by SN sites that favor indiv posts & trended news
SHAREABLE JOURNALISM SITES Buzzfeed, Huffington Post, Upworthy	Viral content for qlty journalism w/social sharing, comments & app viewing				Large readership for highly shareable content	Sponsored content can go viral especially on Facebook	Community contributors must fit tone & native ad pay		Popularity overtaking legacy news like CNN & NY
BLOG & LINK DIRECTORIES ALLTOP, Yahoo! Directory, DMOZ	Indexed directory of blog topics				RSS links content featured in topic listings	Backlinks - content vetting by topic & directory	Shallow indexing hurts content discovery		Technorati lost discovery & news boards
MAJOR CONTENT AGGREGATORS Business 2 Community, AllBusiness, Social Media Today	Business sites that syndicate blog feeds & content to 3rd parties like Yahoo!			Through Author	High qlty stds. with contributor backlinks.	Sites of this type where shares are topic influence specific (e.g., selections social media)			Quality stds & topic specificity fit timely & useful
PR DISTRIBUTION SERVICE PR Newswire, PRWeb, Help a Reporter Out (HARO)	Wire services for distributing press releases, news sites, journalists & bloggers			Through	Search, PR fit & attractiveness overrides unfair media agendas	Quick/broad release if PR found through search & social	No control over media spin		Growing mobile use & popularity of smart discovery
NEWS AGGREGATOR APPS Feedly, Linkedin Pulse, Fark	User tailored news app w/ability to organize & share content				Trending from social engagement & followers	Fair shot for article display on highly visible sites	Need to be community active for likes & influence		Engines for user tailored news display
ARTICLE DIRECTORIES Ezinearticles, ArticleBase, Buzzle	Website collection of articles solicited from anyone with unique and qualied			Limited	Author link to site. Tags & categories for organize/search	Straightforward article acceptance after 1st submit	No backlink SEO credit or embedded links to blog		Content farms losing ground as SEO benefits subside
PAID CONTENT SYNDICATION Outbrain, Taboola, Zemanta	Recommenders of sponsor content placed in front of relevant audiences				Placement from behavior, context & personal factors	Mainstream visibility with smart readership fit	High cost of sponsored content		Suits growing mkt for native ads & branded content
SELF PUBLISHING PLATFORMS LinkedIn Publishing, Medium, Examiner	Long form posts on social network content management systems				Metrics + distribution beyond social ntwk if popular	Builds reputation & web exposure w/email CTAs	Restricted acceptance of contributors		Best of high social exposure & content ownership

Figure 8.1 Content Discovery and Syndication Alternatives

6. reputable content aggregators;
7. PR distribution services;
8. news aggregator apps;
9. article directories;
10. paid content syndication networks; and
11. self-publishing.

Really Simple Syndication

With RSS, you can publish frequently updated information from your blogs, podcasts, or video channels. These feed readers enable audience subscription to your content as it is released. In essence, subscribers take content directly from a feed you provide them. They can then share this with their audiences.

The process for syndicating via RSS is very straightforward. Having readers subscribe to the RSS feed merely involves the installation of a chicklet that noticeably places the RSS feed icon alongside a blog post or podcast episode. Figure 8.2 demonstrates how readers of your post merely click on the RSS feed icon (step one) to have it added to their aggregation of abbreviated posts or drop-down menu of bookmarked sites (step two). Your syndicated content then gets displayed as *read* or *unread* links for anyone subscribing to your feed. Clicking on a blog post or podcast episode link (step three) then takes your RSS subscriber directly to the content.

Content readers in essence benefit from timely updates without having to manually check your site for new content. Moreover, they can aggregate data from many sites in one convenient location. In turn, content providers benefit from displaying content to anyone willing to subscribe. This bypasses the contributor-vetting process or active community engagement required of many social bookmarking and social news sites, respectively, as a condition for prominently displaying your content.

Figure 8.2 Syndicating Content Through RSS

What Content Discovery and Syndication Platforms Do to Boost Your Exposure

As described in Figure 8.1, content discovery and syndication platforms aggregate news mainly for avid readers of business topics and entertainment. In the case of social news and social-bookmarking sites, exposure of your content is based on its popularity within the social community housing or sharing your content.

Some social news websites like Buzzfeed, Upworthy, and the Huffington Post are dominating the online news aggregation landscape. These sites lend themselves well to viral content reach through social sharing. Recent surveys, in fact, show that they rank among the highest in Facebook likes and Twitter shares per article posted. In deciding what, when, and where content gets published, these outlets typically use an editorial staff to vet article acceptance as well as their placement prominence.

Other social news syndicators include community-voting sites like Digg, Reddit, StumbleUpon, and Newsvine. These aggregators encourage content providers to share their blog posts, videos, and other media with a community of subscribers. But unlike the case of major online news aggregators (e.g., Huffington Post), community subscribers themselves determine which content gets more prominently displayed. This is often determined by the number of up and down votes it receives.

In some cases, content providers benefit from the added authority perception of the syndicated site especially when the topic area is the one where the provider has limited credibility. Overall visibility is then based on direct readership, views from socially shared actions, and downstream boosts in SERPs due to higher overall readership. This assumes, however, that procedures are in place (e.g., canonical tags) to ensure that the same amount of SEO link juice is passed on to your original content. Without these steps, your content runs the risk of being seen as duplicate content where the SEO credit is at least partially passed on to the syndicated source.

How Content Discovery and Syndication Platforms Work

As described earlier in Figure 8.1, content discovery and syndication platforms vary based on their requirements for sourcing, accepting, and displaying content. Depending on the platform, some syndicated sites include community-authored articles and blog posts as well as community-selected content from other members. More reputable aggregators, however, use contributors vetted from a pool of high-quality journalists.

Acceptance of your content is handled in a number of ways. Some platforms conduct a onetime vetting of viable contributors, where acceptance allows future articles to be streamlined through an RSS feed and with minimal oversight. In other cases, every contributed post must be vetted by an editorial team much like the acceptance of journal publications. Still others vet the article based on its trending in social networks. Once accepted, the criterion for display dominance ranges from community member votes and reader preferences to smart algorithms that learn individual reader's interests much like that of Netflix.

When received, the content may be displayed as an excerpt, a thumbnail and link, or as the full article. And like self-publishing (e.g., LinkedIn, Medium, and Examiner) or newswire services, the content may be a retake on a previously published post.

Why Content Syndication Outweighs Your Own Posting

Unless your blog site is amassing traffic that qualifies it for an Alexa rank under 100K, it may be worthwhile to capitalize on the far higher exposure given to social news sites. Many are becoming widely popular apps for news aggregation, suggesting that the rapid migration to mobile news will continue to favor syndication over blog sites not optimized for mobile.

Many of the larger news aggregators listed in Figure 8.1 have loyal readers accustomed to sharing content on a regular basis. And as the Google algorithms are expected to consider social signaling, this bodes well for your rankings as well. At minimum, these more established social-bookmarking and social news sites are known to be more quickly indexed since they are crawled by search engines on a more regular basis.

When and Where Content Syndication Should Be Considered

The choice to use syndication is often based on a trade-off between distribution and search engine ranking. Where search could be particularly jeopardized is when automated and large syndications are used without oversight. Experienced bloggers often recommend using only a few reputable players when syndicating content. And they typically advise against a reliance on automated syndications that seem to raise the most issues over SEO rankings.

But even reputable syndications could easily siphon off the search engine credit due your original content to the point where the syndication scores higher on SERPs. For many, this trade-off is reasonable if the main goal is to extend the distribution of particular content pieces as far as possible. Where the choice becomes questionable is when syndication is used primarily to build author credibility for new audience capture. In this case, it is advised to eventually withdraw the supporting RSS feed after the content has received sufficient exposure through the syndicated site.

In general, the choice of when and where to consider syndication should be based on the following:

1. *Industry fit*: The authority of the syndicator in an area of interest to your readers should weigh heavily on your decision to syndicate as well as who to consider.

2. *SEO impact*: Although the main purpose for syndicating should not be to bump up search rankings, the choice of syndicator should consider the procedures in place to avoid their ranking higher than you in SERPs. This will have much to do with their willingness to support backlinks, your prescribed anchor texting, and permission for you to withdraw your content after a certain period of time. The latter is often done to recapture excess SERP losses to the syndicator.

3. *Credibility*: Some sites like Business 2 Community and Social Media Today have reputations for stringent vetting and high-quality contributors. Coupled with higher social proof from their widespread audiences, readers may credit your content as being more newsworthy and credible.

4. *Attracting unique and more qualified visitors*: To reach a new audience, the syndicator should be scrutinized for its readership potential. Much like reviewing media kits, insights could be gained from readership that helps position the content along new audience

interests. Some of the niched directories and bookmarking sites may be closer to what you need as a qualified prospect. Especially in the beginning stages of growth, your ability to target specific audiences may be limited to how well you capitalize on keywords. Syndicators, on the other hand, may have well-defined topic indices or tag categories that better hypertarget your audience of interest. Moreover, sites like StumbleUpon offer paid advertising options that could jumpstart your content reach to well-target audiences.

5. *Overall exposure*: Weight should also be given to the amount of overall traffic (i.e., check Alexa rank) and social-media viewership garnered by the syndicated site.

In addition, the choice should consider the stage of content maturity. Note in Figure 8.1, for example, that some platforms are more suitable to first-stage content growth. The syndicated blog, in this case, will offset the slow SEO gestation period with a broad audience reach. As readers become aware of your site mainly through author profiles, they may subscribe to your own RSS feed. Later in your blogging maturity, you may find the more reputable syndication networks as an excellent resource to boost your influence as well as to kick start a new readership following.

Unified Keyword Strategies

From Chapter 1, we have focused on content that addresses our target audience's pain points. In effect, we have outlined topics that could help our audiences solve problems in a manner that is relevant and timely to their situation. But having topics that are essentially *user friendly* does not mean they are *search friendly*. Consequently, content marketers often miss the mark on content terms that are not synchronized with the keywords used by our target audiences. Moreover, the selection of keyword phrases may not be unified across your

1. domain name;
2. authority signaled across other indexed pages; and
3. linking strategies.

Selecting Content Topics that Match Search Behaviors

To synchronize pain points and keyword phrases, your content has to address a narrow enough audience to appreciate the pain point subtleties of individual personas. An effective mapping of pain points and search terms should include the following:

1. a long-tailed niche approach to persona identification, i.e., get specific;
2. an examination of persona passions or pain points from business challenges; and
3. a candidate word search that matches pain points (e.g., using negative terms like *broken* teeth vs cosmetic dentistry).

Consider the three case examples shown in Figure 8.3: a residential realtor, a wholesaler of quail eggs, and an accounting firm. From specific personas, pain points and passions were identified and used as a baseline for discovering tips and solutions. This leads to a list of keyword phrases as candidates for search engine optimization (SEO).

From this list of candidate subjects, blogging expert, Stan Smith, suggests you brainstorm nine search phrases depending on where your

Example 1: Real Estate

Audience Persona	Targets	Passions/Lifestyles	Challenges/Pain Pts.	Tips & Solutions	Key Word Candidates		
Temporary Living - Campus Community	University Students	Campus Life	Fitting In	Off-Campus Housing Tips (safety, budget, etc.)	University Housing	Off Campus Living	Student Housing
Temp Living - Career Change & Vacationing	Snowbirds, Job Relocating Families	Florida Lifestyles & Vacations	Acclimation & Temporary Living Stress	Relocation & Destination Guidelines	Temporary Residence	Home Move	Vacation Homes
Golf Communities	Retirees & Golf Enthusiasts	Golf	Getting Around	Golf Community Networks	Golf Communities	Active Adult Communities	Country Clubs
Equestrian Communities	Equestrian Enthusiasts & Horse Farmers	Polo, Jumping & Riding	Horse Care Facilities	Polo Club Activities	Horse Farms	Polo Grounds	Equestrian Properties
First Time Home Buyers	Newlyweds	Weddings & Home Decorating Ideas	Dollar Stretching	Wedding Planning	Homes for Sale	Affordable Mortgage	Wedding Planning

Example 2: Quail Egg Wholesaling

Audience Persona	Targets	Passions/Lifestyles	Challenges/Pain Pts.	Tips & Solutions	Key Word Candidates		
Inflammatory Diseases	Allergy Prone	Outdoor Engagement	Out of Breath, Itch & Drowsiness	Natural Allergy Relief	Antioxidants	Natural Allergy Treatment	Free Radicals
Gourmet Chef Recipes	Chefs	Cooking	Worry Free, High Value Appetizers	Exotic Recipes & Gastro-Pub Pairing Items	Canapes	Master Chef	Food Safety
Adult Youthfulness	Seniors	Active Adult Living	Sexual Vitality & Health	Natural Aphrodisiacs	Anti-Aging	High Protein Diets	Sexual Performance
Child Development	Moms	Mommyhood	Kid Friendly Nutrition	Child Hair, Brain & Skin Care	Brain Food	Choline	Baby Development

Example 3: Accounting Consultation

Audience Persona	Targets	Passions/Lifestyles	Challenges/Pain Pts.	Tips & Solutions	Key Word Candidates		
Property Management	Residential Property Managers	Property Renovations	Cost Control & Operational Efficiencies	Software Reviews & Property Operation Planning	Property Managers	Property Management Software	Home Owners Association
High Income Wealth Management	Medical Professions, Executives & Celebrities	Golf, Fitness, Cars & Club Lifestyles	Investment Returns	Trusts, IRAS & Investment Leverage	Accounting Services	Asset Management	Wealth Management
Real Estate Accounting	Real Estate Investors	Business Growth & Playing the Market	Tax Exposure	Market Tips & Tax Planning	Real Estate Accounting	Buying Real Estate	Property Accounting
Small Business Services	Start-ups	Business Ideas	Operational Funding	Cash Flows & Tax Planning	Operating Budgets	Small Business Accounting	Software Accounting

Figure 8.3 Identifying Keyword Candidates from Persona Pain Points and Passions

	Information About Your Subject	Key Topics in Your Area	Decide to Do Business
Real Estate	University Housing	Off Campus Apartments	Rental Properties
Accounting	Asset Management	Undervalued Assets	Real Estate Property
Quail Eggs	Master Chef Canapes	Safe Gourmet Appetizers	Quail Eggs
Cosmetic Dentistry	Makeovers	Cosmetic Dentistry	Dental Implants

Figure 8.4 Examples of Search Phrases Across Buying Cycle

audience is in their buying cycle. Using Figure 8.4 as an example, consider three phrases your readers use to

1. find information about your subject (3 terms);
2. research key topics in your area (3 terms); and
3. decide if they should do business with you (3 terms).

Selecting Topic Titles for Blogging

Continuing with the accounting firm example, shown in Figure 8.3, we could begin structuring newsworthy blog topics from these candidate terms. Each topic should be trending upward if it is to attract the attention of audiences and the search engines. To discover what topics are current, checkout what is trending on:

1. Twitter (e.g., viewing tweet popularity on Topsy or viewing hashtag trails on HootSuite or TweetDeck);
2. syndicated blog directories and news aggregators listed in Figure 8.1;
3. personalized content discovery platforms and social analytics tool like Swayy, BuzzSumo, and Klout; and
4. Google (e.g., Google Trends or Google's auto-keyword suggestion tool when typing in the search box).

In addition, key audience topics can be discovered from a review of your blog comment trails or discussion boards in LinkedIn Groups. The latter, in particular, raises a lot of questions from members seeking serious professional solutions to their business challenges.

Once a trended topic has been discovered, keyword phrases should be filtered based on their

1. degree of competition for the term;
2. reach in monthly inquiries (using Google's AdWords Keyword Planner);
3. relevance to your business expertise, URL domain name, and persona pain points; and
4. specificity and context precision (e.g., a cosmetic dentist counting on "dental" for search may find the term too broad as it includes dental schools, dental plans, and dental research audiences as well).

Note from Figure 8.5 how this process for screening keywords from candidate topics led to nine blog titles. A good starting point in crafting titles from these screened terms is to use one of the free blog topic generators. Hubspot, for example, generates some effective titles after you insert three keywords as nouns (http://bit.ly/1A4KeVN). From the initial draft of titles, terms could then be added or modified to better reflect the expertise, keywords, and context.

Optimizing Blog Posts around Keyword Strategy

Once an examination of candidate topics and content titles is complete, your blog content is ready to be optimized. On the basis of Google's Panda, Penguin, and Hummingbird algorithms, care should be taken to

Example 3: Accounting Consultation

Audience Persona	Targets	Passions/Lifestyles	Challenges/Pain Pts.	Tips & Solutions	Key Word Candidates		
Property Management	Residential Property Managers	Property Renovations	Cost Control & Operational	Software Reviews & Property Operation Planning	Property Managers	Property Management Software	Home Owners Associations
High Income Wealth Management	Medical Professions, Executives & Celebrities	Golf, Fitness, Cars & Club Lifestyles	Investment Returns	Trusts, IRAs & Investment Leverage	Accounting Services	Asset Management	Wealth Management
Real Estate Accounting	Real Estate Investors	Business Growth & Playing the Market	Tax Exposure	Market Tips & Tax Planning	Real Estate Accounting	Buying Real Estate	Property Accounting
Small Business Services	Start-ups	Business Ideas	Operational Funding	Cash Flows & Tax Planning	Operating Budgets	Small Business Accounting	Software Accounting
TALKworthy Blog Titles	Operative Phrase	Reach (Monthly Inquiries)	Trend (Google Trends)	Competitive (Adwords)	Target Relevance	Business Relevance	
Top 10 Reasons why HOA Special Assessments favor HOA Due Increases	HOA Dues	Moderate (27K)	Rising	Low	High (Property Management Issue)	High (Accounting Expertise)	
8 Tips for Generating Residential Rental Property Income Beyond Rents & Dues	Residential Rental Property	High (550K)	Falling	High	High (Property Management Issue)	High (Accounting Expertise)	
5 Ways to Minimize Community Property Security Expenditures	Property Security	Moderate (65K)	Steady to Falling	Medium	Moderate (Property Management Issue)	Moderate (Accounting Expertise)	
How to Account for HOA Management Reserves in Economic Downturns	HOA Management	Moderate (15K)	Rising	Medium	Moderate (Property Management Issue)	High (Accounting Expertise)	
7 Residential Property Management Steps for Running Profitable Community Socials	Residential Property	Moderate (50K)	Falling	Medium	Moderate (Property Management Issue)	Moderate (Accounting Expertise)	
Top 10 Reasons Why Property Managers Fail to Balance Annual Budgets	Property Manager	High (246K)	Steady	Medium	Low-Moderate (Incl. Commercial Properties)	Moderate (Accounting Expertise)	
6 Reasons Why HOAs Lose Their Grip on Delinquent Collections	HOAs	Moderate (50K)	Steady	Low	Moderate (Property Management Issue)	Moderate (Accounting Expertise)	
How to Boost Residential Rental Property Referrals and Renewals	Residential Rental Property	High (550K)	Falling	High	High (Property Management Issue)	High (Accounting Expertise)	
Property Manager Checklist: Accounting for Hurricane Preparation Expenditures	Property Manager	High (246K)	Steady	Medium	Low-Moderate (Incl. Disaster Prep)	Low-Moderate (Accounting Expertise)	

Figure 8.5 Real-Estate Accountant Example Process for Rationalizing Content Title Search Terms

avoid blatant keyword stuffing. Your goal is to apply the targeted keywords and phrases in a natural way so as not to signal the algorithms that you are gaming the system. This starts with creating quality content that is measured by its reading popularity. The more your content resonates with popular conversations and invites legitimate links to your post, the more the search engines will credit you as an authority on the subject.

Consider the case shown in Figure 8.6 of a blog post written to attract social-media marketing educators. Starting with a pain point analysis like the one displayed in Figure 8.5, the analysis discovered a number of keyword phrases that scored high on search-ability. Included in the screening of suitable terms was the volume, trend, competitiveness, and relevance of each term.

Popularity and Competitiveness of Terms

Although the search volume is fairly low, these long-tailed terms ensure a more precise fit with a target audience of social-media educators. The fact that many of the keyword phrase inquiries are either rapidly rising or tapering in growth (e.g., abrupt rise in 2010 and steady through 2014) suggests that a number of keyword candidates qualify for popularity. A concession made at this point, however, is the choice of candidate terms having a history of high competition in paid search. This would imply stiff competition at the organic SEO level as well.

Relevance of Terms

Relevance starts with the targeted audience. A question asked at this point is whether the intended keyword phrase truly reflects a pain point relevant to your target audience. Note from Figure 8.6 that those phrases marked *moderate* have too broad a context. Searches for the phrase "Social Media Marketing Class," for example, may include inquires for the local availability of course offerings or seminar approaches to training. Neither would benefit from a blog post on how social media is taught at the MBA level.

Two other aspects of relevance relate to the content provider. One deals with domain names and the other with authority claimed on other indexed pages. Notice from the domain name "blog.socialcontentmarketing .com" that more weight is given to phrases including the terms *social* and

Unified Keyword Selection	Google Trend	Monthly Searches	Competition	Topic Relevance to Target Audience	Topic Relevance to Domain & Other Posts[1]	Topic Relevance to Authority	Keyword Usage	Key Phrase Usage in Top Paragraphs	Key Word Density in Top Paragraphs
Social Media Marketing Courses	Tapering	170	High	High	High	Very High	Primary Term	3	2%
Social Media Education	Tapering	260	High	High	Moderate	High	Primary Term	3	2%
Social Media Courses	Rapidly Rising	390	High	Moderate	Moderate	High	Latent Semantic Content	1	1%
Social Media Marketing Education	Tapering	30	High	High	High	Very High	Latent Semantic Content	1	1%
MBA Social Media	Tapering	20	High	Very High	Moderate	Very High	Latent Semantic Content	4	3%
Teaching Social Media	Tapering	40	High	Very High	Moderate	High	Latent Semantic Content	1	1%
Social Media Curriculum	Flat	50	Medium	Very High	Moderate	High	Latent Semantic Content	1	1%
Social Media Marketing Classes	Tapering	170	High	Moderate	High	High	Context Too Broad[2]		
Social Media Marketing Training	Tapering	210	High	Moderate	High	High	Context Too Broad[2]		
Learn Social Media Marketing	Tapering	110	High	Moderate	High	High	Context Too Broad[3]		
Social Media Classes	Rising	590	High	Moderate	Moderate	Moderate	Context Too Broad[3]		
Social Media in Higher Education	Rising	140	Low	Moderate	Moderate	Moderate	Context Too Broad[4]		

1) Domain blog socialcontentmarketing.com, related blog posts, social media books approved for academia
2) Includes non-Higher Ed classes (e.g, seminars) and availability of course offerings
3) Includes social media technology and other non-marketing aspects of expertise
4) Includes the use of social media in classroom teaching

Figure 8.6 Selecting Keywords for Blog Post on Teaching Social Media to MBAs

marketing. The same applies to the authority signaled on other indexed pages. Terms such as social media, for example, include the technology aspects of the field that extend beyond the content providers area of expertise.

Selecting Primary and Latent Semantic Content

A common mistake made by many bloggers is to optimize their page around too many terms. As a rule of thumb, no more than two primary terms should be selected. Too many terms tends to confuse the algorithms. Once decided, however, a number of root derivatives should be selected in line with what the search engines expect to see when claiming authority for a phrase.

This latent semantic content can boost rankings if the terms consistently show up in Google Adword analyses when sorted by relevance. For example, Figure 3.6 suggests that the term "teaching social media" is related enough to "social media education" to be credited as a root derivative of the latter. Much like the outline of a good paper, the use of semantic latent content could signal to the search engines that your authority is backed by a comprehensive list of terms often used by others claiming authority on these terms.

Optimizing the Page

Once the terms are established, a goal of around 2–4 percent keyword density should be established for the primary and latent semantic terms. A lower density may not justify authority, but a higher density could trigger black hat tactics that ultimately jeopardize your standing with the search engines (e.g., penalize your search results). When applying these terms, emphasis should be placed on the following to ensure a unified keyword strategy:

1. domain URL
2. titles
3. headers
4. tags
5. top paragraphs of visible text
6. anchor text.

Shown in Figure 8.7 is a display of how this was done for my blog post on teaching MBA social-media marketing courses. Notice the emphasis

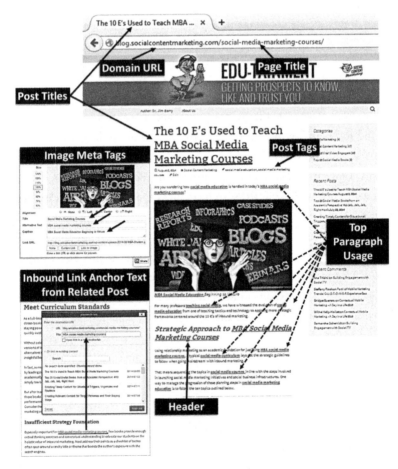

Figure 8.7 Using Strategic Keywords in a Blog Post

on primary terms in the domain URL, page title, and post title. The domain URL is believed by most SEO experts to far outweigh any other tactic. Next in line for SEO priority are the titles for the page and post. The former merely requires an edit of the gobbledygook default names otherwise assumed in your hosting software.

Like titles, headers and tags are also given weight to the authority claimed for SERPs. Tags include labeling for any embedded graphics or photos. As shown in the far left of Figure 8.7, image tagging allows a significant amount of search-rich descriptions to cover photo titles, alternative text, captions, and detailed descriptions. Similarly, popular blogging software programs like WordPress permit page tagging and a complete SEO package to streamline the entire SEO process across all posts.

Finally, terms should be applied throughout the body of the text but without butchering the conversational tone and readership of the post. Although Google in particular keeps their ever-evolving algorithms a secret, SEO experts seem to agree that far more weight is given to headers and the first paragraphs than the remaining body of text.

Native Advertising to Seamlessly Promote Content

A common prediction for 2015 was the mainstream arrival of native advertising or the purchasing of sponsored content on social networks and online news sites. Pushing this trend is *banner ad blindness*; the *viral brand lift* gained from native ads; and a user *migration to mobile platforms* that do not accommodate traditional display ads. Add to that the pressure publishers are feeling to fill the gap of declining display ad revenue, and it is no wonder that native advertising continues to grow in popularity.

A clear grasp of native ad trending first requires an adequate definition of what constitutes native advertising especially since a universally accepted definition is still in the making. But for now, let's define it as "the use of content-based ads that match and live within the stream of editorial-type content, while contextually following the experience of the publisher's platform." Common to most definitions is the dual objective of native ads to (1) "stand out" for reader awareness and (2) "fit in" with nondisruptive, opt-in content, i.e., finding the sweet spot between advertising and publishing content.

But finding a sweet spot in this convergent media (placement paid, content owned, and sharing earned) has been quite a challenge for brands and publishers confronted with issues like transparency and disclosure described further. The mere fact that the ads are created to blend in with content often confuses the reader with what is being promoted and what is editorial.

Where this becomes especially problematic is when the native ad is featured in mainstream news sites (e.g., Forbes.com, BuzzFeed, Mashable, and The Atlantic), advertorials, promoted social-media content (e.g., sponsored stories), and content recommendations.

Another issue to resolve before fully embracing native advertising is the uniform standards to adopt for the various media formats they represent. In their Native Advertising Playbook, the IAB identifies and provides examples of six types of ad units most often described as native:

- in-feed units;
- paid search units;
- recommendation widgets (e.g., "From Around the Web");
- promoted listings;
- in-ad with native element units (e.g., banner with text or preceding a post); and
- custom campaigns.

The wide variance in formats has much to do with the ad's fit to form (e.g., in-stream vs out of stream); its match to function (e.g., video on a video or story among stories); its match to surrounding content

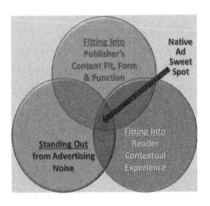

(e.g., mirrors page content behavior); its target specificity and guarantee of location placement (e.g., narrowly vs broadly targeted placement); and its metric objectives (e.g., views, likes, and share for top-of-funnel brand engagement vs sale, download, register for bottom-of-funnel direct response).

What Constitutes Native Advertising?

In its most limited form, these ads could include social-sponsored posts much like those shown in Figure 8.8. At the other extreme are long-form narratives (Figure 8.9) including featured news article or videos hosted in major publications. Although the publications were once the domain of social news aggregators such as *Buzzfeed, Gawker, Mashable, Forbes, The Wall Street Journal, The Atlantic, Business Insider,* and *The Huffington Post,* an estimated 90 percent of publishers are now offering native ad offerings.

Why All the Hype Behind Native Advertising

No doubt the content-marketing craze has reshaped a marketing landscape once riddled with digital display ads. According to Patrick Albano, cochair of IAB Native Advertising Task Force, "this renaissance in digital advertising is driving brands, publishers and consumers to communicate with each other in more personal and natural ways."

What has likely delayed a more widespread adoption of native ads are the mechanisms to scale and integrate them into editorial content

Figure 8.8 Examples of Short-Form Narratives

Figure 8.9 Examples of Long-Form Narratives

acceptable to publishers. The pace of adoption is likely to increase, however, due to revenue pressures. Many publishers are feeling the pinch of ever shrinking display ad margins as a greater number of blogging sites, social news sites, and social platforms are staking claim to available ad space. This oversupply of inventory, coupled with consumers being clobbered with overwhelming ad noise, is forcing publishers to adopt some form of native advertising.

Brands see these content-based ads as a far superior approach to brand affinity lift and consumer engagement than can ever be realized under traditional display advertising. Banner ads, in particular, are not conducive to social sharing or to mobile usage. And it is this lack of mobile adaptation that is most concerning to traditional display advertisers since mobile is expected to overtake desktop web viewing in the not too distant future.

In a detailed evaluation of the native ad landscape, Altimeter Group's Rebecca Lieb highlights the many reasons why brands, publishers, social networks, and advertising agencies stand to gain from a widespread adoption native ad formats. Common to all parties is a drive for

1. new revenue streams;
2. a potential for deeper behavioral/contextual data; and
3. target audience opt-in to content.

How Far Native Advertising Will Advance

Among the holdups barring parties from embracing native ads more extensively is the potential of native ads to deceive its readers. In particular, the Altimeter Group study cites transparency and disclosure as major concerns especially in light of the ethical sensitivity toward ad content that is mistaken as editorial content (i.e., separation of Church and State analogy). This issue came to a head in the infamous publication by *The Atlantic* of David Miscavige's salute to Scientology. *The Atlantic* posted an advertorial package for the Church of Scientology, which was subsequently inferred by many as an editorial piece endorsed by the publication. Perhaps no one sheds light on this concern better than the hilarious John Oliver in his HBO Native Advertising feature that went viral (http://bit.ly/1owOWTw).

Another issue suggesting a more limited rollout of native ads is its scalability to so many diverse publication standards. Compared to banner and other display ads, native ads are not portable across platform formats. To scale them optimally across publications, a great deal more is required to make them contextual relevant while also having them fit seamlessly into a publication's form, fit, and function. Banners, on the other hand, merely require compliance with universally accepted placement standards, something yet to evolve for native ads.

Much progress has been made in this area, however, as technology companies jump into the fray. Sharethrough, Outbrain, Taboola, and Disqus are among the 40 technology firms listed in the Altimeter Group's review. To date, these predominately software companies have been able to sort and configure the many content, creative, and social metric elements associated with native ads to where they are becoming increasingly programmatic across multiple publishing platforms.

How the Landscape Will Ultimately Shift toward Native Ads

According to Figure 8.10 forecasts from BIA/Kelsey and eMarketer, U.S. native social advertising revenues are forecast to grow from $1.6 billion in 2012 to $4.6 billion in 2017. The near 23 percent/year compounded growth reflects the higher engagement results seen from native ads. It also attests to the rapid adoption of native ads by publishers, many of which are finding engagement rates of native ads to approach those of their editorials.

Even the more minimal in-feed native ad placements and promoted listings we see on social networks are demonstrating the efficacy of native

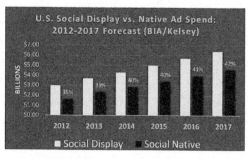

Figure 8.10 Forecast of Native Ad Revenue (BIA/Kelsey)

ads. According to a study by Interpublic Group's IPG Media Lab and Sharethrough, consumers looked at sponsored content 52 percent more often than banner ads. The same study showed native ads generated 9 percent higher brand affinity lift and 18 percent higher purchase intent response than banners. Finally, the study found that 32 percent of respondents said the native ad "is an ad I would share with a friend or family member" versus just 19 percent for display ads.

This bodes well for what seems to be a welcomed attraction to the marketing landscape. Consumers can now view marketing messages as part of an overall brand story told in the context of something relevant to what they are reading. Brands benefit when the consumer shares the content-ad. The more the engagement, the greater the brand affinity lift especially when the ad is seen as relevant and useful. Finally, publishers benefit from a new source of revenue to offset a dismal decline in display advertisements.

When Small Businesses Will Embrace Native Advertising

So far the momentum behind native advertising has mainly benefited large brands that have the resources and relationship with news publishers. The scalability issues have been reasonably addressed to date with tighter brand/publisher collaboration. Publishers, in some cases, have even hired dedicated staffs to manage native ad content.

Minimums to play in this arena, however, are quite high given the growing demand for premium placement of native ads. Add to that the time-consuming collaboration required of this convergent media to represent both brand and publisher interests, and you can see why smaller businesses may not be so quick in their adoption of native ads.

But with the growing adoption of big data into contextually relevant platforms, expect to see a rollout of limited in-feed native ads for small businesses. Although not as customized as the multiplatform narratives used by big brands, these more affordable alternatives are being aggressively promoted by native ad integrators (e.g., ShareThrough.com) and news sites. BuzzFeed, in particular, has had recent success in building a native advertising ad network on other publisher homepages. Should they and others elect to broker their native ad placement capacity, small businesses may have an answer. This assumes, however, that these native ad integrators or publishers can autoconfigure content-ads to suit the standards of multiple platforms.

But the adoption by small businesses of native ads may be hindered more by a mindset than technical solutions to scalability. Small businesses may be slow to embrace the true essence of native advertising. For example, it's one thing for Coca Cola, Chipotle, and Dell to piecemeal powerful brand stories over numerous branded content placements. They have the vision and appreciation for content strategies that justifies a long-term investment. But it's another thing for small businesses to embrace this type of narrative especially where results in brand buzz and brand affinity lift may not be so readily measurable.

Small businesses will have to be courted, in part, by publishers and agencies willing to train them on native ad scaling as well as in making content contextually relevant. In essence, these small businesses will have to understand that native advertising has as much to do with complementing editorial content as it does with catching the eye of a waiting prospect. This perceptual shift from fitting in over standing out will undoubtedly require a new leap of faith. As best said by Patrick Albano of Yahoo!, "The challenge with native is finding that sweet spot between fitting in and standing out."

Developing Link Building Strategies for Traffic and SEO

Besides syndicating, optimizing, and seamlessly promoting content, marketers can spread their reach by distributing their content through link building strategies that invite new traffic sources while bumping up SERPs. In fact, one of the most critical components to any unified keyword strategy involve the tactics used to essentially garner votes via links on your keyword authority.

One way to validate this vote is through links to your content where the linking source (e.g., a syndicated site or guest blog host), your landing page (e.g., blog post), and the anchor text describing this link uniformly support your claimed authority around certain keywords. Add to that a high page rank from the linking site and you stand a good chance that the search engines will boost your SERPS. But here again, gaming the system with black hat techniques (e.g., link baiting) will only lead to penalties and potentially site banning.

To legitimately garner links that earn SEO credit, content marketers often focus on the following:

1. earning links from reputable sources backed by high page ranks and site content related to the landing page content;
2. applying anchor text terms consistent with page source and landing page content; and
3. rewarding back-linkers.

Care should especially be given to the consistency or terms used throughout. For example, search engine algorithms will consider the consistency of terms applied from the source page, the link defining anchor text, and the content destination. Key to achieving this objective is to have content worthy of a link. This invariably favors blog content over static website landing pages as the former is typically more relevant to your audience's pain points.

And more than just incentivizing your readers to share your content, attracting links requires you to provide something of value to the one linking to your site.

This value could include a source of validation for some of their expert claims or positions taken on a subject. This is why the display of study results in your blog post from new empirical research can attract links. The same applies to product/service ratings, awards, top rankings, and reviews that validate someone's credentials.

Guest blogging also offer an opportunity to attract links to your content. Guest authors posting on your site often link to these posts as a way to validate their own expertise or popularity. The same could apply in reverse. Much like that discussed in syndication, your original content posted on someone else's site could invite backlinks. But different from syndicating your content, however, you are giving away your content to another site when you guest blog. Unless you retain rights to repost the content on your site at a later date, you are essentially donating your SEO value to the site hosting your content. This is why it is imperative to at least get permission to embed links in the body of the guest post or through author profiles.

Atomizing for R-E-I-M-A-G-I-N-E-D Content

The mass audience has atomized; that means you have to 'atomize' your content—customize it to different media, in different places, at different times to make it meaningful to the greatest number of individuals.

—Andrew Susman, CEO, Studio One Networks

Up to this point, an assumption made for exposing content is that it is adequately *atomized* to handle different media types. In their *Content Rules*, leading content strategists Ann Handley and C.C. Chapman refer to this as having to *reimagine* your content for various platforms and formats.[1] To be effective, a content strategy should be developed that anticipates where and how the content collectively addresses your target audience's pain points. Without this perspective, your content is merely addressing the challenge of platform compatibility. Ideally, the reimagined content will build a trail of expertise and customer orientation in the process.

A great place to start the process of crafting content is to ask why folks buy your product or service in the first place. From these spending motivations, a further examination of the subtleties in personas should reveal new insights into their pain points as well as the questions raised in response to these problems. It is at this point that content marketers should consider how the question could be diced into individual blog posts that are subsequently consolidated into deeper content that addresses the problem more completely. This allows you to build a trail of trustworthiness posts for your audience to examine before digesting a more complete and time-consuming solution to their problems.

But more than just recycling your content, R-E-I-M-A-G-I-N-E-D implies content that is:

1. *Repurposed to Macrocontent*: The reuse of blog posts and other top-of-funnel content recast for downstream webinars, e-Books, and other mid-of-funnel content allows readers to examine a trail of trustworthiness. As an example, Figure 3.11 shows how a nine-blog series of tutorials was subsequently recast into an e-Book addressing *property cash flow* issues. By maintaining a consistent focus on their condo and HOA cash flow issues throughout the blog series, the accounting firm demonstrates an appreciation of the property manager's pain points. This allows a reader to judge the firm's customer orientation before digesting the more time consuming e-Book.

2. *Expertise driven*: Repurposing content from blogs to more in-depth elements like webinars and e-Books also permits target audiences to examine your subject matter expertise as a qualifier for deserving 30 minutes to an hour or more of their attention. Note in Figure 8.11

Real Estate Accountant	Targeted Personas	Influencers	Passions	Challenges	Tips & Solutions
Audience #1	Property Management	Residential Property Managers	Homeowners & Other Community Associations	Property Renovations	Cost Control, Operation Efficiencies	Software Reviews, Cash Flow Solutions
Audience #2	Real Estate Accounting	Real Estate Investors	Realtors, Real Estate Agents/Brokers	Business Growth, Playing the Market	Tax Exposure	Market Tips & Tax Planning
Audience #3	High Income Wealth Mgnt	Medical Professions, Executives, Celebrities	Asset/Wealth Mgmt Advisors, Investment Bankers	Golf, Fitness, Cars & Club Lifestyles	Investment Returns	Trusts, IRAs, Investment Leverage
Audience #4	Small Business Services	Entrepreneurs	CFOs, Lawyers, Executive Clubs, Chambers of Commerce	Business Ideas	Operational Funding	Cash Flow & Tax Planning

Potential Blog Topics for Audience 1	Pain Point	Expertise	Repurposable Content (e.g., potential eBook)
Top 10 Reasons why HOA Special Assessments favor HOA Due Increases	Property Cash Flow	Accounting	Maximize Property Cash Flow
8 Tips for Generating Residential Rental Property Income Beyond Rents & Dues	Property Cash Flow	Accounting	Maximize Property Cash Flow
5 Ways to Minimize Community Property Security Expenditures	Property Cash Flow	Accounting	Maximize Property Cash Flow
How to Account for HOA Management Reserves in Economic Downturns	Property Cash Flow	Accounting	Maximize Property Cash Flow
7 Residential Property Management Steps for Running Profitable Community Socials	Property Cash Flow	Accounting	Maximize Property Cash Flow
Top 10 Reasons Why Property Managers Fail to Balance Annual Budgets	Property Cash Flow	Accounting	Maximize Property Cash Flow
6 Reasons Why HOAs Lose Their Grip on Delinquent Collections	Property Cash Flow	Accounting	Maximize Property Cash Flow
How to Boost Residential Rental Property Referrals and Renewals	Property Cash Flow	Accounting	Maximize Property Cash Flow
Property Manager Checklist: Accounting for Hurricane Preparation Expenditures	Property Cash Flow	Accounting	Maximize Property Cash Flow

Figure 8.11 Relevant Content Evaluation for a Real-Estate Accountant

how the sequencing of light blog posts allowed the accounting firm to demonstrate their financial expertise before releasing a more comprehensive e-Book on maximizing property cash flow. This middle-of-the-funnel content further opened an opportunity for the firm to request an e-mail opt-in, an option not available for the less valuable blog posts.

3. *Integrated into content platforms*: As discussed in Chapter 1 under *embracing omni-channels*, considerable traction can be given to content that readily blends into the form, fit, and function of fast-growing social content networks like SlideShare and LinkedIn's own publishing platform.

4. *Miniaturized for microcontent*: A similar opportunity applies in the other direction. Recasting long-form posts into shorter-form microblogging platforms like Twitter and Tumblr, as well as native advertising space, can significantly expand your target audience reach from an already crafted blog post.

5. *Adapted to media formats*: In light of the growing trend toward audio and visual formats, experience content marketers take every opportunity to convert text-based content into scripting for podcast episodes and storylines for videos.

6. *Google search friendly*: A common practice to follow in any content strategy is to map out the use of keyword phrases across all channeled content outlets. Whether it's for video metatags, photo gallery descriptions, or microcontent, the repurposing of content around these phrases will substantiate your keyword authority in a consistent manner.

7. *Integrated in mobile platforms*: As discussed further in Chapter 12, a challenge faced by content marketers is repurposing content for smart device viewing. But this takes more than abbreviated content. It requires a format that allows the content to be more responsive to a mobile customer experience. For example, mobile users often favor photo-based and app-oriented content aimed at bottom-of-funnel decision making.

8. *News feed friendly*: A similar challenge is faced when blending content into the news feeds of Facebook, LinkedIn, and Google+ as well as that of major news aggregators like *Forbes*, *Buzzfeed*, and the *Gawker*. Oftentimes, an existing piece of content can be readily

adapted as native advertising that blends in well with the news feed objectives of these online publications.

9. *Engaged with others' content*: Another practice followed by experienced content marketers when finishing a blog post or more in-depth content piece is to relate the information as comments on the blogs of influencers.

10. *Discussion framed*: Similarly, comments could be posted as answers to questions posted on popular question-and-answer websites or a social-network group. Rather than reinventing content, existing blog posts can be adapted to craft an answer to a popular question on Quora or a LinkedIn Group. Regularly applying this practice assures the right choice of group or discussion forum in which to be engaged.

Pinning and Posting

Next to SEO, the role of pinning and posting content on social networks often represents the greatest opportunity to expose content. In its most basic form, the posting of abbreviated links via URL shorteners (e.g., bit. ly) offers a straightforward method for broadcasting your latest content releases.

Posting links through Twitter still remains among the most common practices followed by marketers in promoting new content. The key to tweeting links for your new content releases is the assignment of hashtags that build new followers in the process. Especially for those Twitter followers that filter their content interests through hashtags (e.g., via Tweet-Deck or Hootsuite), finding the right hashtag category to park your content becomes critical to attracting new followers. Tools like hashtag. org can help identify which hashtag terms resonate the most with your target audience as well as your area of expertise.

But developing a visually intensive post can also lend itself to pinning your content on platforms like Pinterest. Note in Figure 8.12 how a link to a blog post on social-media marketing courses was tweeted, updated in a LinkedIn feed, and pinned for Pinterest viewers. The latter often leads to the highest amount of referred traffic to a site, making it essential

Figure 8.12 Pinning and Posting Links

for blog posts to accommodate pinnable images. Moreover, extensive descriptions supporting the pin contribute to its discovery and potential engagement with Pinterest followers.

Social Sharing

Besides pinning and posting content to your existing followers, all content should incorporate sharing buttons that allow readers to share it with their own friends, fans, connections, and followers as well. Although the practice has been widely adopted for blog posting, many content marketers neglect to incorporate these widgets into e-mails and mid-of-funnel content.

For example, once e-Books are created and hosted, they can be easily shared across your audience's social-media channels. Shown in Figure 8.13

*Figure 8.13 Sharing Downloaded e-Books
and Other PDFs*

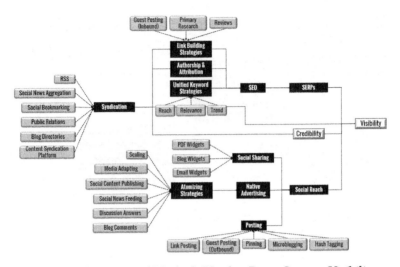

Figure 8.14 Summary of Methods Used to Boost Content Visibility

is an example of how an embedded Twitter widget allows a PDF-based e-Book to be shared once it's let loose as a downloaded document. For instructions on how to incorporate retweet buttons into PDFs, checkout Social Media Examiner's blog post at http://bit.ly/1nMye2k.

R-U-N-L-A-P-S to Expose Content

Shown in Figure 8.14 is a model of the ways your content can be made visible when you R-U-N-L-A-P-S through RSS and other syndication, Unified keyword strategies, Native advertising, Link building strategies, Atomizing your content, Pinning and posting, and Social sharing.

Note

1. Ann Handley, Ann, and C.C Chapman. *Content Rules*. New Jersey: Wiley. 2011. p. 15.

PART 3

Getting Audiences to R-E-A-C-T

With our content developed and reaching audiences through search, syndication, social networks, and influence, we need to get them to R-E-A-C-T. The next five chapters will discuss ways to engage our fans, turn them into proprietary audiences, and meet them on the device of their choice. Once engaged and subscribed, we could begin the process of courting them through the sales funnel in the following way:

1. R-E-S-O-N-A-T-E your brand as ambassadors (Chapter 9)
2. Engage them through C-O-N-V-E-R-S-A-T-I-O-N (Chapter 10)
3. Advance them through the sales funnel with email marketing (Chapter 11)
4. Contextually relate to their mobile C-U-S-T-O-M-E-R experiences (Chapter 12)
5. Test trial your Freemiums (Chapter 13).

CHAPTER 9

Empowering Brand Ambassadors to R-E-S-O-N-A-T-E

Advocacy happens when customers talk favorably about a brand or defend it without being asked to do so. They just love the brand, what it stands for and how it makes them feel.
—Ann Tran, *Forbes* top social media influencer

The acceleration of social media and content marketing has done more than usher in an era of inbound marketing. In fact, many predict that advocate marketing will be as mainstream in a few years as e-mail marketing is today.[1] Brands and small businesses are recognizing its power in cultivating fans that can serve as brand ambassadors. But more than just brand advocates, these ambassadors are formally assigned to a brand's marketing efforts typically in return for some compensation. And unlike brand influencers, these ambassadors need not be incentivized for every action. Instead, this special class of fans includes existing customers and other loyalists who are happy with a brand and willing to evangelize on its behalf.

By using existing customers on social media as ambassadors, brands are well positioned to expand their reach and boost loyalty while facilitating valuable customer insights in real time. And because of social media, brands can now exploit the following:

1. a media in which to collaborate with communities of similar interests;
2. a vehicle in which to easily share brand content and sentiments; and
3. a tool for brands to acknowledge those spreading the word and contributing to causes.

What Ambassadors Do for a Brand

Advocates on social media serve as a catalyst for the profit growth brands have always recognized from word of mouth referrals. Much like what May Kay, Tupperware party plans, The Pampered Chef, and multilevel marketing companies have done for years, these fans provide a cost-effective way to lead discussions while influencing the brand opinions and even purchase intentions of brand followers. And by capitalizing on the testimony of real users of the product or service, targeted audiences now hear from people they trust.

Lacking in these pre-Internet models, however, was a practical way to spread the word beyond parties or brand-sponsored content riddled with their own propaganda. Now with the addition of easily shared social content, any company today can enable its fans to share their own stories of brand experiences. In fact, research done from over 1 billion mentions on the web found that word-of-mouth marketing has grown exponentially on social media.[2] Moreover, the extensive reach of social media now lets these fans feel like they are part of something big especially when the brand mission is tied to a worthy global cause.

When you add the emotional impact of shared imagery, as well as the growing demand for video content, firms can now take advocacy to a new level. Organizations are now recognizing the power of video testimonies and other content that allows their mission to be conveyed as a story. Instead of managing campaigns that connect the dots of promotion tactics across social-media channels, campaign elements and content can be assembled into a narrative around noble themes surrounding a brand's values. In so doing, fans can visibly benefit from acts of generosity or contributions to a better world. Without this piece, companies can only bank on fans to endorse their features or service experiences. Not only is this word-of-mouth short lived, but it is also likely to diminish over time as merchants flood the social channels with their content and voices.

When managed effectively, brand ambassadors can have significant impact on a brand's bottom line. Some notable statistics captured by Joe Chernov, VP of content for Hubspot, are the following[3]:

- "Customers referred by other customers have a 37% higher retention rate." (Deloitte)
- "Offers shared by trusted advocates convert at a 3x-10x higher rate than offers sent by brands." (Zuberance)
- "Brand advocates are 70% more likely to be seen as a good source of information by people around them." (Marketingcharts)

Why Brand Ambassadors Tell Your Story

Research shows that there are certain conditions that make a brand more appealing to their potential ambassadors. In his book, *Think Like a Rock Star*, Mack Collier equates the attitudes of these folks to that of fans following rock stars.[4] The author builds a solid case that brand advocates don't become fans because of the brand but because of how they see themselves. This means that the brand has to inspire and enable something in themselves. Consequently, the sentiment expressed by them on social-media channels has more to do with their involvement in the mission espoused by the brand.

Besides having certain emotional attachments to a brand mission, however, research demonstrates that, under the right conditions, these ambassadors exhibit some attributes that make them more predisposed to sharing your story.[5] Advocates are far more willing than typical web users to:

1. share information about a product;
2. solve problems that help others make better purchase decisions; and
3. share great product experiences and opinions with someone they don't know.

More than just brand loyalists who incessantly hit the "like" button, chatter from advocates shows an inordinate number of comments that endorse products or reference promotions across a variety of channels. The great news for brands is that chatter indicative of these predisposed sentiments can be picked up by social-media monitoring software.

How to Empower Brand Ambassadors

Once discovered, it behooves brands to empower these ambassadors and get out of the way. After all, we have more than enough evidence to suggest that social-media audiences listen more to their peers than to brands. In academia, we see this in high-school recruiting efforts. College-bound candidates are far more interested in hearing from existing student ambassadors than members of administration. Student ambassadors are seen as more candid and credible. Consequently, they are better positioned to sway opinion as candidates finalize their enrollment decision.

Knowing this power that brand ambassadors have, brands are accelerating their efforts to empower ambassadors that resonate their voice. But as captured in the acronym R-E-S-O-N-A-T-E, a certain environment is needed to cultivate the influence these fans have on recruiting, swaying opinions, and facilitating feedback loops. According to leader social-media expert, Michael Brito, brand ambassador programs have to "mobilize and empower people who already love your brand, and then amplify their voices continuously over time." In essence, "the goal is to empower them to tell your brand story."[6]

Getting Ambassadors to Rally Around Your Mission

In his lectures, leading branding consultant, Simon Mainwaring, builds a compelling case for conveying a story that is exciting and clear enough for ambassadors to tell others.[7] By witnessing the contributions of their voiced support, brand ambassadors can now rally around your mission. This rally point starts with owning a property like Coca Cola's "Open Happiness," P&G's "Change that Matters," Starbuck's "Shared Planet," Nike's "Better World," IBM's "Smarter Planet," or Unilever's "Sustainable

Living." Common to all of these properties are the underpinnings of a story representing the companies' purpose, values, and mission.

Simon points out that what really gets fans to rally around this mission is a brand that:

1. is the celebrant, not the celebrity, of their customer community;
2. makes the customer the hero of the brand story; and
3. assumes what you want to prove (explained further) and dramatize the benefits.

Recall from Chapter 3 the example of Nike celebrating the achievement of an overweight jogger as part of their "Find Your Greatness" campaign. Like Subway's story of Jared Fogle, who lost 245 pounds that he kept off for 15 years, stories like these get fans to rally around the customer—not the brand—as hero. Common across most of these stories are regular people portrayed as heroes instead of elite athletes or glamorous models whose performance or looks are beyond our reach.

Consider the case of Black Milk, an Australian fashion brand known for their form-fitting tights, that never advertises. Instead, their fans, called Sharkies, support more than 60 private Facebook communities. The firm found a way to mobilize these Sharkies by creating hashtags for them to park photos showing off how they wear the tights. This user-generated content inspired other women concerned about fit to join the community. Black Milk then gives the Sharkies a chance to be part of the bigger story with a storytelling sales receipt and gift voucher that starts with "Once Upon a Time."[8]

Getting Ambassadors to Embrace the Story

The aforementioned third point (assume what you want to prove) means that connectedness through values cannot be preached. Instead Coca Cola's Open Happiness assumes the benefit, thereby allowing fans to embrace the theme on their own. Coca Cola reinforces this theme by having fans select three individuals who ultimately travel the world inquiring about how happiness is perceived by others. This is an example of how the customer can then become the hero while the brand serves as celebrant.

Successful brands usually lead with a social purpose by expressing a distinct point of view on matters that people care about. For example, stories surrounding a sector philosophy, cultural movement, a sustainability vision, or some form of eco-consciousness seem to get the most visibility as fans of the theme, according to Simon Mainwaring "will rise to the conversation you create around them." Each engagement with this super fan then boosts the story impact with an audience motivated to spread the word. But to sustain this motivation, the story has to be consistent and worth telling.

Getting Ambassadors to Share Content

For content to be worth sharing, it has to transcend technology and include compelling experiences. Stories like that of Nike and Subway gain momentum not because of Instagram or YouTube, but as fans live vicariously through their hero's struggles. To make it worthy of sharing, however, fans have to be enthusiastic enough to create their own stories through photos, videos, and blog posts. This implies that your brand should first resonate with your community based on a common purpose and a singular message. It is at this point that ambassadors will be willing to work with you to promote the brand.

When the shared content involves community giving, employee volunteering, cause-based marketing, or a foundation, every piece of content can be treated like another chapter in the story. The Coca Cola and Subway examples show the journey of their heroes where each point of progression (e.g., weight point or new visiting part of the world) offers an opportunity to contribute to the mission. And by taking away the focus from their product to their fans, brands are better positioned to build trust and inspire others to share their content.

For companies like H&R Block, which operates a network of independent tax consultants, content sharing is a way to keep these ambassadors in the loop after tax season. The company now allows corporate-approved tax advice to be shared across the ambassador network, thereby capitalizing on the closer relationship developed between consultants and clients than what clients have with the corporation. On the other hand, the easy of sharing helpful tax tips from content sanctioned by the corporation allows the consultant to mobilize their community while building social currency in the process.

Independent of a successful story to motivate content sharing, any content should first focus on why people use the product or service instead of the offering itself. A manufacturer of flour, for example, would gain far more traction with food recipes than dialogues about flour. Fiskars, a scissors manufacturer, found this when they stopped talking about their product and instead had their community talk about scrapbooking.

Others like P&G and Walmart connect with their fans through dialogues involving community personalities resembling that of a typical customer. For example, both host videos or blogs that express opinions on a variety of matters from a mother's perspective. Sharing content from these trusted individuals or product applications becomes more a matter of adding to the collection of story elements. And when the content is entertaining and gives reasons for people to laugh, ambassadors have all the more reason to talk about the brand.

Getting Ambassadors to Offer Insights

For technology companies like Dell and Microsoft, running ambassador programs are essential to their gaining insights from users far more versed in the brands' product potential than perhaps the best of engineers employed at these firms. These are the folks who struggle with and stretch the potential of the brands' offerings. Some are even involved in resolving problems through their own forums, thereby giving them a closer ear to the ground.

Smartphone accessory company, OtterBox, regularly taps into their ambassadors for design opinions as well as for insights on pop culture. In turn, they sponsor contests and provide sneak previews of new offerings. The key to these companies capturing insights often to the point of crowdsourcing new features is to let these ambassadors know you are listening and applying their insights. This requires an atmosphere of candor and open lines of communication with the brand's development teams.

Getting Ambassadors to Neutralize Negative Sentiment

Even the best of brands know that brand sentiment will not always be positive. And most of them have experienced a negative news storm that required either a crisis response or a team of advocates to defend their honor.

While working at Trimble Navigation as a marketing director in the mid-1990s, I faced this situation as missed deadlines kept us from rolling out our next-generation GPS navigator on time for a major trade show. But I marveled over the influence pilots had on the sale of our aging technology. At the time, Garmin was cleaning our clock with their color moving map displays that dazzled a lot of sports aircraft enthusiasts. But to the serious pilot, this negative criticism was taken personally. Avid fans of our brand took pride in the founder, Charley Trimble's, pioneering spirit to the point of pitching our more outdated product throughout the trade show event. They literally took over our booth and animatedly demoed the less exciting, but more accurate and reliable, features of the Trimble offering as the rest of us took notes.

Consider how United Airlines could have been spared from their humiliation when a video amassing over 15 million views disclosed their carelessness and uncaring service over a broken guitar (http://bit.ly/1obSDPx). Unfortunately, the folks at United Airlines reacted too late and too insincerely in their response to the complaint. Rather than immediately addressing the complaint, the airline was counting on the issue to disappear. Instead, social-media channels went wild with advocates of the complainer rallying around his complaint. Just a few key advocates could have come to their defense had they been passionate enough to rally around their mission. Instead, United was seen as a thoughtless bureaucracy that had few friends.

Getting Ambassadors to Act on Your Behalf

But this case representation goes beyond the handling of negative criticism. Whether it's answering questions or using content to promote the brand, successful brand ambassador programs let their brand ambassadors operate autonomously. Fiskars doesn't run their blog, for example; they turn it over to their scrapbookers. Moreover, these Fiskateers regular visit shops and sponsor scrapbook workshops.

Others like Stonyfield operate a team of over 60 Yo-Getter ambassadors and 30 Clean Plate Club ambassadors who collectively blog on a number of organic lifestyle topics. These parent bloggers share their tips and recipes all in one place on the website. In exchange, the brand enlists their help to educate people on improving their eating habits. And since the brand does not pay these groups, they make sure to highlight and promote their ambassadors' posts so as to help boost their readership.

This requires brands to transfer ownership of the brand to their ambassadors. In essence, you are letting fans define the brand. By providing the content-sharing tools, networks to connect with each other, and free access to senior management, they will recognize your sincerity in letting them run the show. In return, brands often gain the participation of these fans in guest blog posts, case studies, and testimonials.

Getting Ambassadors to Tap into Their Communities

As brands struggle to reach their audiences on all relevant platforms, their ambassadors offer opportunities for you to tap into their communities. This could help turn a monologue into a conversation. And by leveraging the personal connections of ambassadors, brands can extend their story to new audiences as well as new platforms for communicating their theme. But unless the content is scaled to suit the ambassador's channel preferences, these ambassadors have little to support their claims or back their opinions. To accomplish this, brands often have to extend their media offerings and content formats to fit new channels.

Back in 2000, Maker's Mark launched a brand ambassador program as it was losing its ability to talk directly to its customers. The program now allows its most passionate fans across the country to run the show.

Getting Ambassadors to Enlist Others

This transfer of ownership could payoff in recruiting as well. Companies like Fiskars and Maker's Mark recognize that empowerment leads to ambassadors attracting new members. As the network of advocates grows, ambassadors are often in a better position to scout others willing to tell their story. Their ownership of this recruiting process further validates the brand's willingness to relinquish brand control.

WhattoExpect.com does this well with their mothers-to-be baby registry. Future mothers gain advice from a community of moms that have been through the trenches.[9] In turn, these expectant moms are inclined to pay it forward, thereby enlisting others to join the community.

How to Motivate Brand Ambassadors

For brands to capitalize on the passion and benefits from ambassador programs, they must R-E-S-O-N-A-T-E as well. Key to any successful ambassador program is the tools, support, and behaviors that will

1. *Reward ambassadors*: Not all ambassadors are paid monetarily. Some benefit from the brand promoting their blog posts, thereby improving the readership of the ambassadors. Others accept rewards like advanced viewings of new products. This can also build a brand buzz around a product launch.

2. *Entitle them*: Ambassadors must feel like they are part of an exclusive club. By giving backstage passes like access to senior leadership or authority to communicate advanced knowledge, these programs can create an atmosphere of privilege.
3. *Simplify their job*: The task of sharing content and facilitating a feedback loop has to be painless and seamless for ambassadors to stay motivated. The same applies to storytelling. Stories have to be easily grasped by your ambassador for them to convey it to their own followers.
4. *Operationalize the program*: Many brands collaborate around brand advisory and customer advisory councils chartered with organization tasks that fit within the infrastructure of the brand's operations. This ensures that voices are not only heard but also adopted into the brand's planning process.
5. *Network them*: In order to networking ambassadors to collaborate on ideation and community outreach, they need platforms like Facebook that are conducive to engagement. But for more established brands,

it often takes more than a Facebook Group. Many are adopting platforms like Social Chorus, Expion, Lithium, Influitive, and Branderati to facilitate brand advocate networking and content sharing.

6. *Acknowledge them*: Just like bragging rights, advocates need to be celebrated. Instead of celebrating their best jeans, Levy celebrates their fans by crowd sourcing the best-fit jeans on their fans. Knowing they have a global voice in which to share their interests and product ideas, this could be a big deal. Other brands provide official recognition of their ambassadors as in the case of Maker's Mark where they have their names branded on a six-year-aged barrel of whiskey.

7. *Train them*: To be an effective ambassador, brands like Fiskars train them to keep up with advances in their trade as well as ways to articulate their story. According to Michael Brito, the key to telling your story correctly is "a solid editorial framework that determines the content narrative, tone of voice, content and platform priorities and the content supply chain (workflows that facilitate content ideation, creation, submission, approval and distribution)."

8. *Engage them*: Much like the success of rock stars who passionately engage with their fans, brands need to engage regularly with their ambassadors or risk having fans feel exploited or ignored. This means regularly providing interesting and relevant content for ambassadors to share.

Shown in Figure 9.1 is a summary model of factors driving effective brand ambassadorship programs.

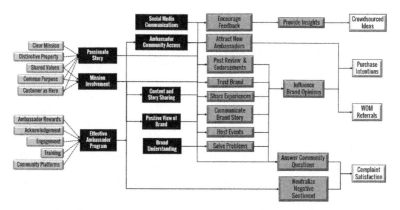

Figure 9.1 Summary Model of Empowering Brand Ambassadors

Notes

1. "Are You Harnessing The the Power of Brand Advocates?" contributed by Kristen Matthews to Convince & Convert (http://bit.ly/WqI0AV).

2. "New Research Shows Social Media Word-of-Mouth Rising" contributed by Kiera Stein to Social Media Examiner (http://bit.ly/1lH7Zjs).

3. Abstracted by Joe Chernov from CMI's "The Complete Guide to Influence Marketing, Content Marketing Institute" (bit.ly/1tneWYt).

4. Mack Collier. Mack, *Think Like a Rock Star*. New York: McGraw-Hill. 2013.

5. "The Actions, Motivations and Influence of Brand Advocates" by Brian Covelli to BzzAgent (http://bit.ly/1o98Ipe).

6. "Leaders in Advocate Marketing: Q&A with Michael Brito" contributed by Dan Sullivan to Social Media Today (http://bit.ly/1lyyxDs).

7. "How to Build a Self-Sustaining Customer Community" by Simon Mainwaring. Presented to Social Media Marketing World in San Diego. March, 2014.

8. "Brand Storytelling: Turning Casual Fans into Passionate Followers" contributed by Sarah Mitchell to CMI (http://bit.ly/1lKN5Qz).

9. "Six Ways to Maximize Brand Advocates on Social Media" contributed by Aimee Reardon to The Punchbowl Trends Blog (http://bit.ly/1AkepwO).

CHAPTER 10

Engage Communities through
C-O-N-V-E-R-S-A-T-I-O-N

*Social media sparks a revelation that we, the people, have a voice, and
through the democratization of content and ideas we can once again
unite around common passions, inspire movements, and ignite change*
—Brian Solis, author of Engage

As great attention has been placed on getting followers, brands are
finding that it is not about reach and impressions anymore. It's about
engagement, which can boost your brand lift by over 300 percent.[1] For
followers to stay followers, they need to play a role. And if our content-
marketing approach is to buy their attention and slam them with content, we have merely participated in a new generation of spam. Only
instead of interruptions with our product ads, we are now interrupting
them with our content.

Social-network engagement is about getting followers to act on your
content and share your stories to those who could benefit from your brand.
Research shows that when a consumer acts upon information shown
about a brand, conversions improve by 70 percent.[2] But this number increases even more when they engage in a conversation about the brand
or are asked to contribute their own content. This is why engagement
has to go beyond clever gimmicks for inviting curious clicks and shares
for rewards. Engagement has to involve a C-O-N-V-E-R-S-A-T-I-O-N,
as shown below, that gives your fans a say in what your brand does.

In many cases, this engagement will lead fans to share their experiences with others, thereby leading to even more followers. And since these new followers have been invited by those they trust, your opportunity to win them over as potential prospects is far greater than can be expected from traditional marketing approaches. But to effectively engage them over a sustained period of time, successful brands are investing heavily in contests, engaging dialogues, and interactive activities.

Developing Contests for Followers and Engagement

One of the best ways to engage fans, while gaining new followers in the process, is to host a contest on social networks. They are effective in having your fans continually return to your page even after the promotion is over. The growing popularity of contests across social networks has much to do with their suitability to photo-based platforms like Facebook, Twitter, Instagram, and Pinterest. When implemented effectively, they provide opportunities to:

1. attract new followers as contest entrants;
2. expose content across a community of fan's friends;

3. build likability from prizes and fan-generated content;
4. sustain engagement as voters and participants are drawn in multiple times for entry contributions and status checks;
5. grow page likes and e-mail subscriptions; and
6. promote products.

More than just sweepstakes, contests normally require some fan input like submitting a photo, essay, photo caption, or video. With sweepstakes, entrants merely enter their name and e-mail where a winner is drawn at random. Contests, on the other hand, involve some form of voting so as to engage your community while letting them know they have a legitimate chance of winning. Ideally, contests should combine voting by the public with judging from a select group of experts so as to reward a relevant audience or ensure valid answers. This is especially important for quiz-based contests that may require expert review.

Facebook remains the largest host of contest activities in part due to their versatility and third-party support. They offer both a timeline contest and Facebook app contests. The former is free and easy to host but lacks convenient ways to capture e-mails, pick random winners, and co-ordinate the overall campaign. Apps aren't required for timeline contests; you only need to solicit a photo or comment and select a winner from best overall response. But timeline contest apps from AgoraPulse, TabSite, Hevo, and Woobox greatly simplify the contest process.

A Facebook App Contest help facilitates the e-mail entry, voting, and winner-selection process often through self-service, drag-and-drop templates. In addition to those mentioned earlier, some popular contest apps suggested by Facebook expert, Andrea Vahl, include Offerpop, Votigo, Antavo, Strutta, and ShortStack.

Running effective contests requires special attention to platform rules, prizes, and voting procedures. Most platforms, like Facebook, are sensitive to pressures placed on entrants to endorse your content. For example, contestants can no longer be compelled to like a page as a condition for contest entry. They can, however, complete an action like an e-mail submission or comment to qualify as an entrant.

To avoid the attraction of contest scammers and other parties not of interest to your brand, steps can be taken to enforce ID validations and select prizes relevant to your business and a specific audience. For example, rather than rewarding contestants with an iPad, a travel business may reward winners with hotel-stay discounts or free airline tickets dependent on the level of contest effort required of the contestant. This may discourage participation from contest scavengers.

As an example of a highly successful contest driven primarily by user-generated video, American Express OPEN hosted their Big Break for small-business owners. To enter the contest, these entrepreneurs had to visit and submit answers to a short questionnaire describing how they would utilize the competition's winnings to better their business.

During the first round of judging, 10 small-business finalists were selected by a panel of prestigious judges. Each submission was judged based on the following criteria:

- commitment to their business and growth;
- overall social-media need where Facebook could improve their business; and
- energy and enthusiasm for small business.

Finalists then competed in a final round of judging where American Express OPEN Facebook fans were then asked to vote for their five favorite small businesses to win a trip and a $20,000 prize.

This contest, like many others, works well in extending reach, exposure, and interaction to your Facebook page. For example, the contestants want votes, so they appeal to their network of friends thereby extending the reach. The fact that you are restricting entrants to those meeting a certain criteria also ensures a more legitimate contest relevant to your target audience. Finally, this type of promotion allows for the collection of user-generated content that, in the case of AMEX's Big Break, started a trend of active fan engagement as well as content later used by the company as testimonies to back their brand acceptance.

Key to any successful contest is its adequate promotion and sustainment. Promotion across all of your social-networking sites with contest hashtags, trailers, and entry highlights can also boost your content exposure with new followers. Although contests are recommended to last no longer than a few weeks for the sake of momentum, postcontest activities will often make or break the contest's success in boosting engagement.

Some ways to keep the momentum going is to allow content additions to a storyline collection. Besides Although the contest may involve involving user-generated video productions, the collection could include less resource-intensive additions to a graphic montage, photo gallery, fan story album, or inspirational commentary.

Creating Engaging Discussions

Social media has to be inherently a social activity if you want fans to stick around. This means more than setting up a Facebook page that allows fans to browse around. It means letting them know you are willing to have a dialogue. And for the dialogue to have real impact, it has to be two way and authentic while having a conversational tone.

Sparking Open and Authentic Dialogues

By now, brands realize that social media remains highly personal for consumers who prefer interacting with other people, not with brands. One way to accomplish this is by having candid discussions with your fans or followers in an open forum. The more your fans see your personal side, the greater trust they have for your shared responses. McDonalds went out on a limb with their "Our Food, Your Questions."[3] They track down reputable sources within and outside their company to answering consumer questions about their food quality. By having the right people answer with very candid answers, the brand has likely boosted its reputation for authenticity.

By itself, however, these question and answer forums are not likely to involve high levels of engagement. The most effective open dialogues often incite a controversial debate or insightful argument. But they do it carefully. For example, if taking a position on an unpopular side of a controversial topic, make sure the argument is backed by fact. Oftentimes, by clarifying your role as Devil's Advocate, your fans will see that you are merely asking them to join in the debate and not necessarily agree with your position. The key is to act more like your fans rather than preach down to them. The more you act like a real person that shares the same values as your fans, the more you can expect them to engage with meaningful commentary of their own.

Dealing with Negative Commentary

Much like we witnessed prior to social media, the satisfactory handling of complaints can often boost brand sentiment. Brands recovering from a service issue will often receive positive sentiment based on their empathy and efforts devoted toward solving a problem. In fact, research demonstrates how satisfaction in a brand could improve to levels above the sentiment felt before a complaint was registered.

In social-media channels, brands are coached not to be defensive in dealing with complaints, ranting, or harsh disparagement of the brand. Instead, negative comments should be treated as an opportunity to boost goodwill and engagement. Depending on the seriousness of the post and the unfairness of the response, most criticism of a brand could be dealt with in the following manner:

1. acknowledge the problem and empathize with the complainer's viewpoint;
2. ask to deal with the issue off-line; and
3. offer to remedy the issue with a reward commensurate with the inconvenience.

Where lifts in positive engagement can happen is when humor or humility is applied. Most of us like seeing the real vulnerabilities of a brand. And some appreciate the light-hearted side as well as when brands poke fun of themselves. Consider how a disparaging comment about Smart Car in Figure 10.1 was dealt with by the folks at Smart Car. When the tweeter claimed the droppings of one bird totaled the car, Smart Car scientifically corrected him on how many birds it would actually take to do that much damage. The post itself was retweeted 581 times. In effect, the humbled and humorous response to a sarcastic comment boosted engagement.

Capitalizing on Visual Storytelling

As discussed in Chapter 3, visuals are key to creating an emotional connection with our audiences. Readers are drawn in by visuals and often decide from the visual whether to engage further on a post. In fact, 87 percent of engagement on Facebook brand posts occurs when a post includes a photo.[4] According to visual storytelling expert, Ekaterina Walters, viewers spend 100 percent more time on web pages with videos. Moreover, there are 94 percent more total views attracted by content containing compelling images than without. Finally, she points out that every minute

1. 208,300 photos are posted to Facebook;
2. 27,800 photos are share on Instagram; and
3. 100 hours of video are uploaded to YouTube.

Much of this she attributes to the creativity brands have applied in using visuals to tell their stories as well as the technologies available for almost anyone to create compelling imagery. Fans with limited graphic and technical

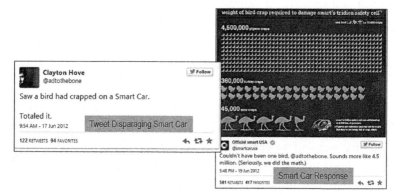

Figure 10.1 Dealing with Negative Commentary

skills, for example, can easily compose GIFs, Memes, Vines, filtered photos, and infographics on photo- and video-intensive platforms like Facebook, YouTube, Instagram, Snapchat, Tumblr, and Pinterest. Once created, tools like Storify can then help you curate the imagery and build social stories into a coherent narrative. When compiled, this richer media will help address the decline in average modern adult attention span now slipping to 2.8 to 8 seconds. But it will also raise the bar in creating the emotional connection that statistics show is key to getting your fans to engage.

Telling a story with visuals need not involve a sitcom style of video episodes. A video or photo gallery could spark an emotion that conjures up a deeply rooted sentiment or life story. Back in 1971, a Public Service Announcement from the Ad Council on "Keeping America Beautiful" featured a crying Native American Indian who stumbled across a polluted creek. One captivating photo in this case told the whole story. What is key to a successful visual story is to make it interesting and engaging. This can often be done in a single post by overlaying photos with an inspiring quote or alarming statistic.

Especially as consumers migrate toward mobile usage, visuals may ultimately become the only way fans will engage with your posts. Their real-time demands and information overloads will make them tap into the greater context permitted by visuals as well as the fact that 90 percent of information transmitted to the brain is visual.

Creating an Atmosphere of Belongingness and Exclusivity

After examining the feeds of several social-media influencers I later labeled as charismatics, I noticed a distinct behavior. They nurtured their followers in the following ways:

1. they regularly congratulate and share the accomplishments of their fans;
2. they provide meaningful responses to fan posts often explaining why they found the post interesting;
3. they respond to their fans tweets and posts often outside the dialogue of their own platform of exposure; and
4. they provide inspirational messaging that seems to resonate with a great number of followers.

The last point, in particular, shows they listen intently to what their audiences seek and feel. This makes the kudos seem less pretentious while sparking some motivation into those struggling with their routines. It also lets the fans know that their voice counts.

In some cases, I noticed the influencer revealing personal insights and values much like that espoused by fraternities or sororities. This likely leaves the followers with a sense of belonging to a club managed by a leader they admire. The same affinity could develop when a brand reveals behind-the-scene insights. Fans, in this case, will sense their acceptance into an exclusive club that could nurture their passions or inspire them to reach higher.

Maintaining Relationships with Responsiveness

In this world of 24/7, consumers expect instant replies to their comments on social media especially if it involves a complaint. Social media has become the new service channel. A study by The Social Habit found that 42 percent of consumers contacting a brand for customer support expect a response in 1 hour, three quarters of which expect an answer in 30 minutes. Moreover, according to leading social-media expert, Jay Baer, well over half expect the same response time at night and over weekends as they do during the day.[5]

This responsiveness carries over to your social-networking dialogues as well. When your fans see trails of unanswered comments in your feed, you are sending a signal that no one is home. Social media is about discussion and sharing. Given that many willing to comment on your posts are often your best leads, the attention given to your fans' comments replies should match that given to creating and optimizing the content itself.

Engaging in Interactive Activities

Besides engaging in dialogues, brands and small businesses can now entertain their fans with games, quizzes, and other interactive activities. Whether it involves soliciting their opinions or asking them to share stories, the more they see you value their input, the greater they will respond and encourage others to join the community.

Sharing Customer Stories

Big brands recognize that the key to engagement is inviting their fans to submit their own stories. Walmart and Starbucks regularly feature photos of their fans or samples of their content. Others will incorporate everyday life adventures into their promotions. Dunkin' Donuts did this very well in a series where they asked their audiences to describe in a tweet how their coffee fit into their everyday lives. After scouring through tens of thousands of responses parked under the hashtag #mydunkin, the brand featured the best in their commercials and YouTube videos.

When community members feel you care about their stories, you can win fans for life. And as demonstrated by Dunkin' Donuts, the story can be made to fit under 140 characters or blended into a montage as is often done by Walmart. What is important is that the story told on Pinterest, Instagram, or Facebook allows fans to share their passions. And what better bragging rights to have with your friends than to be featured by a major brand.

Ask Questions or Fill-In Blanks

These story-sharing exercises don't have to be elaborate productions. To make a photo engaging, for example, it helps to have your fans add something to it. Brands often do this in crowdsourcing their new ad concepts where respondents are asked to supply a caption or fill in the blanks. In effect, they are contributing to your story while providing you some useful information for future campaigns.

Fans are likely to engage routinely when you simply pose questions or invite them to fill in the blanks. Pringles, Zappos, and many universities take this route in their chat-ups to fill the space between more substantive campaigns. Filling in the blanks about how something makes you feel, what you enjoy the most, or how you tackle issues are great ways to trigger commentary from others.

Asking as opposed to telling separates a post from one of
preaching to facilitating. Remember that fans love to share their
opinions. Posing questions helps
in engagement by soliciting feedback from those we should be embracing. Over time, the answers
themselves should provide insights
for future posts. But to boost engagement, it helps to narrow your fan's
focus to a select few words. For example, asking fans to explain their best
memories with their first love is not likely to muster up as many responses
as having fans describe what best two words describe their first love.

William & Mary's Ampersandbox campaign was highly successful in
recruiting students. Participants are asked to create or contribute to pairs
of terms, like William & Mary, which reflect what the school means to
them. An extensive gallery of experience boards has accumulated over
time on term pairs like hide and seek, dollars and sense, pomp and cir-
cumstance, leaps and bounds, and ebb and flow. In the process, student
candidates get a broad perspective of the university's mark of distinction
and campus experience without having to wade through stacks of generic
looking brochures.

Trivia questions, ice breakers, and quizzes are also great ways to keep
your fans hanging around. Companies can exploit this method of engagement while highlighting more about their story in the process. Coca Cola,
for example, is known to host trivia questions surrounding their history
or products. Their "Which of the following is worth the most Scrabble
points?" invited fans to research certain brand names. After completing
their research and posting their response, fans returned later to check on
answers and even comment again. By awaiting answers in subsequent
updates, fans get accustomed to visiting your site on a more regular basis.

Facilitating Twitter Chats

A great way to stir conversation on a passionate topic is through Twitter
Chats. By simply specifying a date and time, a hashtag, and a topic, you
can start a dialogue with your fans that builds thought leadership in the

process. These chats now number in the thousands as brands find Twitter to be an excellent channel to mobilize folks around short-form conversations.

The key to a successful chat is to be passionate about the topic. Much like I notice in classroom sessions; if I am pushing through material that does not interest me, it shows. On the other hand, when I get excited to cover new ground, it spurs far more participation. Chats work the same way. Over time, you begin to reveal your own personality, thereby adding to your authenticity that will characterize you on other channels as well.

Advice from social-media pros on hosting an effective chat tends to consistently include the following:

1. include guest thought leaders;
2. stay on topic to avoid conversation derailing and ranting while allowing enough flexibility to encourage multiple participants and viewpoints;
3. transcribe and curate the comment trails for SEO and follow-up blog appeal; and
4. pick a distinctive hashtag that reflects the topic and scope of dialogue.

If handled effectively, these chats will attract new followers seeing you as an authority. The scheduled arrangement and promotion of the chat also provides additional opportunities to engage with your existing followers while conveying your commitment to the topic.

Designing Interactive Infographics

Publishers who use infographics enjoy a 12 percent lift in traffic.[6] But by itself, visuals can only go so far. We know humans are wired to visualize, but even the most digestible and succinct infographics can overwhelm audiences. When visuals are combined with our kinetic learning tendencies, however, you have a great combination for engagement. That is why interactive infographic infographics have become so popular. Brands are now turning static infographics into dynamic visuals that allow a variety of click-throughs and roll-overs for more information. This not only allows them to skip over irrelevant information, but it also appeals to their sense of curiosity and exploration.

Similar concepts are being applied to YouTube videos that allow viewers to formulate their own story. In Pepsi's "Now Is What You Make It" #FutbolNow, you can expand on the narrative at parts that most pique your interest. Especially at a time where audiences are being inundated with content, these self-navigation schemes provide short-cuts to data visualization while allowing fans to participate in your content.

Conducting Opinion Polls

Asking your fans for ideas is often the most neglected part of an engagement strategy. Our greatest assets are our customer, and yet many of us fail to see them as our greatest fans as well. Successful brands regularly ask their customers what they want. But they tap into their inputs normally in a

sincere and often entertaining way. Sincerity requires evidence that the crowdsourced inputs are indeed applied to either product changes, product names, or marketing concepts.

Companies like Modify Watches regularly solicit their customers for ideas on watch design and product naming often incorporating the inputs into their designs. Similarly, for a special version of their Juke NISMO, Nissan asked its customers to share their technology ideas through the hashtag #Jukeride. In the process of collecting ideas, the brand shared some behind-the-scenes videos on how many ideas were being adopted.

More Twitter chats are now being used for crowdsourcing as facilitators use the forum to conduct online focus groups. The real-time interaction also avoids moderator bias when participants are given leeway to freely chat. And because of the anonymity, audiences may not feel as intimidated or self-conscious as they might otherwise feel in live sessions.

Another feature of social-media sites is their ability to host surveys and pools. Especially when a real-time histogram displays your results relative to other voters, many fans are excited to register their vote. Besides allowing a potential fun exercise, brands benefit from the polling insights.

Participating in Social-Networking Groups

Brands that regularly engage in LinkedIn groups, Facebook groups, and Google+ communities make a statement about their genuine intentions to help others. By moving their conversations away from their newsfeeds and into community forums, they are letting potential followers know it is about your target audience's business challenges and not your brand. LinkedIn, in particular, has made great strides in allowing brands to contribute to hypertargeted topics of interest to business professionals. When used effectively, it becomes a Holy Grail for building channel relationships and thought leadership.

Selection of the groups you decide to join should consider the influencers in your industry to whom you want to mingle and spread the word. Once decided, you will find postings submitted by the group leaders that invite commentary later scored for "likability." The more your content is liked, the greater your exposure as an expert as well as the popularity of the subject matter.

Engagement in these groups works much like that on your own social-media properties except that the dialogues are controlled by your topic popularity and the moderator in charge of the group. The key to getting engagement is to spark a conversation that enlightens others anxious to share their inputs and curious to find what others experience. In the process, business connections are often made as discussion contributors recognize joint interests and even partnering opportunities.

In deciding a strategy for group involvement, the choice of group often starts with a design of channel relationships leading to your target audience. From there, the type of relationship you expect to develop determines the nature of your dialogues and content postings. Consider how this was done in the services sector for a company known as "Landscapes-to-Go," a start-up venture of garden and landscape improvement kits.

The venture launched a ready-to-go assembly of floral products derived from its patent-protected designs. The company initiated this business in response to Floridian gardeners seeking backyard tranquility and hobbies that contribute to home-appreciation value. The kit approach further addressed a growing trend toward "do-it-yourself" home improvements coupled with time restrictions that prohibit gardening from scratch. Finally, a growing problem among nurseries to reduce plant and other inventories called for complex business arrangements with landscape marketers that pull-through excess farm capacity and aging inventories.

As demonstrated in Figure 10.2, the selection of LinkedIn Groups first required an understanding of the channel relationships between the owners and their target audiences associated with their new housing, commercial real estate, and consumer markets. Knowing the role of each channel provided a better picture of their likely hangouts and business interests. For example, new housing construction was best addressed through strategic alliances with commercial landscape architects and landscape construction contractors.

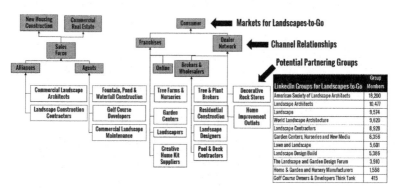

Figure 10.2 Example Selection of LinkedIn Groups

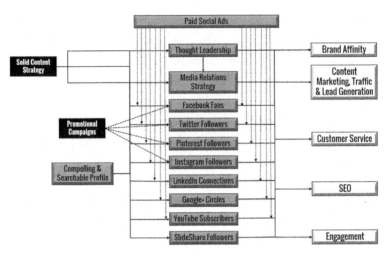

Figure 10.3 Summary Model of Enlisting Followers with a S-T-A-M-P

This channel partner could be reached through the LinkedIn Group known as "American Society of Landscape Architects." Some of the consumer channels, on the other hand, could better be reached and influenced through LinkedIn Groups such as "The Landscape and Garden Design Forum."

The key to using LinkedIn Groups is not to market directly to your target audience, but to build relationships by collaborating with those who seek the same audience recognition. To gain their attention, it is important to reach their group discussion feeds with topics that show your credibility and thought leadership (Figure 10.3). This could include advisory tips, but more than often includes market research and other data relevant to industry trends.

Notes

1. BuzzFeed Case Study: Virgin Mobile (http://bit.ly/1vmjZXE).
2. "Engagement Marketing: The Future of Brand Advertising?" by Paul Dunay to *Forbes* (onforb.es/12lEEm6).
3. "Our Food. Your Questions" by McDonalds (http://qmcd. ca/1phNl5G).

4. "Photos Are Still King on Facebook" contributed by Phillip Ross to Socialbakers (bit.ly/1ozjT0o).
5. "42 Percent of Consumers Complaining in Social Media Expect 60 Minute Response Time" contributed by Jay Baer to Convince & Convert (http://bit.ly/1omrVUU).
6. "12% Traffic Growth: Why You Should Give Infographics a Try" by ePublishing (http://bit.ly/1vg8G5n).

CHAPTER 11

E-mail Engaging and Perpetuating Proprietary Audiences

If you aren't building, engaging and activating proprietary audiences of your own, you're falling behind.
—Jeffrey Rohrs, author of Audience

Constant changes from Facebook and other social networks have made brands wean off these networks as a source for audience correspondence and content marketing. But only to a point. The organic reach restrictions obviously infuriate many brands now forced to pay for reach. But wise brands see the advantage in blending the viral capabilities of social networks with the messaging control of e-mail and phone text.

Having access to e-mail and SMS contact information is vital to the process of escorting audiences through the sales funnel. Just having content go viral, for example, does little for brands seeking intelligence on who is interested in their offerings and where they are in their buying journey. But the social networks play a key role in expanding the funnel.

Why E-mail-Engaged Audiences Require Social Media

Facebook, in particular, provides one of the greatest sources of audience development at the top of the funnel (ToFu). Their custom audience and look-alike audience features administered through their Power Editor shows great promise in building databases for lead generation. For example, the web custom audience feature allows you to capture the ID of your website visitors where Facebook finds this person when they arrive on the social network. At that time, they could be served a retargeted ad. Better yet, a strong welcome incentive invites them as a fan, where they may submit an e-mail. And the cycle continues as shown in Figure 11.1.

Using social networks to attract followers—and e-mails to correspond with them directly–is a great way to jumpstart e-mail campaigns that could track downloading behaviors; store this intelligence in CRM or marketing automation systems; and tailor a response appropriate to the prospects buying stage. Now imagine Facebook fetching more contacts for you from their look-alike audience features as you acquire more opt-ins from blog subscriptions, apps, webinar registries, or downloaded e-Books? Your funnel gets wider and your leads get more qualified.

Why Social Media Requires E-mail

As discussed in previous chapters, there are many effective approaches for leveraging social media and SEO to extend the visibility of your content. But sales nurturing goes beyond ToFu lead generation. Nurturing requires the following intelligence on your target's needs and buying stage:

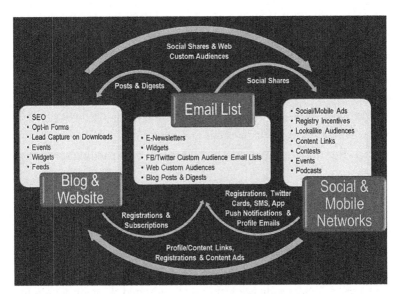

Figure 11.1 Combining Social And E-Mail To Build Proprietary Audience

1. Who downloaded the content?
2. What topic areas about the content piqued the interest of your target?
3. What follow-up response would be appropriate?
4. How urgent is their need?

Without some sort of e-mail-marketing guidance, social media would merely serve as a viral marketing tool leaving your hard-earned content wandering in space. Yes, a high-populated social community or well-SEO blog can spread the word about your brand. Your friends and followers can even endorse your brand or content through likes, shares, or comments. But with only SEO and social media to promote your content, you are essentially limited to the spreading of brand awareness (the ToFu stage).

Even the best of social-media newsfeed posts, retweets, and other communications cannot tell you much about your target audience's intended use of your content. The target simply gets educated through your content. They may even grasp the manner in which it addresses your problem. But you are left with no evidence of their interests in your content talking points let alone your ultimate offer.

When coupled to e-mail campaigns, however, you can now guide and track your content delivery. Why is this important? Without knowing the problem-solving urgency or stage of buying for your target, your content is aimlessly bouncing off wasted eyeballs. Left without any tracking intelligence, you will likely end up pummeling your targets with even more ToFu content. Moreover, you may end up pre-empting your content sequencing with premature bottom-of-the-funnel offers.

Either way, you lack a vehicle for tracking download behaviors. And without tracking what piqued their interest, your follow-up is not aligned with their buying stage. You are left instead with an intrusive broadcasting style of content since you have no way to reel in your leads.

E-mail 2.0 Serves to Educate as Opposed to Promote

This is where e-mail 2.0 plays a vital role. E-mail 2.0 is essentially e-mail in the world of social media and mobile. But unlike prior generations of e-mail used primarily for broadcasted offers, e-mail 2.0 is aimed at sales nurturing. This nurturing starts with a "permission only" process—preferably double opt-in—for legitimately obtaining an address. It then educates your audience as opposed to selling them on untimely marketing messages. In essence, you are escorting your sales leads down the social sales funnel.

For example, most well-crafted middle of the funnel (MoFu) warrants an e-mail address in exchange for what your target perceives as a gift. This gift may include a free white paper, e-Book, or webinar registration. Not only do you get the address in exchange for rich content, but your target should also not feel intruded or bombarded with irrelevant information.

E-mail 2.0 Provides Intelligence to Steer Your Content

Some of the objections with prior generation e-mail blasts and social media is that they were promotional in nature. With only 5–25 percent of your site traffic ready to do business and 50 percent of qualified leads not ready to buy immediately, pushing your targets often leads to losing them.

Imagine instead that streams of MoFu content are tracked across every e-mail call to action. In her book, *eMarketing Strategies for the Complex Sale*, Ardath Albee points out several examples of how e-mail, CRM, and social behaviors collectively provide powerful tracking insights.[1] Consider the case of the real-estate accounting firm targeting property managers.

Over the course of newsletter deliveries, webinar hosting, and podcast releases, the following information would be captured by the e-mail's associated CRM system.

We know from the CRM system that the target:

1. is a property manager;
2. is highly interested in the topic with some sense of urgency based on the fast response to e-mail and webcast activity;
3. has a high level of interest in the accounting services; and
4. is late in the buying cycle.

Email Campaign Objective	Sales Goal	Campaign Objects	Forum or Content Topics
Product or Service Announcement	Introduce the company	Link to a FREE downloaded whitepaper posted on website	Downloaded Whitepaper for Improving Property Cash Flow
Opt-in registration to your eNewsletter	Build loyalty & gain trust (via thought leadership)	Articles on skill building, industry activity or local networking activities	Understanding the Tax Consequences of Lease Options
			Maintenance vs. Capital Improvement: A 3-Part Test
			Recent Tax Law Outlines Depreciation Guidelines for Common Property Amenities
"Special offer" emails	Increase sales and maximize exposure	FREE Consultation	Q&A on 1031 Exchange Strategies for Rental Real Estate
Educational and/or networking event invites	Drive traffic to a specific event your organization is hosting or participating	Keynote addresses and speaking engagements	Luncheon speaker for FL Chapter Speaker at National Association of Residential Property Managers (NARPA) on Property ROI Enhancement
		Conference seminar or workshop	Seminar on Cost-Effective Neighborhood Watch Setup
		Sponsored community event	Hole sponsor for Annual Habitat for Humanity charity Golf for Property Managers
		Webinar hosting	Long-term strategic financial planning for real estate asset managers
		Speaking and/or exhibitor at a trade show	Customized accounting software exhibit for Florida Multi Housing Association Conference

Figure 11.2 Sample E-Mail Campaign for Real-Estate Accounting Firm

Setting Campaign Objectives

The key to effectively utilizing e-mails in lead nurturing is to adopt a plan for campaigns, digests, or follow-up correspondence that keeps your audiences engaged. The following campaign objectives are most often considered by heavy users of e-mail marketing:

1. introducing your firm's offerings through product or service announcements;
2. enhancing your brand reputation, building trust, and renewing relationships through e-newsletters;
3. informing and educating your audiences through speaking engagements, workshop events, and webinars; and
4. generating more sales through special offers.

Once the campaign objects are considered, content topics or event forums should be defined in line with these objectives. Notice how this is done in Figure 11.2 for the case of the real-estate accounting firm.

Note

1. Ardath Albee. Ardath, eMarketing Strategies for the Complex Sale. New York: McGraw-Hill. 2010.

CHAPTER 12

Enabling Mobile C-U-S-T-O-M-E-R Experiences

If you're not using mobile marketing to attract new customers to your business, don't worry—your competitors are already using it and are getting those customers instead.

—Jamie Turner, 60SecondMarketer.com

As the number of smartphones well exceeds 1 billion, it is not surprising that mobile has rapidly overtaking desktop access to the Internet. One obvious consequence of this trend is the growing number of online marketers embracing a "mobile-first" design philosophy. But more research is suggesting these intentions are not materializing into a distinct mobile-customer experience. Instead, efforts are often limited to screen optimizing and mobile-friendly interfacing.

The good news to marketers is that efforts to convert on online-marketing initiatives become more promising. The buying stage of a mobile user tends to be closer to the bottom of the funnel (e.g., shopping checkouts). And with mobile-message responses averaging around 15 minutes as compared to 48 hours for a desktop-delivered e-mail, marketers should have more opportunity to stay engaged throughout the buying cycle. This should translate into more personalized messaging, relevant mobile apps, and responsive mobile websites. But we are not seeing this.

A Vibes study, for example, found that 89 percent of consumers want personalization, but only 18 percent see it frequently from retailers. And the mainstream adoption of local context has yet to materialize, leaving a gap between what consumers have now come to expect and what mobile marketers are actually providing. The criticality of this gap in mobile attention becomes an even greater concern as trends support a predominantly mobile world in years to come.

Mobile Users Want Less and Expect More

So what is keeping marketers from addressing these mobile-experience demands? Experts attribute most of the sluggish response to the following:

1. a desktop first, "mobile-second" design philosophy;
2. a failure of marketers to adequately understand and map a mobile customer's end-to-end journey; and
3. continuing technology maturing across mobile-payment apps, geofencing, and in-store shopping infrastructures.

What should be an alert to all mobile marketers is the damage done when consumers have a bad mobile experience. According to Compuware and IAB, an estimated 40–61 percent, respectively, will visit a competitor's site when this happens.

Addressing Unique Experience Expectations

At the same time, consumers are clamoring for less functionality to accommodate their smaller screens and reduced attention span when on mobile devices. This often goes beyond the obvious reduction in links and text required for a mobile display. The more simple and direct end-to-end journey of a mobile user typically translates to far fewer navigation steps as well. Overall, the unique experience expectations of a mobile user can be defined in an acronym that spells C-U-S-T-O-M-E-R.

Convenience of Payments, Calls, and Directions

Consumers expect quick-and-easy mobile experiences. This includes having instant access to product and service research, locations triggers, and the ability to make mobile payments in hassle-free steps.

Mobile consumers expect far more in real-time research and context relevance in comparison to their desktop counterparts. And with a growing number of apps primarily aimed at simplifying the mobile experience, these expectations will become greater. Steps like linking local addresses into contact listings, or automatically mapping directions, will become commonplace as mobile users experience this elsewhere.

Mobile payment, in particular, is one area where users have been enamored with the convenience of merging coupons, loyalty cards, and credit cards into one Near Field Communication (NFC) swipe. And while Apple and Google work out the differences in their proposed payment technologies (e.g., Bluetooth LE/iBeacons vs NFC), mobile marketers need to gear up for some type of iWallet. At stake are the many pull-through loyalty perquisites and behavioral tracking that come with mobile wallets.

Utility for Real-Time Self-Help

In his book, Youtility, Jay Baer builds a strong case for utility as the future of marketing. Utility marketing is defined here as "putting content and information in your marketing material that your target audience can utilize."[1] One way to accomplish this is through mobile apps. By using apps to help consumers with useful problem solving in real time, mobile marketers stand to gain far more in brand loyalty.

Imagine, for example, an app offered by a grocery chain that provides free advice on dieting habits or by a bleach manufacturer helping you decide the best way to remove a wine stain. The key to applying this "friend-of-mine" marketing approach is having brand credibility in the area of advice offered to the mobile user.

Showrooming for Better Deals

Perhaps the most demanded mobile-user experience relates to showrooming or the practice of examining merchandise in a traditional brick and mortar retail store often with the intent to purchase the merchandise elsewhere. Mobile users can now get ample research in-store on competing prices as well as on ratings and review. It is at this point that retailers in particular should consider personalized offers as a way to thwart away any temptation to buy elsewhere.

According to a recent Vibes Study, the number of consumers who purchased a product from a competitor while in a retail store has increased 156 percent since 2012. The study further demonstrated that

1. 47 percent move onto complete a transaction;
2. 45 percent go elsewhere to purchase items; and
3. 7 percent do not make purchases.

But these timely offers apply to more than just showroomers. Mobile users "on the go" are far more prone to look elsewhere in dealing with any online task at hand. And with the average adult will now spending over 5 hours per day in mobile activities, expect an "instant response" mentality to become increasingly important.

Timely Mobile Marketing

The same applies to timely alerts outside of, but in proximity to, store shopping. Mobile users in close proximity to a marketer's place of business often don't benefit from local offers out of their reach. So timing becomes everything especially in light of the high number of users in shopping mode. And when done proactively, as in the case of reminding customers of upcoming events or appointments, mobile users will often credit the mobile marketer with a convenience benefit as well.

Special Offers and Rewards for Mobile Efforts

Much like the case of rewarding social-media fans for the privilege of accessing their news feeds or inbox, mobile users expect something for their efforts. After all, marketers are asking for time spend downloading apps. They are also asking to interrupt a mobile user's journey with SMS messaging and other alerts often when the mobile user is in the mid of pressing business. So special compensation is should be expected in the form of exclusive mobile rewards.

The good news to mobile marketers is that 90 percent of users who enroll in an SMS loyalty program feel they gained value from it. Why? When you send timely, relevant, and useful information to them during the shopping stage of their buying cycle, you may be credited with expediting their decision. An even more surprising statistic is that 70 percent of them say they would actually like to receive offers on their mobile phones.

Mobility in Addition to Mobile

As the global workforce become more mobile, consumers and employees will count on devices like tablets and smartphones to do their work at the office, at home, and while traveling. Conceivable, more workplace information will be transferred from desktops to tablets as portability becomes

critical to workplace efficiency. This same portability is also gaining favor among mothers needing to multitask when on the run. And when packed with photo-messaging apps, mobile devices provide them more real-time social networking as well.

Ease of Use for Shorter Attention Spans

In his podcast interview with Amy Porterfield, Greg Hickman shares some startling statistics on mobile-user intolerance for unresponsive web designs. For example, he points out that 74 percent of consumers will wait 5 seconds for a web page to load on their mobile device before abandoning the site. Perhaps even more startling is that 46 percent of them are unlikely to return to a mobile site if it didn't work properly during their last visit. Among the ways to optimize mobile sites for friendly user interfacing are the following:

1. touch interaction that avoids "fat thumb syndrome";
2. video and other imagery that replaces text; and
3. shorter route "calls to action."

Relevance for Space, Time, and Opportunity

On a more positive note, retailers, brands, and even small businesses have made strides in developing mobile-friendly websites compatible with the multitude of smartphone and tablet configurations. Progress is also being made with mobile wallet solutions that expedite in-store shopping experiences while enabling cross-device loyalty programs. And with more advanced audience targeting and cross-platform retargeting underway, mobile users are rarely greeted as "Dear Valued Customer."

Fulfilling customer experiences on smart devices, however, goes well beyond loyalty programs and personal greetings. Mobile users expect far greater context relevance that taps into who they are, where they are, what they are doing, and when they need help. This is why the role of native ads has become even more important to mobile users than to desktop users. And if marketers know why they need help, the mobile user can further benefit from anticipated needs as well.

The mad dash toward mobilizing our marketing efforts is well justified. Mobile has traditionally taken a back seat to desktop Internet marketing. But as mobile access surpasses desktop access, marketers seem to be dragging their feet in designing customer experiences that are meaningful to a mobile consumer's journey. Statistics show that many marketers still see mobile simply as an optimization exercise. Some are indeed stepping up to responsive web designs as a top priority. But missing from many mobile-marketing strategies is a very different customer experience that extends beyond the demands of a desktop user.

As SoLoMo matures to SoLoMoNative and SoLoMoVideo, don't be surprised if mobile-web access becomes the de facto standard for Internet access in retail, at home, and in workplace settings. Those who embrace this "mobile-first" philosophy have a significant advantage in light of the higher receptivity of mobile users to personalized messaging and offers. The key to implementing a responsive mobile strategy is a recognition of the distinct customer experiences expected by mobile users.

Geo-Fencing and Location-Based Mobile Marketing

Almost every year since 2012, social-media marketing predictors say this is the year of context marketing. How real is this trend toward context-based mobile marketing? For starters, consider that consumers allocate more than 25 percent of their mobile time to social-networking apps, each of which has some local element. The notion of context-based marketing itself is not new; it's just not meaningful enough without including location in the context.

Consider how behavioral marketing currently works. Through a browser cookie, we can be presented with ads that fit our browsing history and essentially represent our lifestyle interests. Now imagine adding location to that "context." You can now approach some *geo-fence* and be informed of nearby deals that suit your taste and buying preference. Only instead of your profile data coming from a browser cookie, the background information may be integrated from a multitude of social-media sources.

For some time we have been familiar with location-based services (LBS), where geo-fencing allowed Apple Passbook, Foursquare, SCVNGR, and others to promote local establishments by encouraging check-ins, offering incentives for reviews, and building engagement on their Facebook Pages. Foursquare, in particular, was known for their tips and their algorithm of things that might interest us in an area of interest.

But many believe that the original intent to award badges and engage us in social gaming has caused LBS to likely run its course. Or has it? Apple's Passbook has become a major player in the mobile-commerce space. And with continued development in geo-fencing and low-energy Bluetooth, many predict hyperlocal technology to take hold with retailers. More than some ego-driven badge of gamification (e.g., mayorship titles for repeat check-ins), however, this new era of LBS is likely to use "context" that allow us to market smarter For example, by incorporating reward programs with check-ins, social currency, and real value (e.g., search efficiency) to our targets, we improve our target's experience while still capturing a lot of data.

With LBS, we more than likely enrich this experience by providing real-time (more like "right-time") useful information in the proximity of where our target is ready to buy (i.e., BoFu content). But this experience will quickly erode if it does not bring real value to our target audience.

But consider how such value is provided by some major brands today. Dunkin' Donuts, for example, describes their "Runner" program where multiemployees can assemble their donut orders through a runner. Imagine the data gathered at Dunkin' Donuts with follow-ups like "we have fresh blueberry bagels" to the patron who normally orders that item.

Similarly, Subway teamed with O2 Media to launch their "You Are Here" campaign using a scannable smartphone discount voucher. Consumers, in this case, are able to redeem the MMS discount vouchers by scanning their smartphones or tablet devices in Subway stores. The technology works using "geo-fences" that are set up around Subway outlets. That is, when a customer enters the O2 More target area, they automatically receive an MMS.

American Express has perhaps the most innovative use of them all. With their "My Offers" program, they blend LMS and preference-based context marketing. For example, they recommend and rank merchant offers based on your spending history and location. Much of this data is gathered from Twitter, Facebook, and Foursquare.

A real challenge for marketers in this field will be the optimizing of your context-based mobile marketing for "search, engagement, and discovery" at the local level. Lee Odden stresses this concept throughout his book, *Optimize*.[2] In the case of mobile LMS, you can encourage your target audience to engage with your locations through check-ins, recommendations, and likes while also maximizing the opportunities for discovery.

The concept here is that your target audience engagement not only enhances your profile, it will ultimately drive more folks to your business. Think of this as a direct "BoFu" offer. Hopefully, your trail of ToFu content has earned the trust of your target. Your MoFu content then collects enough data to serve this target with personalized offers (BoFu content) at the "right time."

Many believe this is why Instagram became so successful (e.g., second to only Facebook on time spent in apps). With the release of Instagram 3.0, they are now putting location at the center of the experience. And by using Foursquare's venue data, place-tagged Instagram photos went up by 50 percent. Now consider what can happen with the addition of WhatsApp to Facebook's crowned jewels.

Notes

1. Jay Baer. Youtility. New York: Portfolio/Penguin. 2013.
2. Lee Odden. Optimize. New Jersey: Wiley. 2012.

CHAPTER 13

Enrolling Trial Users with Freemiums

I'll do anything for free stuff.

—Sandra Bullock, Actress

Freemiums are often the content of choice today for company's seeking to advance their customers through their social sales funnel. But do they help more than they hurt revenue generation? With an estimated 90–99 percent of the 1 million+ apps downloadable free of charge, consumers are quite accustomed to receiving free services. So businesses see this as a content-marketing strategy for the bottom of the sales funnel (i.e., BoFu) content. The intent here is to engage customers through trial use of a business solution that allows service providers to showcase their competence while getting sales ready prospects to consider an offer.

In the mobile-app business, freemiums are generally applied in the following manner:

1. feature limited—start with a reasonable set of functions;
2. time limited—free trial typically of entire feature set that expires over a 30-day time period; and
3. capacity or subscription limited— free offering applies to a limited set of subscribers.

Freemiums have been employed very successfully in social-networking arenas. Popular examples include Skype, Hoovers, LinkedIn, Dropbox, and most e-mail service offerings.

Proponents of the freemium model suggest that providers of apps and other digital offerings deliver a base set of services free of charge in order to reach high Internet traffic. A fee is then charged for specialized services or future activation of paid service (e.g., time-limited trial subscription).

Trial use apps, along with free audits and assessments, are widely used in BoFu content strategies where users need a free look before purchase. During this trial period, suppliers can collect significant research information in a social CRM database.

In total freemiums offer the following benefits:

1. *Rapid customer acquisition (click away)*: If you can convert trial users without forcing them into a purchase decision, you can build a customer base fairly rapidly and efficiently. Some research supports the notion of simplicity in purchase, i.e., users are adverse to pulling out credit cards or even completing registration forms. It is, therefore, suggested that these actions be deferred until after initial interaction.

2. *Promotional tool with reduced marketing expenses*: The freemium model can be an especially effective promotional tool online because customers easily spread the word throughout social-media outlets. When offered free of charge, the free product can be easily recommended to friends via Facebook, blogs, LinkedIn, Twitter, and industry forums. Moreover, if the download link goes viral, marketing expenses are drastically reduced.

3. *Validation of business model*: Freemiums provide opportunities to prove market potential for a company's offering as well as to prototype the offering for product research.

4. *Search engine effectiveness*: Freemiums provide far more valuable and popular blogging content as users link to the site hosting the free download. Consequently, more opportunities are provided to bump up search engine results (e.g., through fresh content and greater audience reach). In addition, research shows terms like "free" to significantly boost the effectiveness of Pay-for-Click (PPC) ads as well.

5. *User confidence*: Much like a money-back guarantee, a giveaway is often perceived as an expression of confidence on the part of the service provider. That is, by offering a freemium, a company is essentially expressing its confidence in product effectiveness while imparting

some goodwill to its sales-ready audience. In effect, the introductory price is a signaling mechanism. A low entrance price signals that you are confident that your product will create value for the customer.

6. *Overcoming customer reluctance for untested experience goods*: Many digital products or services need a period of use before the customer can determine its usage value. Since customers tend to underestimate the value of a product, the optimal pricing for an untested experience should include a low introductory price, which is then increased when the customer realizes the full value of the product.

7. *Tiered pricing rationale*: Freemiums also provide a rationale for premium offerings. For example, if priced by the number of shared app users or the number of activated features, users have a baseline in which to justify pricing from the most basic to enterprise-level platinum support.

8. *Valuable research*: Freemiums allow early research of a product's or service's feature demand. And by tracking downloads from their source, information can also be gathered about target audience characteristics as well. Finally, freemiums are normally provided at the bottom of the sales funnel. As a result, the downloading of a free app provides a trail of conversion data often missing from middle-of-the-funnel content (e.g., blogs, e-Books, Podcasts, webinars, etc.).

But despite their growing popularity, freemiums typically suffer from the following:

1. *Slow time to monetize*: The conversion from free to paying customers can take months to years for freemiums to be profitable. Statistics show that paid adopters typically range from 1 to 10 percent of total app downloads. This would imply that a freemium model often hinges on an aggressive up-sell of feature upgrades or user base expansion.

2. *Competitor imitation*: The more viral a freemium offer spreads, the more exposure it has to competitive scrutiny.

3. *Psychological perception of perpetually free*: Free is a huge accelerator of adoption. The flip side of this is that after using the product for free, it is very hard to get the customer to start paying for it.

FUTURE

Social Content-Marketing Predictions from a Strategic Planning Perspective

After combing through scores of predictions on what will happen with social media, the following is clear. Social media and content marketing will be more about honing strategies, leveraging big data, hosting microvideos, and getting serious about ROI. But how can we distill from these predictions a manageable set of planning inputs to our operating budgets?

To begin, let's consider what impacts the planning process. Many of the predictions relate to strategy development across marketing, advertising, and brand development. Other predictions cover the environment as it relates to user expectations, media ecosystems, and changes to expect in our operating infrastructures. The rest provide insights as to what business models are likely to succeed.

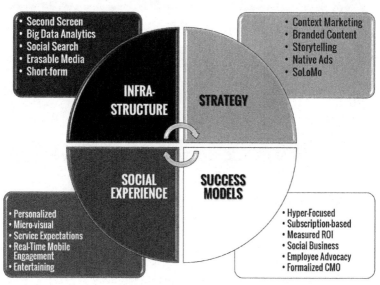

- Second Screen
- Big Data Analytics
- Social Search
- Erasable Media
- Short-form

- Context Marketing
- Branded Content
- Storytelling
- Native Ads
- SoLoMo

INFRA-STRUCTURE

STRATEGY

SOCIAL EXPERIENCE

SUCCESS MODELS

- Personalized
- Micro-visual
- Service Expectations
- Real-Time Mobile Engagement
- Entertaining

- Hyper-Focused
- Subscription-based
- Measured ROI
- Social Business
- Employee Advocacy
- Formalized CMO

Strategic Predictions

Strategy in this social media Zeitgeist can be summed up as one of streamlining and seamlessly blending into our audience's social experience. Consider the streamlining in your plan as the typical steps taken by companies during a lean recovery state. During these maturation stages, we begin to prune away the experimenting of shiny new objects and focus more on the most likely to payoff.

This usually leads to greater attention on integration and execution and less attention on experimenting. For many brands and small businesses, there will likely be heightened attention on what really contributed to lead generation and conversion. As a result, the merits of content that shows promise in stimulating engagement will weigh more heavily in budget decisions than the merits of content reaching the largest audience.

Consequently, engagement metrics like *comments* and *shares* will be more important than vanity metrics such as *likes* and *followers*. The seamless blending of content into our user experience streams has much to do with separating ourselves from the clutter. One way to do this is by adding value to the content our audience is actually seeking. This should

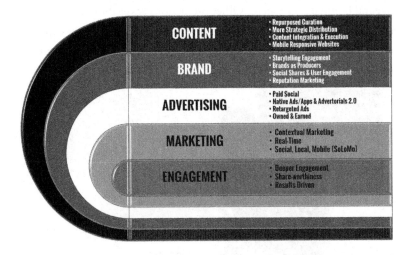

translate into more purposeful content pieces that reach our audience in the right way, at the right time, and in the right mood.

Content Strategies

Content-marketing strategies will have to be more justifiable and hyperfocused. The goal here is to boost conversion rates at the expense of more fans and followers. One way to start on track is to repurpose curated content. For example, consider how you can regularly reach a targeted audience at many points in their buying cycle by recasting your content into several blog pieces, podcasts, and videos. Not all of the content has to be original.

Your audience merely wants a reliable source that answers the mail briefly and immediately. The latter suggest you repurpose the content on whatever platforms your audience prefers at the time. This leads to another planning adjustment. The next few years may be more about smart content distribution than content development. In order for conversion rates to go up, budgets will have to shift more toward channel placement.

With pay-for-play social advertising on the rise, this will mean more investment in reaching your targeted audience. Finally, nearly every social-media and content-marketing expert agrees that "creating for mobile first" should be foremost in our content-marketing thinking. With mobile access to social media already exceeding desktop access, expect successful brands to invest heavily this year in responsive mobile websites.

Brand Engagement Strategies

Many predict that over the next few years real-time mobile-customer engagement, brand storytelling, influence marketing, and share worthiness will be the central focus of marketing investment into deeper audience engagement. With noise levels skyrocketing, more brands are recognizing that engagement will require more than promised benefits. Brands will have to inspire and entertain more than ever.

By storytelling, brands have an opportunity to develop a loyal following that is far more interested in stories than brand messages. In addition, more brands will be expected to adopt their own media studios and newsrooms as tight control of the brand story requires a more immediate response and authentic voice to their target audience. Although the cost to operating plans seems onerous at this point, longer-term savings are likely to result as in-house control of the brand story leads to a more reliable boost in engagement.

Advertising Strategies

Here is where we see a great deal of consistency among predictions. Paid social ads will be adopted reluctantly by brands as perhaps the only way to maximize their reach in social-network news feeds. At question, however, is the timing of native advertising as a core element of content-marketing plans.

Sponsored or branded content will be key to separating brand stories from the noise of too many brands now competing for diminishing social ad attention. Much of this content will likely be niche specific and of high enough quality that followers recognize immediate value. And to provide this value, brands may have to consider longer-form content. Jay Baer even suggests this will be the year that Advertorial 2.0 takes hold.

But perhaps the biggest breakthrough will be the widespread use of native apps. As more brands witness the success of Clorox, Charmin, Ortho, and Columbia in advising us how to remove a stain, find a clean restroom, identify a weed, and tie a boat knot, respectively, native apps in particular will capitalize on this trend toward real-time "self-help."

Marketing Strategies

As the quality of data surrounding our prospects has drastically improved, more brands will likely exploit the ability to know what audiences are doing at a certain time and place. Add to that the knowledge gained from behavioral tracking and social profiles, we have an excellent formula for hypertargeting. And much of the technology is here to pull it off.

At minimum, expect brands to be ramping up for the use of predictive analytics in retargeted advertising. Experience in this level of behavioral targeting can then lead the way for contextual marketing that supports a real-time and locally relevant shopping experience. Another trend to expect soon is the growth in agile video marketing. Expect brands to embrace their own newsrooms as mobile users become accustomed to getting rapid response news on breaking stories.

Infrastructure Predictions

As in any plan, a survey of our surroundings helps us understand the landscape of competition and technology constraints. Most likely to materialize this year is the following:

1. A technology that is analytical and possibly wearable.
2. Data that are important for ROI.
3. An audience tweeting with TV.
4. A referee, called Hummingbird, that will level the playing field for true content contributors.
5. Content platforms meant for the short-lived and easily escapable.

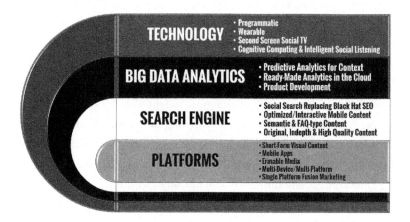

Technology

Much to the credit of big data, an estimated 20 percent of U.S. display advertising will involve programmatic ad buying. The rapid growth of brands flocking to the programmatic buying process will likely continue as overstretched marketing resources seek efficiencies from automation. Social networks are dramatically changing the landscape of TV marketing and will certainly impact planning. The market for second screen for global social TV is expected to reach $250 billion over the next 3 years.

As the sale of iPads and smartphones continue to skyrocket, expect the same growth in TV viewers interacting with live-show content. One area still in question is the role of wearable technologies. Glassware, smart watches, wrist-ware, and Facebook's Oculus Rift are still serving the early adopters in an application seeking mode. Although Google Glasses is often sported in the media as the high-concept wearable tech product of the year, its future remains uncertain. To reach high levels of adoption, it will likely need the endorsement of critical diagnostics applications in the military and medical fields. Small businesses, in particular, may be wise to holding off any plans to gear up for wearable device optimizing.

Social Search Engine

Google's Hummingbird is being greeted with mixed responses. It is good news for legitimate content providers and bad news for black hat SEO spammers. We finally have a search engine that is penalizing SEO link spamming and magical keyword stuffing. Hat's off to Google and their semantic-oriented search algorithm for coming pretty close to a fair measure of legitimate content.

Content marketers would be wise to provide high-quality, in-depth content that resonates with topics most sought after by their target audience. And think video first, video second, and video third. The same will apply to search algorithms inherent in the social networks and their tagging or hash-tagging formats. Those that provide engaging and highly shareable content will ultimately win out on exposure.

Platforms

Here also is where there is a great deal of consistency in predictions. Brands should devote an inordinate share of resources to short-form visual content. Video content will benefit search. Short videos in particular will appeal to the limited attention span of today's audience. And perhaps more than before, we are seeing evidence that consumers expect content to fit the platform.

So think erasable video on Snapchat, GIFs on Tumblr, 6-seconds videos on Twitter Vine, infographics on blogs, and photo-rich content on Facebook. At the same time, brands inundated with multiplatform involvement are turning to fusion marketing to integrate their traditional and digital marketing tools.

By working off one platform or dashboard, they hope to manage and benefit from multiple campaigns launched from one place. Investments should also be considered for the development of niche-oriented apps. This growing field of Friend-of-Mine apps is likely to materialize this year as more consumers recognize the value and handiness of self-help mobile apps.

Success Models

A successful business model could be summed up as serious and laser focused. Successful brands over the next few years will likely attribute their success to hypertargeting. Rather than seeking new ways to acquire fans and followers, this will be a year of measuring, recalibrating, and reloading.

Common to most business models will be a subscription-based approach to engagement. This bodes well for e-mail marketing services and will likely put in question the need for RSS. Brands will be looking at courting highly qualified leads with pinpointed solutions to each need across the entire buying stage. Big data and closed-loop analytics will then validate what tactics worked best toward conversion. And if not conversion, expect brands to measure retention and influence as a proxy for business to come.

This will also be the year that brands formalize their involvement in content marketing. The arrival of more chief content officers and more formalized social business setups will likely pave the way for new social talent and enterprisewide collaboration on social intelligence gathering and social listening. More importantly, we will likely see PR and customer service finding their way into social-media marketing.

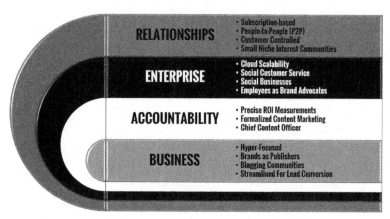

Companies will capitalize more on the power of employees as brand advocates. And with this greater commitment to a social business, more pressure will be placed on marketing, in particular, to validate a greater amount of budget requests with hardcore ROI measurements now available from online tools and cloud-based databases.

Social Experience

Of all the crystal ball predictions, this area of planning is perhaps the least suspect. Here is what we know for certain. Millennials, in particular, are flocking to ephemeral media sites in droves. Facebook's offer of $3 billion for Snapchat was topped by Google for $4 billion. So it is safe to say, Millennials and Gen Z want erasable media.

We also have ample evidence to suggest that the deteriorating attention spans of Millennials will accelerate the arrival of contextually relevant content. So expect location-based services to rapidly adopt social context as well. And as the momentum of early adopters builds, inside shopping assistance will become an expectation.

In the interim, many predict that Twitter Vine will continue to flourish as applications for "how-to's" and "where to find" will augment the earlier and more limited functions of geo-targeting. Now imagine what this does to our customer service departments as target audiences become addicted to getting what they want now.

Finally, consumers will recognize all the more in years to come that the power of conversation rests in their hands. Brands will have to compromise their desire for storytelling with allowing fans an opportunity to share their experiences. In return, fans will expect to be inspired and entertained if brands want their continued involvement.

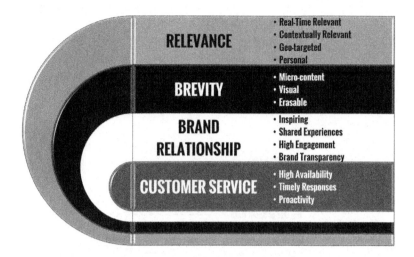

RELEVANCE
- Real-Time Relevant
- Contextually Relevant
- Geo-targeted
- Personal

BREVITY
- Micro-content
- Visual
- Erasable

BRAND RELATIONSHIP
- Inspiring
- Shared Experiences
- High Engagement
- Brand Transparency

CUSTOMER SERVICE
- High Availability
- Timely Responses
- Proactivity

Summary

Arguably, we have had a few lackluster years of new technology. Wearable technologies have been a disappointment so far, and perhaps the only shiny new object warranted our attention Snapchat. Instead, we witnessed the maturation of content marketing and how the social dominion went from publishing to sharing to repurposing curating content. Much of this new wave emerged from the media fatigue that forced many brands to adopt smarter and more proven approaches to their social-media marketing efforts.

That is why many experts are predicting the next few years to be less about breakthroughs and more about hypertargeting, optimizing, and fine-tuning strategies. What's more, plenty of evidence is mounting that marketers will be less concerned about reach and more about impact as executives press them for measured results. Much of this impact will likely come from legitimate, high-quality content as Google's Hummingbird algorithm makes it increasingly more difficult for SEO spammers to muddy the waters.

What is clear is that social content marketing has evolved into an entirely different philosophy of marketing than envisioned just a decade ago. The role of publishing, subtle SEO, storytelling and consumer involvement has created an oxymoronic inversion of marketing conditions as captured below.

Index

DIGITAL AND SOCIAL MEDIA MARKETING AND ADVERTISING COLLECTION HAS MANY FORTHCOMING TITLES, INCLUDING. . .

Vicky Crittenden, Babson College, Editor

- *Digital and Social Media Marketing: Keeping it Real* by Nathalie Collins
- *Online Consumer Insight* by Geraldine Rosa Henderson
- *Corporate Branding in Facebook Fan Pages: Ideas for Improving Your Brand Value* by Eliane Pereira Zamath Brito, Maria Carol Zanette, and Benjamin Rosenthal
- *Mobile Marketing: A Plan For Strategic Success* by J. Barry Dickinson
- *A Beginner's Guide to Mobile Marketing* by Karen Mishra and Molly Garris
- *Digital Privacy in the Marketplace: Perspectives on the Information Exchange* by George Milne
- *Digital Consumption and Fantasy Football: Lessons For Marketers From America's 'Virtual' Pass Time* by Mujde Yuksel, Mark A. McDonald, and George Milne
- *Mobile Commerce: How It Contrasts, Challenges and Enhances Electronic Commerce* by Esther Swilley
- *Electronic Word of Mouth for Service Businesses* by Linda W. Lee
- *Digital Marketing Management: A Handbook for the Current (or Future) CEO* by Debra Zahay
- *Mobile Advertising: Moving from SMS to Mobile Applications* by Aikaterini C. Valvi
- *Presentation Evaluation: How to Inspire, Educate, and Entertain Your Audience* by Michael Weiss
- *M-Powering Marketing in a Mobile World* by Syagnik Banerjee, Ruby Roy Dholakia, and Nikhilesh Dholakia
- *Using and Managing Online Communities* by Edward Boon

Announcing the Business Expert Press Digital Library

Concise e-books business students need for classroom and research

This book can also be purchased in an e-book collection by your library as

- a one-time purchase,
- that is owned forever,
- allows for simultaneous readers,
- has no restrictions on printing, and
- can be downloaded as PDFs from within the library community.

Our digital library collections are a great solution to beat the rising cost of textbooks. E-books can be loaded into their course management systems or onto student's e-book readers. The **Business Expert Press** digital libraries are very affordable, with no obligation to buy in future years. For more information, please visit **www.businessexpertpress.com/librarians**. To set up a trial in the United States, please contact **Adam Chesler** at adam.chesler@businessexpertpress.com. For all other regions, contact **Nicole Lee** at nicole.lee@igroupnet.com.

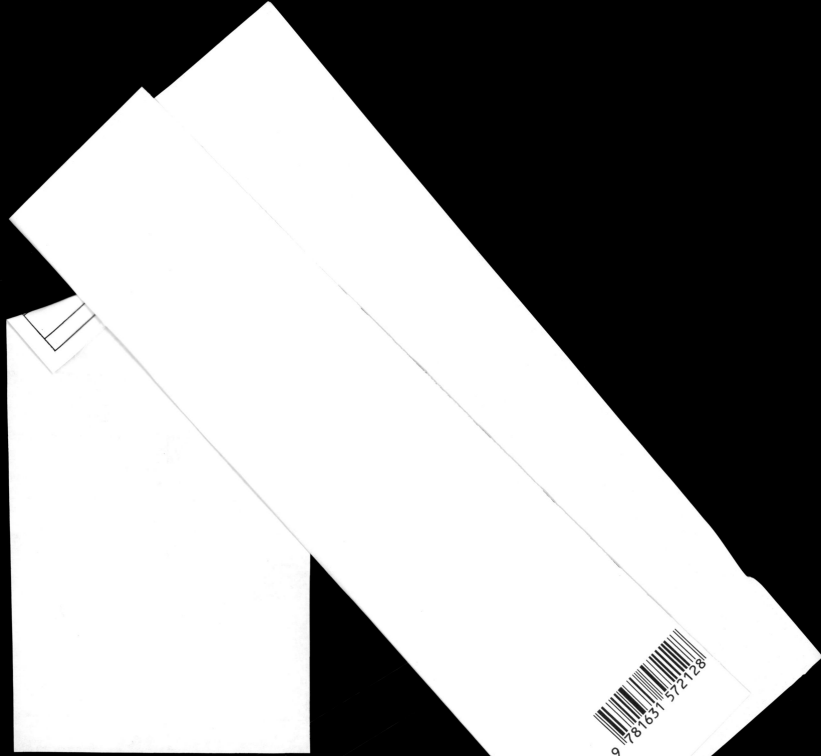

0 1341 1487786 0

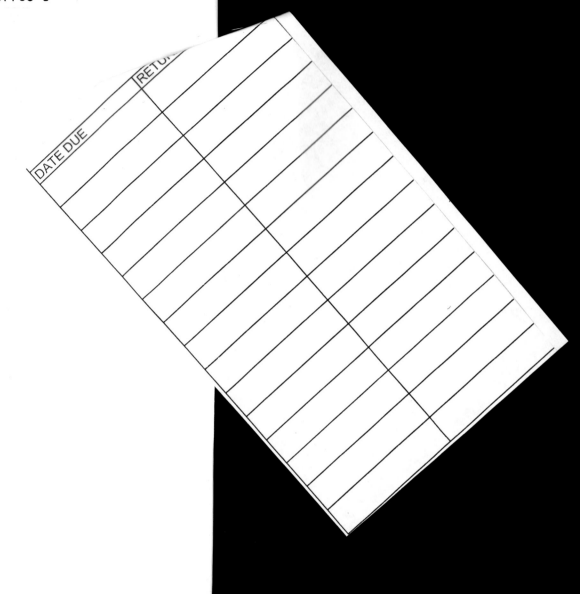

CPSIA information can be obtained at www.ICGtesting.com
Printed in the USA
LVOW/Ms1630211015

459781LV00017B/764/P

0 1341 1487786 0

CPSIA information can be obtained at www.ICGtesting.com
Printed in the USA
LVOW04s1630211015

459181LV00017B/764/P

9 781631 572128